LISA ASCH AND
PETER BLACKWELL

TRAVELLER'S GUIDE TO
TANZANIA

NEW
HOLLAND

First published in 1997 by
New Holland (Publishers) Ltd
London • Cape Town • Sydney • Singapore

24 Nutford Place
London W1H 6DQ
United Kingdom

80 McKenzie Street
Cape Town 8001
South Africa

3/2 Aquatic Drive
Frenchs Forest, NSW 2086
Australia

ISBN 1 85368 704 9

Managing editor: Annlerie van Rooyen
Editors: Mariëlle Renssen and Lesley Hay-Whitton
Design manager: Janice Evans
Designer: Shane Smitsdorp
Cover designer: Darren MacGurk
Cartographers: Caroline Bowie and Paul Marais
Picture researcher: Maryann Shaw
Indexer and proofreader: Sandie Vahl

Reproduction by cmyk Prepress
Printed and bound by Tien Wah Press (Pte.) Ltd, Singapore

While every effort has been made to ensure factual accuracy in this book, with the rapid changes that are
taking place in Tanzania, it is inevitable that information in this book will become outdated. The author and
publishers invite any comment or suggestions for future updates. Please write to: The Editor, *Traveller's Guide
to Tanzania*, Struik Publishers (Pty) Ltd, P O Box 1144, Cape Town 8000, South Africa.

Lisa Asch and Peter Blackwell currently reside and work in Kenya. After spending many years coordinating safaris and working at a permanent tented camp in the Masai Mara National Reserve, they now devote the majority of their time to living in and discovering the African bush through freelance writing and photography. Peter, who was born in Kenya, is also an accomplished wildlife artist having held successful exhibitions in London and Nairobi. Enthusiastic explorers, they have travelled extensively throughout Sub-Saharan Africa and beyond. Lisa co-wrote *Great Game Parks of Africa – Masai Mara National Reserve*, a Struik publication. Peter's pictures have been used in various Struik titles, including *Great Game Parks – Ngorongoro Conservation Area* and *Great Game Parks – Masai Mara National Reserve*; *Globetrotter Travel Guide Tanzania*; as well as *This is Kenya* and *Kenya the Beautiful* (both New Holland Publication titles) and various articles in *Getaway* magazine.

PHOTOGRAPHIC CREDITS

Copyright © for the photographs rests with the photographers
and/or their agents as listed below.

ABPL = Anthony Bannister Photo Library **PA** = Photo Access **SIL** = Struik Image Libary

All photographs copyright © Peter Blackwell (SIL) with the exception of the following:

Daryl Balfour: 23 **(SIL)**; 92 **(SIL)**; 93 **(ABPL)**. **Andrew Bannister (both SIL):** 75 (top); 151. **Alan Binks (both ABPL):** 61; 97. **Gerald Cubitt (SIL):** 135 (top). **Roger de la Harpe (SIL):** 125. **Nigel Dennis (all SIL):** Cover spine; 59 (bottom); 79 (bottom); 87 (bottom). **Corrie Hansen:** 175. **Stefania Lamberti:** Front cover (middle right); 172; 175 (right). **Jackie Nel (both PA):** 72 (bottom); 157. **Peter Pickford (both SIL):** 107 (top); 135 (bottom). **Peter Ribton (all SIL):** Front cover (top left; middle left; bottom left and right); 6; 15; 50; 60; 71; 77; 81; 91; 154; 166. **Anup Shah (ABPL):** 107 (bottom). **David Steele (all PA):** 29; 53 (bottom); 89; 176 (left). **P Wagner (all PA):** Front cover (top right); 58; 62; 65 (bottom).

Front cover: Top left: Bahari Beach Hotel, near Dar es Salaam; Top right: Mount Kilimanjaro, from Amboseli; Middle left: Maasai people; Middle right: Ngalawa, Zanzibar, viewed from Prison Island; Bottom left: The base of the Ngorongoro Crater; Bottom right: Marahubi Palace, Zanzibar. **Spine:** A lioness. **Back cover:** A pristine beach along Zanzibar's coast at Matemwe. **Half-title page:** Sunrise on Zanzibar. **Title page:** Elephants in Game Reserve.

ACKNOWLEDGEMENTS

The author and photographer thank the countless people who offered information, advice and assistance whilst they were compiling this book. Though too many to name individually, their efforts made the completion of this book possible. Special recognition should also go to those individuals who helped us tremendously by acting as trusted couriers in the transport of text and slides to our publishers. We also gratefully thank Mr. Credo Sinyangwe (Managing Director of the Tanzania Tourist Board), the Tanzania National Parks, the Ngorongoro Conservation Area Authority, Chief Warden Moriana (Ruaha National Park), Mr. & Mrs. Sebastian Tham (Serengeti National Park), Dominic Kosen and Brian Payne (Conservation Corporation Kenya) and Oyster Bay Hotels. Special thanks to Darius Bipa and Bob Axten (Conservation Corporation Tanzania), Fran and Chris More (Camels Only), Chris Fox (Mwagusi Tented Camp), Mike Patterson, Richard and Jules Knocker and the staff of Ker & Downey, Tony Christianakis, Oliver Davidson (Hoopoe Adventure Tours), Nomad Safaris, Meserani Snake Park, John & Kay Blackwell, Di Asch, and Dutch, our vehicle who never let us down.

CONTENTS

PART ONE

AN INTRODUCTION TO TANZANIA

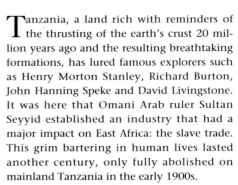

Tanzania, a land rich with reminders of the thrusting of the earth's crust 20 million years ago and the resulting breathtaking formations, has lured famous explorers such as Henry Morton Stanley, Richard Burton, John Hanning Speke and David Livingstone. It was here that Omani Arab ruler Sultan Seyyid established an industry that had a major impact on East Africa: the slave trade. This grim bartering in human lives lasted another century, only fully abolished on mainland Tanzania in the early 1900s.

Today, Tanzania has become better known for its abundant wildlife, unique landscapes and life-giving waters. It is 'the land of the ultimate safari', inviting the adventurous to share in its contrasts – witnessing the thrill of a lion kill and the teeming wildlife on its vast plains, basking in a dramatic African sunset.

LEFT: *Sunrise over Dar es Salaam harbour.*
ABOVE: *Tanzania's coast is renowned for its ruins, among them Zanzibar's Mbweni Ruins.*

THE LAND

Tanzania, the largest country in East Africa, covers a vast area of 945,087 km² (364,898 sq. miles). The unique landscapes of its diverse interior are the result of extensive volcanic activity and tectonic faulting, which created the Great Rift Valley. Tanzania's Mount Kilimanjaro, at 5,895 m (19,340 ft), is the highest on the continent, and the country shares Africa's three largest lakes – Victoria, Malawi (also known as Nyasa) and Tanganyika – with its East African neighbours. Uganda borders Tanzania to the north, sharing Lake Victoria's waters and the prosperous, fertile lands along its shoreline.

To the northeast is Kenya, where the annual wildebeest migration spills over from Tanzania's great Serengeti National Park into Kenya's Masai Mara National Reserve. The western boundary is formed by Rwanda, Burundi and by Lake Tanganyika, the deepest lake in Africa. To the south of Tanzania lie Zambia and Malawi (here the boundary is partly formed by the crystal-clear waters of Lake Malawi's northern shores), while the Ruvuma River separates Tanzania and Mozambique and heads cross-country from the west to the warm Indian Ocean.

Host to three World Heritage Sites – the Serengeti National Park, Ngorongoro Crater and Selous Game Reserve – Tanzania harbours some of Africa's largest and most renowned wildlife parks and reserves. At the same time it is a country that's rich in history and culture, and it has a fascinating architectural heritage left by the cross-cultural exchanges that were brought about via the old trade routes.

The country's vegetation ranges from sweeping grassland plains to original tracts of lush equatorial forest to the coastal shores which boast pristine reefs and offshore coral islands. Tanzania's scenery is immensely

Camels Only Camp in the Arusha area, with Mount Kilimanjaro in the background.

KEY TO REGIONAL AND PARK MAPS

City	☐ ZANZIBAR
Important town	◉ Musoma
Small town	○ Tabora
Large village	◎ Mpanda
Village	○ Kola
Province name	Tanga
Province border	
Country name	RWANDA
International border	across water
National road (tarred)	═A23═
National road (untarred)	═B144═
Main road (tarred)	═B8═
Main road (untarred)	═══
Minor road	───
Track	- - -
Footpath	········
Railway	┼─────┼

Hotel/lodge	Ⓗ
Camp	⌂
Petrol	⬛
Border post	⟋
Domestic airport	✈
International airport	✈
Place of interest	●
Beach	≋
	Isonge
Peak (name and height)	▲1708m
Highlands	
Contour with height	5100m
Crater	⁙
River	∼
Marsh/swamp	
Pan	
Lake	
National Park or Reserve	

TOWN PLAN KEY

Medical centre	✚
Post office	✉
Police station	
Tourist information office	ℹ
Library	
Building of interest	☐
Bus station	
Railway with station	
Place of interest	●
Place of worship	△
Golf course	⚑
Built-up area	▱

9

Breathtaking views can be enjoyed from the Ngorongoro Crater ascent road.

transitional and often changes suddenly from one area to another. Starting with the beautiful coastal sector, this stretches for approximately 800 km (497 miles) and is primarily a flat, low-lying region with gentle breezes from the Indian Ocean gliding across its warm, inviting beaches. The superb diving conditions beckon underwater enthusiasts, while the Arab-Islamic architecture, atmospheric markets and history of the coastal cities and Spice Islands keep the land-bound visitors entranced and fascinated.

Moving inland, the fertile coastline gradually yields to higher altitudes of lush vegetation which receives plenty of rainfall. Progressing deeper still into the interior, the terrain changes dramatically to become the semi-arid Maasai Steppe, which comprises enormous grassland plains that seem to stretch to the horizon. The effects of the Rift Valley on Tanzania's topography are evident here: its eastern arm, embracing the Ngorongoro Conservation Area and Lake Manyara, divides the steppe from the 1,200-m-high (3,937 ft) central plateau which makes up most of the rest of the country. The Rift's western arm splits from its eastern counterpart to encompass Lake Tanganyika. In the east of the country, below Kilimanjaro, a series of mountain ranges curves east, then turns south and eventually southwest to end around the town of Mbeya. Starting with the Pare Mountains, the range becomes the Usambaras, then picks up again with the Ulugurus around the town of Morogoro, moves on to the Udzungwa Mountains, and ends with the Ngurus. This mountainous spine preserves precious traces of equatorial forest that used to extend right across Africa.

The predominant vegetation in Tanzania – that is, on the central plateau and in the southwest of the country – is miombo woodland, composed of a belt of grassland with mainly Brachystegia tree cover. The northeast, including the Maasai Steppe, comprises open grassland with Acacia-commiphora woodland. In southern Tanzania, around Ruaha National Park, the vegetation is somewhat more varied and includes bushland of commiphora, acacias and giant baobabs. Coastal vegetation comprises coconut palms, casuarinas and tracts of mangroves.

Of Tanzania's largest rivers, the Great Ruaha originates in the south of the country in the Buhoro swamp northeast of Mbeya. It flows northwards to form the eastern edge of the Ruaha National Park and is then met by several tributaries, including the Nzombe from the west, after which the Great Ruaha turns eastwards to join up with another major river, the Rufiji, in the Selous Game Reserve. The Rufiji continues east to meet the sea at the Rufiji Delta, opposite the southern edge of Mafia Island.

Other significant rivers are the Pangani which flows south from Kilimanjaro, and the Ruvuma, which creates the country's border with Mozambique.

WHAT TO EXPECT

Whatever your mode of transport, standard of accommodation or personal expectations of your safari, this lovely country should be approached with a relaxed attitude – and patience. Here life is slow and easy – the locals

The road between Dodoma and Arusha will challenge the skills of all drivers.

find no need to rush. Tanzania embodies Africa's true colours, so breathe in the African air, enjoy the scenery in a leisurely fashion, and absorb the richness and variety of its untamed wildlife.

In this part of Africa one should always be prepared for the unexpected: from the treat of watching the swiftly changing colours of a sunrise on an early morning drive, to seeing a lion sprinting through the grass as it chases its prey, to having to endure several punctures in one day. Tanzania is, in the truest sense of the word, an adventure.

Game parks and reserves form a great portion of Tanzania's tourist destinations; however, distances between them are great. The country's road system is a tough challenge. Although some of the major roads have been sealed, the vast majority of secondary roads are gravel, and often riddled with potholes. If driving is your chosen mode of transport, travelling times from one place to another can be lengthy, but driving does at the same time offer many rewards: spectacular landscapes and cameo slices of rural life are offered along the way.

Although Tanzania is considered to be a relatively expensive destination because of its high entry fees into parks and reserves and its often remotely sited accommodation, if one weighs all the factors involved in foreign travel, it can be said that the sheer numbers and the variety of wildlife – some of Africa's largest concentrations – can justify the cost of travel in this country.

Climate
Like most things in Tanzania, the weather is greatly dictated by geographic location. Rains, humidity levels and temperatures vary throughout the country. Most parts of Tanzania (with the exception of the central plateau) experience two rains during the year, separated by a dry season having an average length of five-and-a-half months.

The 'long rains' usually occur from March until May, while the 'short rains' generally arrive around the month of October and continue falling until December.

Large sections of the country are virtually impossible to navigate once the rains arrive (although the scenery, as a result of the luxuriant regeneration of plant life and trees, is magnificent and can be well worth the time and effort); it is advisable to make use of a four-wheel-drive vehicle at this time of year.

The coastal area is hot and humid for most of the year, with temperatures ranging from 20 to 30 °C (68–86 °F). Weather conditions are determined by monsoon winds which blow from north to east from October to February, and south to east for the rest of the year. The average humidity is 78%.

The dry season savanna of Tanzania's central plateau receives rainfall only once a year and is generally warm and dry with temperatures averaging 27 °C (81 °F). Highland zones in the northeast (Kilimanjaro, Pare and Usambara), east (Uluguru) and south (Livingstone, Poroto, Rungwe) of the country are quite pleasant with balmy clear days. March is usually the warmest month, with an average temperature of 21 °C (70 °F), while June is the coolest with an average temperature of 15 °C (59 °F). Evenings and mornings throughout the year can be quite chilly and it is advisable always to have a warm sweater or jacket at hand.

THE LIE OF THE LAND

Formed millions of years ago by volcanic activity within the earth's crust, Africa's Great Rift Valley is a natural phenomenon. It is not, however, a valley in the true sense of the word (usually defined as a gorge created by the erosion and the coursing of water from mountain slopes down towards lower-lying land and the oceans); the Rift Valley was created by subterranean movement, causing sections of the earth's layers to subside into fractures in the earth's crust. It is through this subsidence that grabens, or graves as rift valleys are sometimes referred to, are caused.

The sinking frequently leads to shattering of the layers and the formation of escarpments. It is believed that the simultaneous combination of upward and downward thrusts caused the powerful tearing that has resulted in the extraordinary expanses of the Great Rift Valley.

Stretching for a length of approximately 9,700 km (6,028 miles), the Rift Valley starts in Turkey and, running in a southerly direction, it encompasses the Dead Sea, continues beneath the Red Sea, then reappears on the African continent in northeastern Ethiopia. From Ethiopia's highlands, the eastern arm of the African Rift is a narrow chasm that makes its way southwards through Kenya and on through Tanzania, where it embraces Lake Natron on the border, with its seasonal flamingo population, and Lake Manyara further south. In the southernmost regions of the country, the sheer edges that were the result of the earth's severe upheavals begin to ease away. The western arm of the Rift Valley begins at Lake Albert in Uganda, and curves to the southeast. Inhibited by a range of volcanic mountains, the Rift perseveres and forms part of the floor of Lake Tanganyika which plunges to a depth of 1,4400 m (4,725 ft). In southern Tanzania, the arms of the eastern and now dominant western section of the Rift join at Lake Nyasa (Malawi), a trough similar to that of Lake Tanganyika though not as deep. From Lake Nyasa, the Rift Valley continues, less dramatically, towards Mozambique. Here it fades towards the ocean, where eons ago Madagascar was severed from the mainland.

The Northern Circuit

A journey to Tanzania will no doubt include a visit to one or more of the game parks and reserves in the northern sector of the country. It is with good reason that the Northern Circuit plays host to more travellers than any of the country's other parks.

It offers dramatic landscape features such as the vast Serengeti plains, the impressive Ngorongoro Crater and its highlands and the harsh yet spectacular area round Lake Natron

A lone male lion in the Serengeti, Tanzania's largest national park.

The reception area at Kilimanjaro National Park in Northern Tanzania.

with the still-active volcano Ol Donyo Lengai. The Northern Circuit also offers stunning views and tremendous numbers of wildlife. Woven into this landscape, the Maasai people go about their daily tribal life.

It is here in the north that faulting in the earth's crust and massive volcanic activity have created soaring mountains such as Mount Meru and Ol Donyo Lengai, alkaline and crater lakes such as that at Empakaai Crater in the Ngorongoro Conservation Area, and expansive plains.

In the northeast of Tanzania, at the border with Kenya's Amboseli National Park, Kilimanjaro's snowcapped peak – at 5,895 m (19,340 ft) – looms high above the plains and continues to draw adventure-seekers as it has done for hundreds of years. Blue monkeys and the black-and-white colobus monkey can be seen in Kilimanjaro National Park, which also features interesting vegetation such as giant heathers *(Erica arborea)* and senecios on

its upper slopes, and in the higher alpine zone, strange giant lobelias. Acting as guardian over the land, Kilimanjaro's slopes gently descend to lower altitudes and the eastern arm of the Rift Valley, which cradles the alkaline lakes of Manyara and Natron. These waters play host to thousands of migratory birds throughout the year, which feed, breed and set up seasonal rookeries here. They include Yellowbilled storks and Great white pelicans, but the most spectacular sight is the massive numbers of Greater and Lesser flamingos.

Also in the north, boasting its own form of world renown, is the Serengeti National Park, at 14,763 km² (5,700 sq. miles) Tanzania's largest park. It is famous for its unusual rock outcrops, or kopjes, and teems with a diversity of wildlife, similar to that of Ngorongoro but greater in magnitude, roaming the vast short- and long-grass plains. Serengeti has the largest concentration of ungulates (hoofed mammals) in Africa (major species are wildebeest, zebra, various gazelles, topi, and hartebeest); the park is also famous for its lion, and

sightings of leopard, cheetah and hyena are usually guaranteed. The park contains a number of seasonal rivers which harbour some of the largest crocodiles in Africa.

The Ngorongoro Conservation Area, which has been declared a World Heritage Site, covers an area of roughly 8,280 km² (3,197 sq. miles), and embraces both dormant and extinct volcanic mountains, crater lakes and montane forests. In the lush setting of this protected area, visitors can witness one of nature's greatest accomplishments: nestled in quiet repose in the cool air of the highlands, patiently waiting for morning's misty shroud to unveil, is the world's largest, most perfect caldera, the Ngorongoro Crater. Its floor, lying approximately 610 m (2,000 ft) below the rim, which opens up to breathtaking views, presents a unique and intimate setting for game-viewing; it is possible to see large numbers of wildlife on a single game drive.

It is on the Ngorongoro plains where the great migration plays itself out throughout the year, and comes full circle. In March and April, at the end of the long rains, vast herds

The view of the Ngorongoro Crater from the Ngorongoro Wildlife Lodge.

of wildebeest, plains zebra and antelope migrate from the short-grass plains of the crater and the Serengeti, west almost to Lake Victoria, and then north to the long-grass plains of the Masai Mara in Kenya in search of fresh grazing. Rutting takes place at this time and around eight months later, when the animals complete their migratory cycle and return to Ngorongoro and the Serengeti, it is calving season for the wildebeest herds. Visitors often plan their trips to coincide with this spectacular migration as it is a truly unforgettable experience.

The Ngorongoro Conservation Area has also proved the theories of archaeologist-palaeontologists Louis and Mary Leakey to be correct. Steadfast in their belief that man had his origins in Africa, they spent 28 years relentlessly digging and searching for traces of early man. With little funding they persevered and discovered in Olduvai Gorge, within the Conservation Area, traces of the first

The Maasai giraffe is the only species of giraffe that is found in Tanzania.

upright hominids, their tools, and remnants of their lifestyle. A fascinating museum housing replicas and actual artefacts found there describes the various strata existing in the area (these can be seen when looking into the gorge itself), and the unusual variety of wildlife that made use of the then present lake (Lake Olduvai). Also discussed is Mary Leakey's discovery in 1976 of early man's perfectly preserved footsteps etched into the earth 35 km (22 miles) away at Laetoli. From this valuable discovery and the research that followed, the evolution of present-day man was gradually brought to light.

To the east of Ngorongoro lies Arusha National Park, a small but beautiful area that reveals much evidence of volcanic activity, having Mount Meru within its confines. There are good herds of elephant and buffalo in the park, zebra on the grasslands, Maasai giraffe (the only species of giraffe that occurs in Tanzania) and leopard, and in the forest zone primates such as the black-and-white colobus are visible. South of Arusha is Lake Manyara

National Park, and though it lies in the Rift Valley's path, the eastern wall is absent. The park is known for its hippo, its famous tree-climbing lions and abundant birdlife. Nearby is Tarangire National Park, which contains great elephant herds (depending on the seasons, these can number up to 300). During the dry season there is an abundance of plains game and their predators – lion, leopard and cheetah.

To the extreme northeast, on the boundary with Kenya, Mkomazi Game Reserve is steadily attracting increasing wildlife numbers while undergoing rehabilitation programmes to redress the damage caused by neglect, poaching and overgrazing. Less common animals such as the oryx and gerenuk, as well as predators, occur in the reserve.

The Southern Circuit

At one time considered to be inaccessible, the southern reaches of Tanzania are today easier to reach as a result of the improvement of tarred roads, the completion of all-weather roads and the introduction of airstrips. Admittedly, distances in this area of the country are great, but the breathtaking untouched wilderness, abundant wildlife, superb bird-watching opportunities, and glimpses into the daily lives of tribes such as the Hehe and Maasai are extremely rewarding for the patient traveller.

Ruaha River Lodge, situated on the banks of the Great Ruaha River in Ruaha National Park.

Plains game, like these zebra, are commonly seen in Mikumi National Park, Southern Tanzania.

The Southern Circuit, although visited by few tourists, is a special region, set as it is in an untamed environment. The terrain is characterized by contrasts, starting from the Southern Highlands north of Lake Nyasa (Malawi) where mountain streams, tea plantations and panoramic vistas abound, and moving on to the semi-arid but always magical extents in the Ruaha National Park and Selous Game Reserve. Low-volume tourism and immense expanses of wild, unexploited tracts of land within these game parks and reserves offer visitors a unique game-viewing experience and a great variety of flora.

The Selous Game Reserve, declared a World Heritage Site in 1982, is the largest reserve in the whole of Africa. Its remote expanses of wilderness are inhabited by lion, cheetah, buffalo and some of Africa's highest elephant populations. The great Rufiji River winding through the reserve harbours good numbers of hippo and crocodile.

The accessibility of Mikumi National Park, Tanzania's third-largest national park, makes it an ideal wildlife destination for travellers who have a restricted schedule. Buffalo, elephant, giraffe and a wide variety of plains game are sighted regularly. The country's second-largest park, the Ruaha National Park, offers dramatic terrain that ranges from grassland plains, miombo, acacia and baobab woodland to riverine forests. Greater and lesser kudu, plains game, predators and large numbers of hippo and crocodile are present in the Ruaha.

The Udzungwa Mountains National Park is Tanzania's most recently designated park and offers splendid walks under its forest canopy and has a number of beautiful waterfalls worth visiting. Also of interest in the Southern Circuit are the Stone Age site and Natural Pillars at Isimila, and the rock paintings in the Kondoa region.

Land of Lakes

Situated in the northwest and western parts of Tanzania lie the spectacular lakes of Victoria and Tanganyika. Scattered sporadically between them are several game parks and reserves, where both endemic and introduced fauna exist, but not in great numbers.

17

The brightly coloured lipstick plant (Bicsa aralana) *is found on Zanzibar Island.*

Draining to the north, the waters of Lake Victoria were much sought after by European explorers who came to unlock the secrets of the 'dark continent'. Finding the source of the Nile became an obsession for these 19th-century pioneers, causing much hardship and many mysterious deaths; the numerous tales and memoirs relating their adventures are almost unparalleled. As Africa's largest lake, Victoria is unusual in terms of most of Tanzania's lakes, not so much in size but in the fact that its waters are fresh. The lake is located neither in the western nor the eastern arm of the Great Rift Valley, but in between. Its expansive waters are an incredible sight and yield excellent fishing with their shoals of black bass, tilapia, lungfish and large numbers of the imposing Nile perch. The southern reaches of the lake nurture fertile soils that produce, among other crops, cotton.

Tanzania's largest tribe, the traditionalist Sukuma, work the land on the lake's shores as a type of cooperative society. In an attempt to be self-sufficient, they meet the needs of their community and return any profits to the agricultural cycle. Each village draws up a work plan for cultivation, ensuring that each household becomes part of the collective effort and that all members' plots are planted and harvested. The Sukuma maintain strong beliefs in traditional customs, among which is their enjoyment of music. They also hold an unusual reputation as snake charmers.

Moving southwest along Tanzania's border, Gombe Stream National Park and, a little further south, Mahale Mountains National Park are on the shores of Lake Tanganyika. Secluded and quiet, these two parks are renowned for lush tracts of forest and their resident families of chimpanzees and several other primates. Red and black-and-white colobus monkeys, red-tailed and blue monkeys, and yellow baboons, as well as elephant, buffalo and giraffe – in the eastern woodland areas – occur in the Mahale Mountains park, while in Gombe Stream there are olive baboons, bushbuck, bush duiker and bushpig. As vehicles are not permitted in either of the parks, they are reached by water only (boats are available) and they are ideal sites for walking safaris. Lying to the north of Lake Tanganyika is Lake Kivu, which drains into the Ruzizi River and then, along with numerous smaller streams, empties out into Lake Tanganyika. The world's second-deepest lake (1,440 m; 4,725 ft), Tanganyika is surrounded by a towering mountain range. The gorge within which the lake nestles rises from the lake depths to the mountaintop – a height of 3,048 m (10,000 ft). Filtering through sandy and somewhat acidic soil, the waters of the lake are amazingly clear, and are home to an extraordinary number of endemic fish – cichlids or mouth-breeders.

The Coast and Spice Islands

Along Tanzania's coastline are three large islands: to the extreme north of the country is Pemba, lying about 50 km (31 miles) north of Zanzibar – Tanzania's largest island – which in turn is located north of Dar es Salaam. The smallest island – known mainly for its beaches, snorkelling and scuba diving, and some of East Africa's best deep-sea fishing – is Mafia, approximately 160 km (100 miles) south of Zanzibar. This trio of islands still today conjure up romantic images of dhows gliding softly through warm waters, tropical breezes filling their sails, thus evoking memories of an enchanted past of secret hideaways and furtive journeys made under cover of darkness. The haunting silence of ancient mosques and ruins are reminders of a turbulent past chequered with fierce battles and the rise and fall of Portuguese and Arab rulers. Throughout the coastal area, history infuses the whitewashed buildings and their narrow stone streets with an air of the exotic, synonymous with this part of Tanzania.

For thousands of years, the deep-blue waters of the ocean have enticed traders, fishermen and fortune-seekers. Arriving from far-flung destinations such as Persia, the Arabian Peninsula and the Far East, each group of immigrants left its mark. As a result, the coastal region is a blending of peoples, cultures and architectural styles. The origins of the present-day Swahili stem from the intermarriage that occurred between the local Bantu-speaking tribes and Omani Arab traders and Persian Shirazis who sailed to Zanzibar to settle on its shores.

Zanzibar attained great renown as the world's largest producer of fragrant cloves after the Omani sultan Seyyid Said introduced the crop (indigenous to the Molucca Islands of Indonesia) to the island around 1818. However, Pemba Island now boasts this claim, having roughly three times the number of clove trees. It is through this association with the fragrant crop that the name Spice Islands came about.

However, the industry that probably had the greatest impact on the area was the slave trade, which was introduced by the Portuguese and exploited to a greater extent by the Arabs. The coastline harboured a massive trade in human lives; these slaves were exploited as labourers, not only locally on the clove plantations, but they also fuelled an increasing demand for manual labour in exotic destinations like India and the Far East.

Dhows, the traditional sailing craft of East Africa, coming into Zanzibar harbour.

As the slave trade expanded, European exploration of Tanzania's hinterland began in earnest. German missionaries were some of the first Europeans to risk their lives by venturing into the dark, unknown lands that lay beyond the shores of the Indian Ocean. Later, explorers whose names are famous today for exploits that were both successful and unsuccessful, purposefully penetrated the interior to find, among other goals, the source of the Nile.

Today, Tanzania's coastline and its offshore islands offer sun-drenched tranquillity and panoramic views that are in complete contrast to the rest of the country. Visitors can also immerse themselves in the aura of ancient mosques and ruins that still whisper of long-gone historical triumphs and failures, or they can sink into the tranquil depths of the warm, tropical ocean and marvel at its wealth of marine life.

Cities and Towns

The wide, open expanses of the country make even the smallest of towns important. Throughout Tanzania, people will travel great distances to places that would otherwise be passed by, but these towns act as vital links, keeping local people up to date with current affairs, enabling them to see a doctor or to purchase much-needed supplies. Most cities and towns have telephone communications and postal services.

Dar es Salaam, on the coast, is Tanzania's capital city and the leading centre for commerce, while Arusha, southwest of Kilimanjaro in the north, is the safari capital: a great many adventures begin and end here. There are no large cities in the south, but most supplies can be obtained from the two towns of Mbeya and Iringa. Tabora, Mwanza and Kigoma fill in the gaps in the west and northwest of the country.

ACACIA, TREE OF AFRICA

The image of quintessential Africa is one of golden silhouetted landscapes with the characteristic outline of the flat-topped acacia tree. Acacias are generally thorny and the wood is usually hard, which makes it good for construction, firewood and charcoal.

Many species have a strong, sweet fragrance when in bloom. Classed variously as trees, shrubs and climbers, each acacia species has unique characteristics as its location differs. The number of individual species is too vast to discuss specifically, but many are found in Tanzania. Some of those worth taking a closer look at include:

The whistling thorn *(Acacia drepanolobium)*, found in areas with heavy clay soils, is unique and is named for the large black galls that cover its branches. Holes in the galls create a humming or whistling sound as the wind passes through. These galls are inhabited by a rather fierce ant group that, as a troop, protects the tree from being overbrowsed by wildlife. In a rather symbiotic relationship, the long thorns on the shrubs protect the ant colonies, while the ants themselves use their pincers to ward off overzealous browsers.

The fever tree *(Acacia xanthophloea)* usually occurs in low-lying areas and along rivers. It is easy to recognize as it sometimes grows to great heights, has a yellow powdery-looking bark and white to slightly pink flowers. The fever tree acquired its name from turn-of-the-century pioneers who often set up camp beneath its shade-providing canopy. The travellers regularly came down with fever, and believed it was a vapour emitted by the tree, unaware that the real culprit was the malaria-carrying mosquito which bred in the watery stretches that were never far from the acacias.

The tree that so often epitomizes East African savanna is the umbrella tree *(Acacia tortilis)*. Growing in woodland, grassland and semi-desert areas, this impressive tree can attain heights of 18 m (60 ft). The branches of its gnarled canopy are adorned with slender white spines up to 76 mm (3 in) long and smaller, sharply curved grey spines with black tips. A lush *A. tortilis* woodland of these wide-spreading trees can be seen at Lake Manyara National Park, providing a blessed retreat from the heat. Its inviting branches often play host to prides of sleepy lions.

A street market in Stone Town, the old sector of Zanzibar Island.

Most cities in Tanzania are not noted for their aesthetic qualities and are frequented mainly out of necessity. One can often find a useful – and colourful – market to stock up on water, fuel and provisions. However, it is necessary always to be cautious while visiting the cities. Poverty and crime constantly create risks for the unwary and inexperienced visitor who comes unprepared. The people in the rural areas are generally pleasant.

Vegetation
Due to Tanzania's geographical position, its geological divergence and climatic diversity, many types of vegetation zones are found in the country. Although each vegetation zone is quite distinct, it is not uncommon to see one zone gently merge into another.

The coastal areas feature small patches of pristine and now rare lowland rainforests which continue up the gently rising lower inclines of the Usambara Mountains in the north near Tanzania's border with Kenya. In terms of plant species, this lowland rainforest has the richest variety.

Montane forests are associated with all the larger mountains, such as the Ngorongoro Crater Highlands, Kilimanjaro and Meru. They occur at heights varying from 1,200 m to 3,000 m (3,940–9,845 ft), featuring a great number of plant and tree species in the wetter areas, with a declining array of species as the altitude increases. Montane forest can survive on minimal amounts of annual rainfall as the cooler temperatures characteristic of their location result in lower evaporation rates. Widespread in areas having altitudes of 1,000 to 2,400 m (3,280–7,875 ft) as well as open grassland or forest is the strangler, or wild fig *(Ficus thonningii)*. This indigenous giant begins life as an epiphyte. Seeds of the fig, dropped by birds, often land in the forks of other trees, where they eventually germinate and begin to drop down red-tipped aerial roots. With time these roots reach the ground and grasp hold, eventually developing a more classic root system. Later growing in strength and size, the fig's roots begin to entwine around the host tree which eventually is smothered and dies out. A superb specimen of a strangler fig can be seen on the Mount Meru side of Arusha National Park.

The higher mountain reaches host bands of bamboo forests (up to 3,000 m/9,840 ft) and heath zones (3,000–3,500 m/9,845–11,485 ft) that are rich with giant heather and Philippia. Here, where mist prevails, the vegetation is not affected by the minimal rainfall as the cloud level and shroud of mist offer life-preserving moisture while the cooler temperatures aid the conservation of water through very low evaporation. At even higher altitudes, just below the snow line, moorland of spiky tussock grass is interspersed with abnormally large alpine plants such as giant senecios, lobelias and groundsels.

To the north and northwest of Tanzania, around the Maasai Steppe and the Serengeti, an undulating carpet of red oat grasslands sustains three million head of wildlife during the winter migration cycle. Rivers here support wooded grassland along their banks. Throughout the north of the Serengeti, vegetation is varied. Acacia woodland, equatorial forest and gnarled baobab trees with their characteristic grey wrinkles all occur.

Tanzania's predominant vegetation is made up of acacia savanna and sparse miombo woodland. The savanna undergrowth can grow quite tall, is adaptive and easily regenerates with annual fires. These areas are fringed

A view of the Great Ruaha River, which runs through Ruaha National Park.

by thick bushland which occurs throughout central Tanzania and the western edge of the coastal forest zone. Conversely the savanna bushland, with its thorny and thick shrubs, provides extensive shade and thus inhibits the growth of tall grasses, promoting the growth of low-lying plants such as succulents and semi-succulents. The result is that far fewer fires occur as the fire struggles to establish itself in the thick undergrowth. Visibility for viewing wildlife is limited here and where no paths or roads have been cut through the bush, passage is virtually impossible. To the west, wooded highland mountains experience higher rainfall and nurture black clay soils.

In southern Tanzania, which is lower and drier than the rest of the country and which, unlike most of the country, experiences only one rainy season, the vegetation changes drastically. Reaching across the extent of southern Tanzania, Zambia and Malawi is what is known as miombo woodland comprising mainly *Brachystegia* tree species. The trees do not form a thick canopy overhead as occurs in thick bushland, so sunlight can reach low-level vegetation – thus grasses and plant life flourish in these areas.

The trees comprising the woodland are deciduous, that is, they shed their leaves in the dry season in an effort to preserve water consumption. Characteristic of the miombo belt is the coppery-red hue of their new leaves which unfurl just before the rains, around November.

One cannot fail to notice the enormous variety of vegetation and unique range of habitats as one travels through Tanzania. Particularly pretty are the many wildflowers that bloom in profusion just after the rains, temporarily transforming the lush green of the grassland plains and highlands into fields of riotous colour.

Fauna

As a result of the great diversity of habitats found in Tanzania, it is safe to say that some of the most spectacular concentrations of free-roaming wild animals remaining in the world today occur here. For hundreds of years people have come to Tanzania to experience nature's great bounty – the sheer wild beauty of a land whose highlands and plains teem with a superlative variety and abundance of wildlife.

Of the predators, lion are seen in almost all the parks and reserves, but of special interest are the tree-climbing lions found at Lake Manyara. These animals can often be spotted draped over the branches of trees while they seek respite from the sun's rays. Leopard, although one of the most elusive of predators, inhabit most of the country's protected areas and can be seen in Serengeti's Seronera Valley, as well as in the Selous Game Reserve and Ruaha, Mikumi and Tarangire national parks. For cheetah, the open plains of Tarangire and Serengeti national parks and the Selous should prove the most rewarding. Hunting dogs are spotted fairly regularly in the Ruaha and the Selous, while the golden and black-backed jackals, hyena and bat-eared fox in the Ngorongoro Crater should not be overlooked.

Ungulates (hoofed mammals) can be seen moving between the scrub, open plains and forests as they browse and graze. These include the Maasai giraffe, Burchell's (common) zebra, topi, hartebeest, impala and both Thomson's and Grant's gazelle, of which the latter occurs as far south as the Ruaha. Three species of wildebeest, the 'comical' creature of the plains, occur in Tanzania: the brindled gnu and the more common white-bearded wildebeest inhabit the northern sector of the country, with the Nyasaland gnu occurring south of the Rufiji River.

Buffalo are distributed throughout Tanzania, with enormous herds in the relatively inaccessible Katavi National Park. Easier to see are the smaller though still impressive herds that can be found in Arusha, Tarangire and Ruaha national parks. Of the more

Elephant and zebra are among the abundant wildlife found in the Ngorongoro Crater.

unusual mammal species, look for the rare puku in Katavi, the water-loving sitatunga on Rubondo Island and the gerenuk, with its long, graceful neck, at Mkomazi.

Elephant, quiet giants of the African bush, occur throughout Tanzania. The Selous reputedly has Africa's highest numbers, while the forest of Arusha National Park harbours large herds. Elephant also occur in the Tarangire and Ruaha national parks. The Lerai Forest in Ngorogoro Crater is also good for viewing these gentle giants.

The Gombe Stream and Mahale Mountains national parks are famous for their chimpanzees, while the forests of Arusha harbour the black-and-white colobus monkey. Two endemic primates, the Iringa (or Uehe) red colobus and the Sanje crested mangabey, occur in the Udzungwa Mountains National Park, while Zanzibar's Jozani Forest offers the rare red colobus monkey. Impressive numbers of hippo and crocodile occur in the rivers of the Selous, Ruaha and Katavi, with the largest recorded crocodile population inhabiting Serengeti's Grumeti River.

Wildlife, conservation and tourism are important issues to the government of Tanzania. Programmes are being installed throughout several of the country's conservation areas, not only to initiate a better understanding of the incredible natural resources at hand, but also to help enlighten and educate local communities on the importance of the wildlife.

And, for visitors to Tanzania, the thrill of a classic safari is much the same (although the mode of transportation is now more efficient) – exhilarating sightings are waiting for those curious to pursue them.

THE PEOPLE

Tanzania's population encompasses about 120 ethnic groups, primarily of Bantu-speaking origin. A dozen of these groups together make up roughly half the population, and of them the Sukuma are the largest. But a characteristic peculiar to Tanzania is

A Swahili girl framed in one of the famous doorways of Stone Town, Zanzibar.

that no single ethnic group dominates in terms of size or political influence. This fact, atypical of most African countries, is of great importance as the incidence of conflict amongst distinctive cultures is minimal.

The current population is estimated to be 26 million, with the vast majority dispersed unevenly throughout the rural areas close to the ocean, Tanzania's lakes and the rich, productive highland areas. To the other extreme, insufficient rainfall, poor soil productivity and the presence of tsetse fly have left immense regions of the country's interior void of people.

The majority (98%) of Tanzania's people is made up of two general indigenous groups: the Bantu-speakers whose rural activities today revolve around agriculture and food production; and Nilotic-speakers – pastoralists who originated from the Nile valley, and who are predominantly involved in cattle-keeping. The remaining 2% of the population is made up of Europeans, Asians and Arabs, who generally dwell in Tanzania's urban areas.

The country's lingua franca is Kiswahili, a language of Bantu origin which evolved in the coastal region with contributions from Arabic, Portuguese and English. Kiswahili is spoken by over 95% of Tanzania's population. Although the different ethnic groups may have their own dialects, the use of Kiswahili is widespread throughout the country and is another contributing factor towards the unification of Tanzania's diverse African cultures.

Tanzania's three other major linguistic groups are the Nilotes, Maasai and Luo. After those who speak Kiswahili, the Nilotic-speaking group, who inhabit the north-central highland regions, could be considered second in importance. The Maasai are generally found on the open plains, while the Luo people have established themselves along the eastern shores of Lake Victoria.

Of the various ethnic dialects, the rare Southern Cushitic languages are spoken by the Iraqw people of the northern highlands, which rise south of Lake Manyara. The Khoisan, or 'click', language, linked to the southern African San, is also heard in the volcanic northern highlands where it is spoken by the Sandawe peoples and a smaller group, the Hadzapi.

Though the variety of cultures and ethnic origins throughout Tanzania is enormous, ancient customs and the fundamental ideals and values of the family unit are still widely adhered to. Events marked by the passage of time – birth, puberty, marriage, death and even the passing of the seasons – have great importance and are celebrated with rituals and feasting.

The many ethnic groups within Tanzania make it impossible to discuss each one, but some of the major groups are:

Sukuma (Bantu-speaking)

The Sukuma, or 'people of the north', live in the southern communities of Lake Victoria, though in recent years they have begun to spread outwards. They are heterogeneous: their ancestry is unusually varied as, during the precolonial era, they were arranged into several small chiefdoms which only later unified to form Tanzania's largest ethnic culture. The introduction of trade in the 19th century affected only a small percentage of these chiefdoms, and it was not until well into the 20th century that the Sukuma people showed any outward manifestations of missionary teachings, which tried to establish organized education and the idea of cash crops as opposed to subsistence agriculture. The Sukuma succeeded in mixing their agricultural pursuits, among them cattle herding and cotton cultivation. Working today as a cooperative society, each member of the group plays an important role in the planting and harvesting processes. Dance and music are also an important aspect of traditional Sukuma culture. This tribal group is famous for its 'snake-charming' abilities – members take part in an impressive dance during which they wear a 'live' reptilian costume, that is, the dancers have writhing snakes wound around their neck and shoulders.

Makonde (Bantu-speaking)

The Makonde people of southern Tanzania represent one of the country's five major tribes. They originally migrated north across the Ruvumu River from Mozambique to their present location on the Makonde Plateau, near the eastern shores of Lake Nyasa (Malawi). They are an ardently proud, traditional people who, due to their remoteness, have been able to resist the increasing influence of Western civilization.

The celebrated Makonde wood carvings play an important role in the daily lives of this tribe as they represent more than just a handicraft; they are a centuries-old expression of heritage and culture. The legend of the origin of the Makonde people is based on the tale of a lonely, isolated being, not yet quite human, who carved for himself a female companion from wood and placed her upright in the sun. When night fell, the carving came to life, ending the lonely being's solitary existence. The woman twice conceived and bore a child but on both occasions the child died. After each disheartening event, the woman urged her partner to move to higher ground. Finally, on their third attempt, while living high in the plateau region, a third child was born, and lived. This child, as legend tells, is the first Makonde.

Through the retelling of this tale, the role of women in the life of the Makonde people is highly respected and is often depicted in their fascinating carvings. Usually created from rich ebony, the carvings also portray with great expressiveness the Makonde lifestyle, sometimes as grotesquely unhappy figures, sometimes as forms that are jubilant and full of elation.

Chagga (Bantu-speaking)

The Chagga are a successful group who live mainly on the southern slopes of Kilimanjaro. Here, in one of the most densely populated areas in Tanzania, the Chagga have taken advantage of the richly fertile volcanic soil and prosper economically by growing coffee as their main cash crop.

Receptive early on to ecclesiastical influences both religious and educational brought by the missionaries, the Chagga have succeeded in generating a considerable income from the sale of coffee and from enterprising ventures into cooperative cash crops as a direct result of their higher education levels.

Haya (Bantu-speaking)

The Haya people are found inhabiting the western shores of Lake Victoria. Like the Chagga, they took a relatively early interest in education, which has led to many members of the community, through their higher education qualifications, procuring jobs throughout Tanzania.

The area in which the Haya live is densely populated and necessitates the crop rotation of bananas and coffee in semipermanent settlements. The Haya have successfully grown and traded in coffee since before the arrival of the Europeans, who in turn showed their interest in the crop. Today, using processing plants, the Haya successfully export their product despite being some 1,400 km (870 miles) from the coast.

Nyamwezi (Bantu-speaking)

The Nyamwezi people live in central Tanzania near the town of Tabora. Their origins stem from a cross-cultural blending of many different ethnic groups which started off as a number of small individual chiefdoms. The Nyamwezi were exceptional traders, particularly during the mid-19th century when the flourishing trade routes included their shores. The name given to them by the early Swahili traders along the coast roughly translates to mean 'people of the moon', probably an indication of their emergence from Tanzania's vast interior.

Today, the Nyamwezi lifestyle is a difficult one as the region is heavily infested with tsetse fly and insufficient supplies of water inhibit strong agricultural progress.

Ha (Bantu-speaking)

The people of the Ha culture live in the far western reaches of Tanzania close to the Burundi border, and along the upper edge of Lake Tanganyika in tsetse fly-infested bushland. This tribe still manages to preserve its customs and culture; its members tend cattle and still wear traditional hide clothing.

A strong belief in mysticism and the appeasement of ancestors plays an important role in the Ha people's lives. They are renowned too for their dance celebrations, and often participate in ancient rhythmic dances that require the dancers to tap to complicated musical beats.

Hehe (Bantu-speaking)

The Hehe people have settled predominantly in the Iringa Highlands towards the south of the country, where their current chief lives in an impressive house at Kalenga. Their origins are heterogeneous, but little is known of them before the 1850s. Even the origin of their name has led to some controversy. Some say it relates to the eerie, frightening cry they emitted when they entered into battle; some elders maintain it is associated with their ancestors and place of origin. Whichever tale holds the truth, there is little doubt about the fierce, warriorlike reputation that surrounds these people. The Hehe were already a force to be reckoned with before they gained strength through military expansion in the mid-1800s. Their chiefs held authority sanctioned by supernatural beings and they were reported to possess mystical powers – an allusion to their 'war medicines'.

Probably the most famous of their battles was against the Germans in 1891, which they won; without doubt their most famous warrior was the leader of that battle, Chief Mkwawa. There is a small museum in Kalenga still today, displaying information about Mkwawa. The local caretaker will tell the tale of the intrepid chief's battle with great enthusiasm and passion.

In the early days of the trade routes, the southernmost access route passed through Hehe land and the Hehe lost no time in becoming energetic participants in the fast-expanding ivory business. They traded tusks for guns, fine European cloth, beads and alcohol. Ten years into Mkwawa's reign, the Hehe people had become wealthy and self-confident. Today, they are a peaceful tribe and spend their time overseeing their agricultural interests such as corn, and tending to their cattle and goats.

In precolonial times the Hehe practised many traditional rituals: they were famous for the unique burial ceremonies of their chiefs, in which they marked the chief's grave with elephant tusks. Using all the cloth the chief had received through trade, they would wrap his body into a cocoon. The burial rite then continued with the offering of a live sacrificial member from the chiefdom, whose job it was to hold the cocooned body in his lap. However, education has become an important issue in Hehe society today and they have adopted many Western ways.

A young man transporting charcoal.

Maasai (Nilotic-speaking)

The name Maasai means 'speaker of the Maa language'. Though their true derivation has never been proved, it is generally accepted that the Maasai are Nilotic in origin and that they arrived in Kenya and Tanzania from North Africa around the 17th century by following the Nile River. In the Maasai world, there are approximately 12 different groups defined by their geographical location; the largest group, named Ilkisongo, lives in Tanzania. Most Maasai are dispersed throughout the northern plains and highland areas; however, in recent years they have begun moving further south in small numbers.

Although they still retain relatively similar characteristics, each of the various group tends to have its own dialects, ceremonies and authoritative bodies; the groups even vary the style and colouring of their clothing and beadwork.

The Maasai are a tall, handsome people, and in Tanzania are often seen wearing their traditional clothing in deep, rich tones of purple and indigo-blue. As with many Nilotic cultures, it is not uncommon to see members of the Maasai people with their two lower centre teeth removed, or to meet women who have had their heads completely shaved as a sign of beauty. It is often remarked upon that the Maasai's clothing, known as a shuka, and the accessories of the young Ilmorani (warriors) – short knives and their intricate plaited and woven hairstyles – closely resemble those of the ancient Romans who occupied northern Africa. At one time the Maasai had a reputation as fierce warriors and still today, as the young men undergo initiation rites in order to progress through the ranks of the various age-groups, they must prove themselves as warriors. At this stage, they need to endure many tests of courage and strength before they eventually become junior elders, and so take a participatory, decision-making role in the community. From junior elders, they will progress finally to become senior elders.

The Maasai are pastoralists, believing strongly that all of the cattle in the world were given to them by God. Customs and tradition are of the utmost importance to them, and playing an intricate part in their lives is the oral history of their people, preserved through stories, songs and prayers, and through the enactment of traditional ceremonies. Their daily lives are geared around their children, the security of their community, and taking care of their cattle, goats and donkeys.

The Maasai refer to Tanzania's dormant volcano, Lengai, on the edge of the Ngorongoro Conservation Area, as 'Oldonyo le Engai', or Mountain of God. They believe it is here that God lives and it is also where they will pray for things precious in their lives – their children and their cattle.

Maasai life is semi-nomadic as they move across the plains in a constant search for good water and grazing. The plains, and more so the grass, play an important part in the tribe's existence, best summed up by the Maasai saying: 'God gave us cattle and grass. Without grass there are no cattle, and without cattle there are no Maasai'.

Iraqw (Cushitic-speaking)

Living in north-central Tanzania is a unique group of people whose population is low, but whose history can be traced back to ancient times: the Iraqw. As early as the first millennium BC, individuals were already living in sections of Kenya and northern Tanzania in the Great Rift Valley. Through evidence that they used stone tools, and through linguistics and their cattle-herding tendencies, it is believed that they probably originated in southern Ethiopia. It appears that these unusual people remained in the northern section of Tanzania, not venturing any further south. They went about their daily lives harmoniously sharing the land with the Khoisan-speaking people, who were hunter-gatherers and who had already been settled in the area for quite some time.

Although the Iraqw are mainly pastoralists, the Engaruka area near Lake Natron has furnished evidence that these Southern Cushitic speakers made use of iron and participated in agricultural ventures around AD 500.

Sandawe and Hadzapi (Khoisan-speaking)

Also in the north-central region are two groups of hunter-gatherers believed to be the ancestors of mainland Tanzania's earliest inhabitants. Evidence from skeletal remains, stone tools, weapons, shelters and rock paintings dates their presence to as far back as 3,000 to 5,000 years ago, if not earlier. Today, there are numerous rock paintings that can be viewed in the Kondoa/Kolo area, halfway between Arusha and Dodoma. A widely dispersed cultural group, the majority of the Khoisan-speaking people, known as San (or Hottentot, the early Dutch name for them), are found in southern Africa.

An elaborate Maasai headdress. The dress styles of the various Maasai groups are all distinct.

HISTORICAL BACKGROUND

MAINLAND TANZANIA

The piecing together of Tanzania's history, and its inextricable link with exotic cultures from around the world, creates a unique and intricate puzzle. The lack of written history and the unreliability of oral tradition certainly allow for exaggerations in the ancient tales passed down through the centuries. It is mostly through the remnants of ancient Stone Age sites that we have come to understand where Tanzania's early inhabitants came from and how they used to live. It is believed that Tanzania's first mainland inhabitants had established themselves as early as 3,000 to 5,000 years ago, quite possibly before this. These people who settled in the north and north-central regions were hunters and gatherers speaking Khoisan, or the 'click' language, similar to that spoken by the San of southern Africa.

By the first millennium BC, new arrivals – a Cushitic-speaking people from Ethiopia and Somalia in northeast Africa – settled in the northern regions. They brought with them their cattle and their knowledge of the use of stone tools. Though lifestyles were different, they cohabited with the already present hunter-gatherers.

Then, during the first 500 years AD, small groups of Bantu-speaking peoples began migrating into Tanzania and other central and east African countries; because of the direction from which they came, their pre-Bantu origins are believed to stem from West Africa. Their lives revolved around the subsistence farming of vegetables, millet and sorghum, which was made easier by the use of iron implements. These Bantu-speaking peoples tended to inhabit the wetter areas as they made cultivation easier. They participated in hunting but supplemented their diets by gathering fruits, roots and tubers. In the areas to the north and northwest of Lake Victoria, they are known to have also relied heavily on fishing. Many early Iron Age sites can be found throughout the north.

The Livingstone Stanley Monument (ABOVE AND TOP) *at the Cultural Centre on Livingstone Street (Ujiji) commemorates East Africa's explorers.*

It appears there was little contact between the cultivators and pastoralists, as population numbers were small and the tracts of land separating them vast.

Possibly from the 12th through the 18th centuries, people from the north moved into Tanzania, impacting on the distribution of the already settled Bantu-speaking groups, and in some cases affecting their societal codes and customs. These new arrivals generally were cattle-herders belonging to three cultural and linguistic groups: Cushites who probably originated from Ethiopia, Nilotes from the Nile valley, and the more recent Paranilotic group

EAST AFRICA'S GREAT EUROPEAN EXPLORERS

RICHARD BURTON AND JOHN HANNING SPEKE
Burton, the son of a high-ranking British officer, grew up in France and Italy, but received no formal education and was considered to be unruly and undisciplined. Among his many exploits were a curtailed stint at Oxford University, a short spell with the Army in India, a pilgrimage to Mecca, and sojourns in Brazil, Damascus and Trieste.

Speke and Burton arrived in Zanzibar in 1856 with the hope of finding the source of the Nile. In 1857, they undertook successful expeditions into the interior but, on reaching Lake Tanganyika in February 1858, both were in bad health and needed several days to recover. They explored the lake and discovered the Ruzizi River flowing into its waters. Somewhat disappointed they returned to Tabora, where Speke set out again, this time in search of Lake Nyanza to the north. Burton remained in Tabora to write of their finds, still believing that the Nile's source lay close to Lake Tanganyika.

Speke returned to tell of his discovery of the lake to the north, which he had named Victoria and which he believed was the source of the Nile. An outraged and disbelieving Burton ordered the expedition to return to the coast. A debate was to ensue in England, but first Speke returned to Africa in 1860, going directly to Lake Victoria with James August Grant. However Grant fell ill and was left in Karagwe while Speke continued on.

In July 1862, alone, Speke claimed he had found the Nile's headwaters; he gave the name Ripon Falls to the spot where the Nile emerges from the lake. He arrived back in England to a hero's welcome, but trouble soon brewed, and he was forced into a public debate against Burton in 1864 at the British Association for the Advancement of Science. Speke was found mysteriously dead the day before the debate was to take place.

DAVID LIVINGSTONE AND HENRY MORTON STANLEY Born in Scotland in 1813, Livingstone put himself through medical school, joining the London Missionary Society from 1841 to 1863. He explored the Zambezi River in 1853, and was the first European to see Victoria Falls. Later, he was appointed to 'find the source of the Nile', and he set off in January 1866. After three years, the rough terrain, harsh conditions and malaria took their toll and Livingstone became gravely ill. After being nursed back to health, he continued his journey for several more years. The outside world had heard little of him until November 1871 when his whereabouts were discovered by Henry Stanley, a Welsh-born American journalist commissioned by the *New York Herald* to find the legendary Dr Livingstone.

Livingstone and Stanley travelled extensively together, but the former refused to return to England as he still maintained that the Nile's source had not been found, and that it lay at the headwaters of the Lualaba River. Livingstone decided to travel to Tabora to buy provisions, and await additional bearers and supplies to be sent by Stanley once he had reached the coast. Nine months after leaving Tabora Livingstone was found dead in Zambia. It is said his African companions buried his heart under the tree where he died. His embalmed body was carried all the way back to Bagamoyo on the coast. It was finally laid to rest in England, in Westminster Abbey.

On Stanley's earlier return to the coast, he had carried with him Livingstone's memoirs and documentation of his previous travels, which also told of his horror of and struggle against the growing slave trade. It was Stanley who, after extensively sailing the waters of both inland lakes, Tanganyika and Victoria, from 1874 to 1877, finally agreed with Speke's previous discovery that the Nile's headwaters lay at the Ripon Falls on Lake Victoria.

to which the Maasai belong. Many of the newcomers contributed to existing cultures, but the earliest arrivals appear to have been absorbed by the resident Bantu-speakers. It is still possible, however, to find remnant groups of these early migrant peoples in modern-day Tanzania.

The pastoralist Maasai were some of the later immigrants to arrive in northern Tanzania in the 17th and 18th centuries. Constantly moving their cattle southward as they searched for new pastures, the Maasai fast became recognized for their strength and gained a not unwarranted reputation as fierce

The house in Zanzibar where intrepid explorer Dr David Livingstone lived.

warriors. Some of the Bantu-speakers they encountered slowly adopted some of the Maasai customs, such as their circumcision and initiation rites.

During this period, Bantu-speaking peoples slowly moved towards central Tanzania. Their movement was, however, impeded by the high incidence of tsetse fly, which severely affected their cattle, and the inadequate rainfall levels, which inhibited cultivation. The number of people in these communities, which had tribal governing structures firmly in place, was relatively low until the 1700s and 1800s (unlike those of the ethnic groups found in the northwestern and northeastern territories of Tanzania). Some areas of the interior were still void of people in the early part of the 20th century. Today these areas are generally still sparsely populated.

German Imperialism

During the early 1800s, trade routes to the interior were being established. Essential networks were developing throughout the country, making goods available in remote areas and promoting the exchange of high-demand commodities, such as ivory, from the interior to the coast. Three main trade routes were established: the northern and central routes were geared predominantly for ivory, while the southern route leading to the coastal town of Kilwa supported the existing slave trade (*see* page 39). Slave raiders were extremely aggressive and the southeast areas of Tanzania suffered heavily from this barter of human lives, particularly since the ethnic groups comprised small units and their militant strength was weak.

The first Europeans to enter into mainland Tanzania were Germans Johann Krapf and Johannes Rebmann, representing the British-based Church Missionary Society. At this time, the town of Tabora in central Tanzania became an important centre for the early European traders and entrepreneurs. The 1880s brought an influx of zealous Europeans to East Africa, spurred on by reports of adventurous journeys into the 'dark continent' by Richard Burton, John Hanning Speke, and later David Livingstone and Henry Morton Stanley. This wave of intrepid pioneers arrived on Tanzanian soil, intent on exploration, colonization and Christianization of the indigenous tribes.

An event that was to affect the history of Tanzania for many years to come was the arrival in 1884, under suspicious circumstances, of Dr Karl Peters, who represented the Society for German Colonisation. Making his way through the interior, he met with many local ruling chiefs, signing treaties with them under the guise of promising to place them under German protection. The treaties were approved by Bismarck, who headed up the German government, and who at the time considered these Tanzanian territories as German protectorates. In 1885, Karl Peters led the way for German involvement in Tanzania: he set out to establish the German East African Company.

In 1885, a meeting of British and German delegates formalized Anglo-German interests in the East African territories. The Anglo-German Agreement of 1886 recorded the following: Sultan Seyyid Said, although not included in the meetings, was allotted the islands of Zanzibar, Pemba, Mafia and Lamu in Kenya, and a coastal strip of the mainland that extended from Mozambique in the south as far north as certain towns in Somalia. The British took over what is now Kenya, and the Germans controlled the large portion of land whose borders define what we know as Tanzania today. Two years later, the Germans took a 50-year lease from the sultan on Tanzania's coastal portion, thus strengthening Germany's strategic and economic position in the region.

By the 1890s, faults in the structure of the German East African Company were beginning to show, as well as German mishandling of the local people. The company's trend of financial failure forced the German government to take it over in April 1891 and form the new German East Africa.

One of the tribes in Tanzania's southern central region, around Iringa, was the warlike Hehe. After two years in exile and fierce ensuing battles, Chief Mkwawa had gained power as leader of the Hehe, a position left by his deceased father. The tribe was politically and militarily powerful, and Mkwawa worked at building up their military strength.

By 1883 Mkwawa had had a wooden stockade built in Kalenga, not far from Iringa. From here Hehe power was felt over much of the southern reaches of Tanzania as battles with the Ngoni, Nyamwezi and Gogo groups ensued. Having sufficiently prospered, the construction of a stone-and-mud fort of huge

A crucifix made from the tree under which David Livingstone died in Zambia.

dimensions began. History relates that, by this time, Hehe forces had gained control of the ivory trade, and the transportation of tusks was occurring regularly.

Steadfast in his ambitions, Chief Mkwawa pursued his efforts to forge a path to the north and east. These areas would allow the obtaining of important information pertaining to the ever-growing ivory trade and caravan routes; at the same time local tribes there were smaller and less organized, and thus easy targets for his forces.

However, as the Hehe began to expand their territory further to the east and north, the Germans were at the same time setting up administrative posts deeper in the interior of the country. This initially had little effect on the Hehe, but, when they continually raided people who were under German protection, the Germans decided that Mkwawa needed to be dealt with after attempts to negotiate with subordinate Hehe chiefs failed.

The Germans were pre-empted by Mkwawa on 17 August 1891, when Hehe warriors attacked the German unit, killing the commander and many of its members. Triumphant, Mkwawa confiscated arms and ammunition, but not without a heavy price. Hehe losses were extensive.

Retaliatory battles continued and, on 30 October 1894, the Germans launched a surprise attack on Mkwawa's unfinished fort at Kalenga, where cannon fire quickly brought the Hehe forces down. However Mkwawa escaped, and he continued to wage a guerrilla war against the Germans with his dwindling forces for the next four years.

Finally, in June 1898, legend tells that only two of his loyal men remained with Chief Mkwawa; exhausted and ill from the continuous manhunt, Mkwawa shot one of his guards and instructed his surviving aide to tell the Germans where they could find him. He then built a large fire, shot himself and fell into the flames.

His plan was not entirely successful as only his torso and limbs were burned. When the Germans arrived, his head was removed and sent to Germany. The skull was returned to the Hehe people in 1954 and is now on display at a small museum in Kalenga.

The Maji Maji Rebellion

During the 1890s, the Germans introduced cash crops such as sisal and cotton, but in terms of numbers their administrative capacity was limited. Where they could, they rallied traditional chiefs to act as middlemen in administration, but in many areas, particularly in the southern regions, communities were small and lacked territorial chiefs and strong political organization. To remedy the situation, the Germans began to utilize the strength of *maakida,* or local administrative agents. These agents were given virtually unlimited powers and they made their strength felt. The ethnic groups in the south, already demoralized by the vicious slave-trade raiders, had little recourse.

In 1893 the Germans established the Department of Surveying and Agriculture, making Tanzania the finest mapped region in East Africa before World War I. Transportation became a focal issue, and in 1894 the construction of a road from Tanga, on the coast in the far north of the country, to Kilimanjaro commenced. The railroad followed soon when, in 1896, a line from Tanga to Moshi at the foot of Kilimanjaro was started; it was completed in 1911. In 1905, the construction of a railway line running west across the entire country from Dar es Salaam to Kigoma on Lake Tanganyika commenced and, with its completion in 1914, further opened trade markets.

With the development of transportation, the emphasis was being shifted to the expansion of the agricultural plantations; land was increasingly being taken away from the local people. Labour started to become a problem, so the Germans used indirect methods to recruit the necessary workforce: by using their localized administrative agents, they imposed a hut tax, payable in cash, which made it necessary for the majority of the locals to join the labour force to earn more money. However, the poor labour relations that resulted began to take their toll. Matters worsened with the institution of a cotton scheme in the south by the German governor of the time. All capable labourers were coerced into growing the cotton and working conditions were appalling. In 1905 a gradual yet important resistance movement was started in the south-central regions. Many local African groups united under the guidance of a *mganga,* or 'doctor', who, through his spiritual leadership, nurtured a belief in his people that through the 'power' of a sacred water, *maji,* they would have the strength and ability to deflect the Europeans' bullets.

This resistance movement became known as the Maji Maji Rebellion. By the end of the rebellion, in 1907, the tribespeople had suffered tremendous losses as their spears and the power of the maji proved no match for the heavy artillery used by the Germans. But their point had been made clear. Through this African unity and the significant resistance it achieved, the reform of German tactics was inevitable.

With the arrival of the first nonmilitary governor to German East Africa came considerable change. African land rights began to enjoy some protection, and the local tribes were encouraged in their agricultural ventures. Education was given a new emphasis, although actual government involvement continued to be minimal. However, through the activities of missionaries, religious and educational pursuits increased in importance. At first many lessons were given in the local dialects, but the use of Swahili gradually took over in education, as it was rapidly becoming universally understood.

The number of European plantations was steadily growing however, despite the risks posed by the sporadic rebellions of the locals. By 1912 it was estimated that the number of plantations had grown in the previous seven years from 578 to a monumental 758. At the same time African communities also showed

Sisal, one of Tanzania's main cash crops, growing in a plantation at Pangani, on the coast.

strong participatory roles in the country's agricultural development; the Haya in the northwest accounted for three-quarters of the coffee production, while the Sukuma south of Lake Victoria accounted for three-quarters of the production of peanuts.

The Birth of Tanganyika

With the onset of World War I in 1914, German East Africa was to undergo drastic change. In August of that year, the British began tactical advancements towards the Germans which would prevail for the ensuing three years. German troops held steadfast in their resistance, however. It was only in 1917 that they finally lost their stronghold to the British military.

Under British rule the country became known as Tanganyika. In July 1922 it was declared a mandated territory under the League of Nations, to be administered by the British. All Germans, even those involved in missionary work, were expelled from the country. The war had ravaged Tanganyika. Agricultural interests had petered to a halt while disease and famine were rampant throughout the land. The new administrative body was to prove ineffective in many areas of responsibility. Capital investment from Britain was slow and therefore progress of reform and growth in social, political and economic spheres was sluggish. Tsetse fly infestation, low rainfall and poor soils made the exploitation of the country's natural resources a slow and difficult process.

The British did, however, encourage small farmers and many efficient cooperative schemes were implemented. During the 1920s agricultural ventures surpassed the production levels achieved during German rule. The export business seemed to be rising steadily and the production of gold increased, but little emphasis was placed on transportation, education or other social services. Wage structures and urban residential zoning were biased towards the colonials.

With Tanganyika's second British governor, Donald Cameron, in place, a process of 'indirect rule' was introduced whereby local chiefs became agents for government and administration processes. Funding was still not forthcoming from Britain and the lack of colonial manpower to serve at the local level was an important factor in the application of indirect rule. Unfortunately, the chiefs were used as puppets and, sadly, they began to lose their legitimacy among their own people. Cameron divided the land into eleven provinces to enable the territory to be better governed, and he established the Legislative Council, although there was no Arab or African representation.

In 1925 the ousted Germans were allowed to return to Tanganyika. Soon, alongside the Greeks, they made up the highest numbers of European immigrants, although in the years up to 1931, the Asian population (drawn mainly from the Gujerat region in India) would grow by 15,000 to a total of 25,000.

A revealing report in 1925 by the Ormsby-Gore East Africa Commission on the dearth of education in the country finally sparked an interest which had the effect of several government schools being added to the existing fold of missionary institutions.

Times were difficult, though, in Tanganyika during the 1930s and the depression further inhibited the provision of funds towards new investment or for government use. Until after World War II, it was almost impossible to obtain an education beyond the secondary level, and even then there was only one college available to all of British East Africa.

A push was made to increase the country's exports but, in general, rights for all Africans were making little progress. In 1929 an alliance named the African Association was formed by an increasing number of educated and politically astute Africans, most of whom held teaching jobs or who were employed in low-level civil service positions, and in 1934 an affiliated organization was set up on the island of Zanzibar.

The focus of the organization was predominantly aimed at social and educational issues, but during the 1930s the issues of political imbalances at last began to raise their head.

The Move to Independence

As World War II progressed, Tanganyika focused on becoming self-sufficient, with its strength lying in food crops, and the production of sisal and rubber which made a dramatic yet short-lived comeback. The war produced no conflict in Tanganyika, but approximately 80,000 Africans served under British command during the war. Transportation and road systems underwent some improvement but, by the end of the war, an educational system and medical services were sorely lacking. As resentment grew among the population, the African Association (AA) experienced an increase in its membership. By 1946 Tanganyika was placed under the trusteeship of the United Nations.

In 1948 the African Association split with its affiliate in Zanzibar, becoming the Tanganyika Africa Association (TAA). Based in Dar es Salaam, the organization's interests were steadily becoming more political. Wages, education and fair representation in government continued to be key issues. Under the leadership of Julius K Nyerere, a schoolteacher educated at Makerere College in Uganda and, later, Edinburgh University in Scotland, where he obtained a degree in social sciences, the TAA changed its name to the Tanganyika African National Union (TANU). Nyerere's beliefs strongly rejected the idea of multiracialism and tribalism. His organization called for fair representation in government and for an African majority at all government levels, thereby presenting Tanganyika as an African country. Independence was clearly TANU's goal.

Colonial influences were still powerful during these years, and the administrative bodies worked hard to keep Nyerere and TANU at bay. They passed laws that prohibited civil service employees from becoming involved in political organizations, and even went so far as to prohibit Nyerere from speaking in public. Despite this official resistance, Nyerere was able to claim in 1956 that TANU's membership had grown to 100,000. The struggles of the organization bore fruit when the 1958 and 1959 elections led to

The Askari Monument is a landmark on Samora Machel Avenue in Dar es Salaam.

TANU candidates gaining a majority of seats in parliament. On 15 May 1961, the wheels were put in motion towards self-government, and on 9 December 1961, independence was granted to the country, with Nyerere becoming the first prime minister.

Zanzibar and Tanzania's Coastal Strip

As early as AD500 (if not earlier) the Greeks made reference to the Tanzanian coast. In the 9th and 10th centuries, Arabs from the Persian Gulf were conducting trade with the Tanzanian locals. By the 12th century, Shirazis originally from the Persian Gulf and Omani Arabs, as well as others translocating to Tanzania from trading areas elsewhere along the east coast, had firmly established themselves in the trade business on the islands of Zanzibar and Pemba and

The picturesque 'spice island' of Zanzibar.

Tanzania's coastal strip. The 13th century saw them gain control over two islands which lie to the south of Zanzibar, namely Kilwa Kisiwani and Mafia.

By the 14th century the Bantu language, influenced by Arabic introduced by the traders, formed the basis of what was to become modern-day Swahili. Spoken mainly by the non-Arab communities, it was later adopted by most coastal and island dwellers. At this time, the people of the coastal regions came from three main ethnic groups: the indigenous African people who were already being dominated by the more powerful newcomers and who supplied the labour workforce, the newly translocated Arabs, and the ruling ranks of Afro-Arab origin.

Trading areas were organized into small city-states. Kilwa Kisiwani became a stronghold and gained significant control over the trade routes, in particular certain routes that facilitated the transport of gold. From the 13th through to the 15th centuries, trade rapidly increased due to the fact that Africa contained rich reserves of commodities such as ivory, gold, iron and the steadily increasing need for slaves.

A dramatic change occurred in 1498 when Vasco da Gama arrived on the East African shores. He was followed shortly after by ships of heavily armed Portuguese who stormed through the coastal area and overwhelmed its small city-states. Kilwa Kisiwani fell in 1505, and by 1506 Portugal had seized control of a major portion of the East African coast and its Indian Ocean trade. However, north of the Ruvuma River separating Mozambique from Tanzania, Portuguese rule was not permitted easily. Continuous rebellions plagued their reign and a lack of administrative cohesiveness further aided their eventual demise.

The Portuguese stronghold, Fort Jesus in Mombasa, Kenya, built in 1593, ensured that their rule would last for another 100 years, although their strength and authority were in fact minimal. An Arab attack in both Mombasa and Malindi on the Kenyan coast, which resulted in the fort being held temporarily by the Arabs, helped to weaken Portuguese domination.

The crucial arrival of Omani Arabs in the 1650s provided valuable assistance in the defence of Tanzania's coastal towns. In 1698 the Arabs seized Fort Jesus in Kenya, thereafter establishing a fortified presence on the east coast. Although the Portuguese in Tanzania had been resoundingly defeated, their power in Mozambique would continue for another 277 years. With the departure of the Portuguese and the settling in of the Omani Arabs, Tanzania's coastal communities found themselves under foreign domination once again. Although the Arabs were in the minority, they brought about much change as their strength continued to grow. Local leaders offered resistance and did not willingly surrender their authority, but, when the new Busaidi dynasty came to power in Oman in 1741, intensified pressure led to an increasing number of Omani Arabs heading for Tanzania's east coast.

The Burgeoning Slave Trade

An already established slave industry was now extremely vulnerable to exploitation. Until recent times, the trade had existed predominantly for local markets, but a rising need for foreign labour swiftly increased the demand. The French colonies in particular supplemented this demand, but a large proportion of slaves was also needed by the Arabs for new agricultural ventures along the coastal area, among them the growing clove industry. Zanzibar and the town of Kilwa Kivinje, being well placed on the dhow routes to facilitate transportation across the seas, underwent rapid growth with the mushrooming of the slave trade.

The desire for Africa's other valuable commodities (ivory, rhino horn, tortoiseshell and spices) also continued to grow, and the Arab and Swahili traders negotiated with the indigenous tribes of the interior, so that, by the late 18th century, the Nyamwezi people of the Tabora region were acting as porters for these prized goods.

Sultan Seyyid Said came into power in Muscat, Oman, on the Arabian Peninsula in 1806. During his leadership, Arab control over the east coast area took a firm hold. His introduction of cloves as a commercial crop had a huge impact on the area. Plantations expanded, with many of the locals losing their land and being forced into hard labour. The success of the clove plantations heightened the need for labour, and slaves were brought from the interior to fill this gap.

A large number of European traders, most of whom were British, were also present in Zanzibar. Appalled by the barter of human lives, their influence resulted in the Moresby Treaty of 1822, which was agreed to by the sultan and European representatives. It attempted to curtail the slave trade by prohibiting the purchase of human lives by Christian governments.

The 1820s and 1830s saw the continual expansion of Arab influence. During the twenties, the Oman dynasty seized control of Pemba Island, and in 1837 they took Mombasa in Kenya. By 1840 Said moved his government from Oman to Zanzibar, offering expatriation to the Indian community, which numbered around 2,000 at the time (the Indians were respected for their financial expertise). In 1841 a British consul was assigned to Zanzibar with the main task of monitoring the anti-slavery movement, but the battle waged on. In 1845 another British

The People's Palace in Stone Town (Zanzibar) houses a museum dedicated to the sultans.

This Arab/German fort at Bagamoyo on the north coast was once used to hold slaves.

treaty made an attempt to prevent the Arabs exporting slaves from Zanzibar to the Arabian Peninsula, but the trade elsewhere along the Tanzanian coast and the slipping of the Arab dhows through the coastal blockade were not fully addressed.

Nearing the time of Sultan Seyyid's death in 1856, Zanzibar had prospered to become an extremely wealthy city as a result of its lucrative slave trade and its growth in clove production – it was providing three-quarters of world demand. Sultan Majid succeeded Said and ruled for the next 14 years. Under Majid's rule, continued attempts to abolish the slave trade seemed to have little effect. However, slavery was presented with major obstacles in 1873 when a new treaty called for the total abolition of slave markets in Zanzibar and the exporting of human lives, while in 1876 the gathering of slaves along the coastal mainland and along the caravan routes of the interior was prohibited. Reluctantly, Sultan Seyyid Barghash, who had come into power in 1870, had no choice but to agree to the terms.

German trade with Zanzibar consisted of roughly a third of the island's business during this time. In 1888, the Germans acquired a 50-year lease on the Sultan's mainland coastal strip, which still remained under Arab ownership according to the Anglo-German Agreement of 1886. Later, Zanzibar and Pemba became British protectorates with the signing of the 1890 Anglo-German Agreement on East Africa. In 1891 the sultan ceded the Tanganyika coastline to the German East India Company.

The Omani Arabs, despite being in the minority, formed Zanzibar's wealthy social élite, and, although the sultans ruled Zanzibar, British authority gained a stronger foothold in the ensuing years. The slave trade had supposedly ceased, but it was still ongoing. Change came gradually when in 1897 the British administration put into effect the laws that were written into the earlier proclamations of 1876, which prohibited any gathering of slaves throughout the east coast and interior. Slaves were given the opportunity to apply for their freedom, and compensation was paid to slave-owners for the loss of their labourers. However, no job programmes were made available and freed slaves often fell prey to vagrancy through unemployment. Subsequently, the number of people remaining within the confines of slavery stayed high for some time.

Zanzibar's Independence

In the years preceding World War II, change in Zanzibar's political and social structure was lethargic. Zanzibar was still considered an Arab state, yet most of the high-ranking positions were held by the British with Arabs holding middle-level authority and Asians in the lower ranks. Arabs not involved in administration still controlled the clove industry and other agricultural crops, while the Asian community was involved in commercial ventures. The Africans of Tanganyika's mainland had little representation.

Gradually organizations to assist in increasing the social awareness amongst the ethnic groups gained interest. Zanzibar's arm of the African Association was recognized in 1934 and in 1939 joined forces with the original organization on the Tanganyika mainland. In the same year, the Shirazi Association was formed. Arab and Asian communities, having had to deal with financial issues such as compensation for the loss of slave labour, had already formed their own informal organizations. Political issues only really surfaced after the war, however.

During the 1950s, political, social and religious differences were becoming apparent throughout the islands. The Muslim Arab and Shirazi communities intermarried, although they disagreed on many issues, but both groups had little interest in the local Africans. The fifties saw an insurgence of political dominance.

Anti-colonial sentiments began to brew, and the British found their Arab 'allies' turning against them. The Arabs, though still a minority, were beginning to think about independence. Thus the Zanzibar Nationalist Party (ZNP) was formed, to which the Shirazi, as subjects of the sultan, were permitted membership; however the local Africans were excluded from the organization. The aim of the party was official representation in the Legislative Council by an elective common roll. Constitutional adjustments had been, in the past, initiated by the colonial authorities, but these did not include elections. The Arab community began a government boycott.

The British finally agreed to elections taking place in 1957. The voter's roll included only subjects of the sultan. The Shirazi, undecided on what path to take, eventually combined efforts with a small number of African nationals eligible to vote, and succeeded in denying the Zanzibar Nationalist Party the six seats available on the Legislative Council. With the continuing conflict, the various separate organizations formed by the Shirazis and Africans joined forces to become the Afro-Shirazi Union (ASU).

Discord over finance, a lack of organization and differing attitudes towards the Arabs set in. These problems were made worse by the breaking away, in 1959, of Shirazi ASU members from Pemba. They in turn formed a new association, the Zanzibar and Pemba People's Party (ZPPP). The old ASU became known as the Afro-Shirazi Party (ASP).

During elections held in 1961, the Afro-Shirazi Party won almost half of the newly allotted seats with 40% of the vote, the Zanzibar Nationalist Party took 36% of the vote, and the Zanzibar and Pemba People's Party came in with 17%. A shuffling of the minority ZPPP, allying itself with the other lesser parties, saw the electoral process end in a draw. New elections were rescheduled, with the addition of one seat.

The islands saw considerable unrest over the next two years after the new elections resulted in the Afro-Shirazi Party and the Zanzibar Nationalist Party winning even seats. However, the advantage of the ZNP's alliance with the ZPPP allowed the former to shape government. Riots ensued with many injuries and fatalities.

Support for the ASP increased, and fearing that self-government would be delayed through the continued dispute between ASP and ZNP, the efforts of the Pan African Freedom Movement for East, Central and Southern Africa brought the opposing parties together. Self-government was granted in July 1963, followed by elections for 31 seats. Together the ZNP and ZPPP gained sufficient votes to form the government.

Independence from Britain was finally granted to Zanzibar on 10 December 1963. A period of discontent followed and in January 1964, after much violence and unrest, the ruling sultan and his government were ousted. Major opposition had not been brought on by the Afro-Shirazi Party, but rather by political radical Abdul Rahman Mohammed. His extremist association, known as the Umma Party, received strong backing from various powerful organizations.

Also responsible for the opposition was a Kenyan named John Okello. Joining forces with Umma, the two radicals jointly seized Zanzibar town on 11 January 1964. The Umma Party and radical factions of the Afro-Shirazi Party, assisted by Okello, immediately took control.

On 26 April 1964 Zanzibar, Pemba and Tanganyika joined to become the United Republic of Tanganyika and Zanzibar, which shortly afterwards became known as the United Republic of Tanzania.

The Rise of Julius Nyerere

After Tanganyika became a republic, elections followed in December of the same year and Nyerere became the country's first president. Under Nyerere's guidance, constitutional changes contained moderately socialist leanings. Stronger socialist reforms were detailed in Nyerere's Arusha Declaration, released in 1967, in which he set out his belief in African traditional communities working towards their own common welfare. The Arusha Declaration together with the Interim Constitution of 1962 were to form the basis for Tanzania's intended move towards prosperity. The Declaration called for monetary restrictions on Tanzania's leaders, who were enriching themselves through their governmental positions. In Nyerere's call for the country to become self-reliant, he tried to lessen the need for foreign aid, believing that such aid would inhibit Africans from excelling in their own spheres.

By the mid-1960s, however, the country found itself facing grave problems. Educational opportunities had vastly improved, but graduates left school with no job market to enter into. Agricultural production was

THE GREAT UHURU RAILWAY

The TAZARA (Tanzania Zambia Railway Authority) railway line connecting Zambia and Tanzania was started in 1970 and completed in just five years. The total cost of construction was US$230 million, with around 25,000 Chinese and 50,000 African workers becoming involved. As no aid was forthcoming from Western countries, China supplied the loans for the construction and technical manpower in response to the new, up-and-coming communist social system in Tanzania.

Amazingly, the surveying of the terrain through which the railway was planned to run was all done on foot – by 12 men in nine months. The technical merit to the TAZARA line is commendable since the line passes through some spectacular scenery, crossing rivers and the passes and valleys of the Southern Highlands. The 1,870-km-long line

(1,162 miles) has 23 tunnels and crosses 300 bridges. Although the technology used is now antiquated, at the time it brought hopes of economic relief to the country since it opened up a much-sought-after route to Zambia.

Prior to the railway line's completion, Zambia's copper industry relied on South Africa and Zimbabwe (then Rhodesia) for the export of its ore; now the route to the Indian Ocean had become much faster and cheaper. Unfortunately, the international oil crisis of the early 1970s had serious consequences for the TAZARA line, which fell into a state of disrepair due to fuel shortages and financial constraints. In recent years, the injection of foreign aid and the restructuring of the Chinese loans has seen the TAZARA railway improve, although the trains are notoriously slow and often run behind schedule.

increasing, but at the same time Tanzania's foreign debt was steadily rising. Definite imbalances were becoming apparent in rural and urban wage development.

During the next few years, Nyerere implemented his policy of *Ujamaa*, or familyhood, which he claimed was influenced by traditional African communities and Chinese ideals. The intention was to reshape the already existing rural communities to work as cooperatives which were managed by the village and which aimed to fulfil all the needs of the village. The concept, however, never worked. Restructuring was needed as apathy towards the socialist ideals saw the idea of *Ujamaa* begin to break down. To salvage the situation, a process that became known as 'villagization' was instituted. Under this system, communities were resettled into larger village structures in an effort to consolidate and share resources. But misappropriation and a lack of funds, and often poor implementation of development projects, saw its failure; the country was unable to attain the goals Nyerere had aimed for. Matters were not made any easier with Idi Amin's move during the late 1970s to topple Uganda's government with his armed forces. In October 1978 he invaded Tanzania. Nyerere retaliated with a hastily recruited army and succeeded in repulsing Amin's forces. But the war cost Tanzania dearly with no financial aid from the rest of the world. Julius Nyerere retired in 1985, handing over to the President of Zanzibar, Ali Hassan Mwinyi, as his successor.

The first multi-party democratic elections took place in November 1995, resulting in the ruling party Chama Cha Mapinduzi (CCM) remaining in office but with a new president, Benjamin Mkapa.

TANZANIA TODAY

Government
The United Republic of Tanzania is a sovereign republic with an executive president as head of state and commander-in-chief of the Armed Forces. The Republic is ruled through a National Assembly composed of elected and nominated members from the mainland and Zanzibar. The executive function of the government is carried out by the president, while ministers in various capacities are appointed by the president to handle the administration.

Zanzibar has its own administrative government which is responsible for day-to-day matters and anything that does not fall under Union Government.

The Economy
Recent years have seen a change in the economic policies of the country, with greater investment by the private sector in industry and agriculture. Trade has been liberalized, benefiting the country with the renewed availability of goods and the increase in revenue to the government in the form of sales taxes. The country's present economic policy hopes to establish appropriate incentives for agricultural ventures in an attempt to increase food production for local consumption as well as export potential; it hopes to rehabilitate the country's infrastructure, ensure better utilization of existing industries, and improve the balance of payments by reducing trade deficits.

No recent detailed statistics on Tanzania's economy are available. However, in January 1996, Tanzania's annual inflation rate was reported to stand at 28.1%, with Gross Domestic Product (GDP) for 1995/96 at 4.1%, up from 3.6% in the previous year.

Minerals
The country's mineral reserves now account for less than 1% of GDP. Of that, about 80% of mineral production comes from the Williamson Diamond Mines in Mwadui in the Shinyanga region, which lies in the extreme north of the country, not far from Lake Victoria's southern shores.

Production is slow due to the shortage of proper tools and equipment and the high cost of obtaining the necessary spare parts. Mineral exploration is gaining in importance,

ABOVE: *A fruit market in Stone Town on the island of Zanzibar.*
RIGHT: *Sorting coffee beans at Arusha. Coffee is one of the country's main cash crops.*

with foreign firms looking at the country's gold, coal and diamond potential. Other prospects could include slate, tin, gypsum and phosphate.

Agriculture

Agriculture lies at the heart of Tanzania; over 90% can be classed as farmland. From 1977 to 1985 agriculture formed 50% of GDP and was responsible for approximately 80% of all export earnings.

Tanzania's main food crops are beans, maize, bananas, rice and sorghum. Cash crops include coffee, tea, cotton, sisal, tobacco and cloves, with substantial areas under sugar-cane cultivation. Both Arabica and Robusta coffee beans are a leading export commodity, with Tanzania being one of the world's leading producers of high-quality Arabica coffee. Ninety-eight per cent of the annual crop is exported.

Rural communities raise 99% of Tanzania's livestock. The export of hides and semi-finished leather goods has brought an annual income of over one million US dollars.

Fisheries

Though the potential for a well-developed fishing industry is high, 95% of the country's fish harvest is caught by small-scale fishermen. Most fish are netted in Lake Victoria, with its plentiful Nile perch, and Lake Tanganyika, with its small but prolific dagaa. In the Indian Ocean, fish are caught in certain areas, though in limited numbers due to inadequate equipment. The extensive practice of dynamite blasting by local fishermen has led to severe damage to reefs and entire shoals being fished out. The government has cracked down on dynamiting, although the practice still continues.

Conservation and Tourism

The annual influx of tourists to Tanzania is constantly increasing. The incredible diversity of wildlife, scenery and indigenous peoples is what draws them to the country, although it is considered to be an expensive tourist destination. But, for a true wilderness experience, Tanzania fits the bill.

Conservation efforts are being established throughout the country to preserve the wildlife and Tanzania's threatened habitats; close to 25% of the country is under protection. An infrastructure is slowly being put into place to increase standards in accommodation and tour facilities for visitors, and the improved results are fast becoming apparent.

The parks and reserves of the Northern Circuit are heavily trafficked areas as they're more accessible, and the presence of wildlife can reach staggering numbers; the Great Rift Valley is an explorer's dream, but the Southern Circuit should not be overlooked. Its wild bush and vast expanses are seldom visited by tourists, leaving the natural beauty virtually untouched and the impressive wildlife herds to a select few.

Travelling as part of a tour package can reduce your expenses, or else you can design your safari well in advance to help ease some of the frustrations of an overland trip. Services offered by tour companies range from simply providing a driver and vehicle to supplying knowledgeable guides, making

Fishing is one of the prime industries of Tanzania's coastal towns. A fish market (TOP) *and fishing nets drying in the sun in Stone Town, Zanzibar* (ABOVE).

reservations on your behalf at camps and lodges, and providing round-the-clock expert care and attention. The choice is yours and depends on what your pocket can afford.

There are hundreds of tour companies in Tanzania, of which only a selection are listed in the Visitor's Digest (*see* page 182). It is also advisable to contact any of the travel agents listed in this book to aid you in pinning down exactly what you would like from your safari and how to get your money's worth.

GETTING AROUND TANZANIA

HOW TO GET THERE

As has already been mentioned earlier, the majority of Tanzania's secondary roads are not in good condition, and are often pot-holed. For those who prefer more comfort, airstrips have been established throughout the country, and for certain destinations are strongly recommended in terms of minimizing travel time and for better comfort. However, it should be noted that charter flights can be quite costly.

When planning an itinerary it should also be noted that entry and camping fees within the national parks and reserves are relatively high as a result of government regulations. In addition, because of the remoteness of accommodation and the difficulty in obtaining supplies, hotels and lodges can charge high rates. Despite this, lodgings throughout Tanzania do accommodate a wide variety of travellers. As tourism grows, the differing needs and demands of visitors are being considered, and accommodation now ranges from budget to luxurious. Standards are rising and, for the most part, food and lodging – be it under a canvas tent, a more permanent structure or a guest room – have improved. In fact, lodgings generally are extremely pleasant and comfortable.

By Air

An increasing number of international airlines are flying into Tanzania (Air Tanzania, Air Zimbabwe, Air France, British Airways, Kenya Airways, KLM and Zambia Airways), which has two large airports to accommodate these flights. Kilimanjaro International Airport is situated between Moshi and Arusha, roughly equidistant to both, in the northeast of the country, while Dar es Salaam International Airport lies at the coast, just outside Dar's city centre.

Chartered air services provide an important mode of travel in Tanzania. These can be expensive, but they save a great deal of time and frustration. There are several services

Mwanza, situated on the shores of Lake Victoria, is probably its most important port, with an airport (TOP) and a railway station (ABOVE).

which will fly passengers throughout the country, and some offer scheduled flights into the parks and reserves (*see* Visitor's Digest, page 182).

By Rail

It is possible to enter the country by rail from Zambia, via the TAZARA railway, and from Kenya. The service can be slow and delays are not uncommon as schedule changes and problems with the railway line occur often.

By Boat

Arrival into Tanzania via lakes Victoria, Tanganyika and Malawi (Nyasa) by ferry is also possible. Visitors can also enter the country by boat at Dar es Salaam. Immigration and customs are handled differently for each mode of transport, so obtain details when booking your passage. Be sure to have a valid entry visa before arriving in the country.

By Road

Entry into Tanzania from Kenya, Malawi and Zambia is relatively easy and generally handled most efficiently. Make sure all passports, visas and vehicle papers are in good order before arriving at border posts. Border formalities before entering the country from Burundi, Rwanda or Uganda may take a little longer. Main roads into Tanzania from Malawi and Zambia are in good condition and should pose no problems, while the road from Nairobi in Kenya via Namanga on the border (west of Amboseli National Park) is in fair condition with some large patches of broken tarmac. Four-wheel-drive vehicles are not necessary on the main thoroughfares.

TRAVEL WITHIN TANZANIA

On Arrival

If you have booked through a tour operator or professional organization, you will no doubt be met by one of their representatives upon your arrival in the country. You will most likely make your way to your lodge or hotel, where you will be briefed and given details of your schedule.

If you are travelling on your own, you will need to make your way from your point of entry to your hotel, either by hotel shuttle, taxi, city bus or private bus services. Taxis are generally plentiful at airports and terminals, but be sure to set the price for the fare prior to embarking on your journey. Car hire is available through Europcar and Hertz (*see* Visitor's Digest, page 182) but can prove costly.

Accommodation

Accommodation throughout the country comes in the form of lodges/hotels and permanent tented camps in a variety of shapes and sizes, and of varying quality. Almost all provide en-suite facilities, a bar and dining room, and laundry service. Though there may not always be running water, hot water for showers is readily available. Tents are generally spacious, mostly with twin beds though some have double beds. Where necessary, mosquito nets may be provided.

Give careful consideration to the type of accommodation you would feel most comfortable in. Some travellers prefer the outdoor feel of the tents, while others are not keen on the 'bush' environment and prefer the solid, comfortable protection of a lodge. Units, whether tented or solid structures, can have as many as 100 beds or as few as 10. This

TOP LEFT: *A charter passenger boat at Mwanza.*
ABOVE: *The Dhow Palace Hotel in Stone Town.*

again is an option, although smaller units generally mean higher expense. Some of the accommodation facilities can be extremely remote, while others are easier to reach. Certain lodges and tented camps offer all-inclusive price structures that cover everything from liquor to game drives, while others have individual price structures for meals, activities and 'extras'. City hotels generally offer rates that cover bed and breakfast, while bush accommodation prices usually include all meals. Resident rates are sometimes available, with proof of residency requested.

Safari and Tour Operators

Travellers today may choose from a host of different safari options when planning their journey to Tanzania. Photographic safaris are the most popular attraction, but hunting safaris are also available throughout the country. Guests on photographic safaris can join a group as part of a package tour, create their own tour with a small group, go it alone, or 'rough it' by backpacking.

The booming business in Tanzania has led to many 'fly by night' companies using sub-standard vehicles and accommodation. Get detailed information from each company before deciding on which one to use. Find out exactly what is included and what is extra in the tour.

Be sure the tour company understands the type of trip you are looking for, particularly if you are interested in something specific such as bird-watching or learning more about the indigenous people. Study their philosophies about wildlife, its behaviour and habitat. If you are just looking for the bare essentials, this type of trip is available, but if you are looking for a more well-rounded experience that provides you with information as well as fun and attention to detail, you may have to look a little harder.

Safaris can be arranged to encompass either driving or flying everywhere, or you can settle for a combination of the two. The more exclusive organizers use four-wheel-drive vehicles, while the more moderately priced groups travel in minibuses.

Mobile Safaris

A popular way to experience Tanzania is by mobile safari. This can be an extremely costly way to view the land, but it does often offer some of the finest sites, game-viewing and bush experiences. Mobile safaris are geared to take complete care of the client's needs with the help of efficient, well-trained staff that move the entire camp while guests are out on game drives. Every need is catered for, service is impeccable and the cuisine excellent.

If a particular area proves to be extremely rewarding in terms of wildlife, your guide may decide to stay there longer; on the other hand, you could also leave early if conditions make this necessary. This private mode of travel brings an old-world charm to the ultimate safari experience.

Budget Mobile Safaris

This can be a lot of fun, with relatively lower costs, but guests should be prepared for a no-fuss, sometimes hectic safari. Chores are divided up between the group, and equipment can sometimes be rather lacking. Check out the operators offering this type of safari extremely well. This may be a good option for the backpacker as access into the parks and reserves is provided for (pedestrians are not permitted to enter).

Private Vehicles

Travelling in a private vehicle allows you to move unrestricted around the country, picking and choosing your destination as you see fit. Camping facilities in national parks and reserves are not the best, generally offering lovely scenery but the bare minimum when it comes to ablutions and other facilities. Fees are high, not only to camp but also to get a foreign-registered vehicle into any of the parks, so make your choice of park or reserve carefully. 'Free camping' is possible outside reserve boundaries throughout the country, but one should always take care to try and not be too noticeable.

Make sure your vehicle is in good working order, and check it regularly. Keep a comprehensive tool kit and basic spares. You should

have a first-aid kit as well as a manual. The kit should contain, as basics, bandages, aspirin, general antibiotics, antiseptic creams, anti-histamines, ointment for burns, cold and flu tablets, cottonwool, earbuds, throat lozenges, diarrhoea tablets, eye ointment, malaria prophylactics and cures, painkillers, sunburn lotion, eye drops, a thermometer and simple sutures.

Ensure that you have good, up-to-date maps, a reliable compass and (worthwhile to have but not essential unless you are planning substantial off-the-beaten-track treks)

A camel safari is an unique way to appreciate the beauties of the African bush.

Global Positioning System (GPS) equipment. Remember to check with the local residents what the road conditions are like, how the weather has been and any other pertinent information about the area that you are planning to visit before you begin your journey.

Check that you have plenty of water, fuel and food provisions before you set out. Gerry cans which are attached to the outside of vehicles must be well secured at all times.

EXPLORING TANZANIA

Tanzania's peoples are a diverse, colourful mix, its wildlife abundant. Its landscapes vary from deep, fertile forests of the Mahale mountains at Lake Tanganyika's edge, to the dry scrub of the Selous Game Reserve in the south, to the shimmering waters and breezes of the Indian Ocean. Visitors embarking on a safari often leave one world and enter another in the space of a morning: riverine forests pass into rolling hills, acacia forests or grassland plains, marked by ancient lookout posts or a single tree, inviting to a cheetah or a pride of lion. Despite the harsh sun by day, colour is to be found everywhere. Dawn brings pastels and cool ambers, while dusk surrounds the landscape with gold and spice. The rains transform the highlands as spring flowers make a brief appearance and breathtaking colours flit by on the wing of a bird.

LEFT: *The Ngorongoro Crater is rich in wildlife.*
ABOVE: *The Maasai people were once renowned for their fierce warriors.*

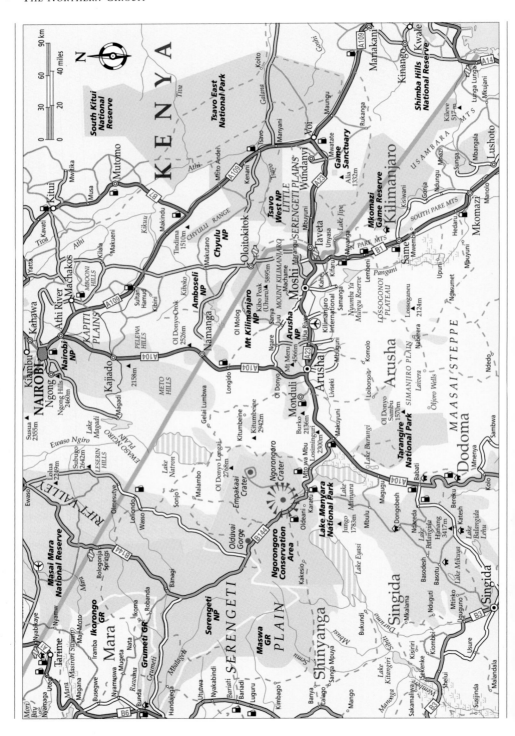

THE NORTHERN CIRCUIT

More tourists visit the Northern Circuit than most other parts of the country, and with good reason. The sprawling landscapes, abundance and variety of wildlife, and fascinating ethnic encounters are facets of northern Tanzania and in particular the Northern Circuit. Drier climates and rocky terrain accompany lower elevations, while misty highlands and cool air complement unusual foliage and forest dwellers.

Ease of travel throughout the region is generally determined by weather conditions. Rain makes most roads slick and slow, while in the dry weather dust is a tough adversary; travel can, however, be quite fast.

Game-viewing is at its optimum in the Ngorongoro Crater and on the Serengeti Plains. The largest animals migration in the world – that of the white-bearded wildebeest – begins and ends here, and, at various times of the year, the alkaline lakes shimmer pink with the presence of millions of flamingos.

ARUSHA TOWN

Arusha is northern Tanzania's centre of commerce and trade, and may well be one of East Africa's fastest-growing cities. It does not offer particularly appealing sightseeing, but is the starting point for many safaris. Arusha has a vast number of safari companies, hotels and curio shops brimming with handicrafts, carvings and gemstones. There are also plenty of shops with general provisions, a city market with ample fruit and vegetables, garages and no lack of fuel. The heart of the business district is marked by the clock tower roundabout, the midway point between the Cape and Cairo. From here the shops, restaurants, banks and city hotels are easily reached.

The city, 1,540 m (5,053 ft) above sea level, is surrounded by fertile lands that nurture crops of coffee, maize, bananas and flowers. Close by, Mount Meru watches over the city, while clear days reveal the snow-capped reaches of Kilimanjaro in the distance. The

TOP: *The reception area, Arusha's Impala Hotel.*
ABOVE: *One of Arusha's colourful street markets.*

locals are predominantly the Arusha, the Meru and the Maasai, who can often be seen dressed in their traditional indigo clothing.

Sights of interest in Arusha

Arusha's National Natural History Museum, near the Arusha International Conference Centre (AICC), is housed in a boma – a garrison built around 1900 by the Germans. Although rather a small museum, it contains information on the evolution of man based on digs undertaken throughout East Africa.

Shopping in Arusha is a highlight as curio shops and street vendors ply their wares throughout the town – local handicraft, batiks, carvings, jewellery and sisal bags. The Cultural Heritage complex can also be visited outside Arusha, on the Dodoma road, while across from the Meserani Snake Park is the Ol Donyo Orok Gallery and Crafts.

The Meserani Snake Park is located 24 km (15 miles) outside Arusha on the main road to Dodoma. Family owned and operated, it

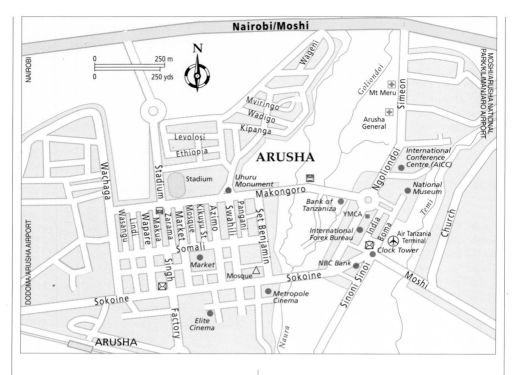

has an excellent display of the reptiles found throughout East Africa and makes for an interesting afternoon. The park also has a friendly bar/restaurant, offers a Sunday barbecue, and has basic camping and ablution facilities. The grounds are well maintained with plenty of shaded tables and benches. The knowledgeable staff are eager to explain about the park's various snakes, lizards and crocodiles. Camel rides are also offered.

ARUSHA NATIONAL PARK

Northeast of Arusha in the eastern branch of the Great Rift Valley is Arusha National Park. Although it covers only 137 km² (50 sq. miles), it preserves a unique world. The name Arusha stems from Warusha, the name given to a people who have long lived in the region. The Maasai are also a major presence and account for the Maasai names occurring throughout the park.

Formerly called Ngurdoto Crater National Park, Arusha changed its name in 1967 when the slopes of Mount Meru were included in its extents. The park is surrounded by densely populated areas, but its game-viewing and natural environment are sure to impress.

Volcanic activity has formed much of what exists today. The park features three distinct landscapes. One is the Ngurdoto Crater – the remains of volcanic activity that once took place within the now extinct volcano, Ngurdoto. It is believed that initially two large ash cones were formed close to each other, but as the molten rock eventually subsided they collapsed, leaving the caldera which is today lush and swampy. The second landscape form is further north in the park. A series of seven alkaline lakes, known as the Momela lakes, these were created in land hollows after Mount Meru experienced violent volcanic activity. The lakes are abundant with birdlife, especially between October and April when migratory birds pass through; it is also possible to see hippo here. Third, the impressive, dormant Mount Meru towers up in the western arm of the park. Magnificent to see, the ash cone is a reminder of the volcanic disturbance that occurred about 100 years ago; traces of lava flow on the northwest mountain slopes are still evidence of this. The dense montane forest harbours a variety of birds and wildlife.

As with wildlife, elevation has a major impact on the flora. The forest floor is often covered with the pink blossoms of touch-me-nots *(Impatiens papilionacea)* – whose ripe seed pods explode when touched – and from December to February the spectacular glow of the fireball lily *(Scadoxus multiflorus)*, a relative of the common onion, can be seen throughout the park. An abundant variety of trees occurs in Arusha, among them the strangler fig *(Ficus thonningii)*, the African mahogany *(Entandrophragma* spp.) and wild date palms *(Phoenix reclinata)*. Acacias grow in lesser numbers in the lower areas where there is sufficient water.

A CAMEL'S VIEW OF EAST AFRICA

An unusual and delightful way to experience the African bush is atop a camel – provided by the Arusha-based Camels Only, owned and operated by Fran and Chris More. Camels have a reputation for being unpleasant and rude, but, through the skilful hands of the Mores and their excellent staff, camel trekking takes on a new light, with passengers gently and enjoyably crossing the plains between Mount Meru and Kilimanjaro. The Camels Only bush base is roughly one-and-a-half hours northeast of Arusha. It is a lovely place to prepare for one's journey, be it a day trip or an extended safari. Bungalows are extremely comfortable with private showers and a separate pit latrine, but boasting the finest 'traditional seating' while overlooking fabulous views. By the end of the trek, guests have not only seen Africa from a completely new viewpoint, but are sure to take away a new outlook on camels! Several itineraries are available, though customized treks are happily arranged.

A camel safari on the slopes of Mount Meru in the Arusha area.

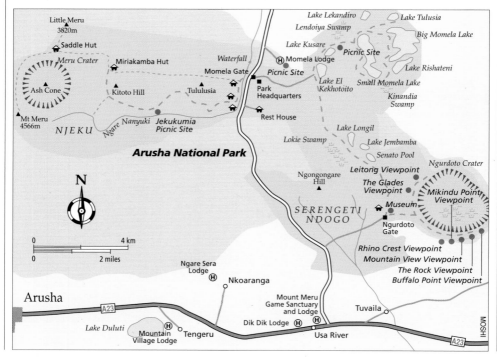

Arusha National Park, with its numerous observation hides and picnic sites, is ideal for a day trip, although lodging and camping facilities are available. The rim of Ngurdoto Crater has seven sites with splendid views not only of the crater but also the surrounding area, as well as Mount Kilimanjaro on clear days. Any walking or climbing requires the accompaniment of a ranger, for which there is a fee. In addition, park fees are due for each 24-hour period spent in the park.

Ngurdoto Crater

Immediately on entering the southernmost portion of the park from Arusha, this section – a grassland plain – is known as Serengeti Ndogo, or 'little Serengeti'. Look out for Burchell's zebra as this is the only area in the park where they can be seen. There are two options here for travelling within the park. At Serengeti Ndogo there is a fork in the road: if you keep to the left and continue northwards through the park to the Momela Gate, you will head for the Mount Meru side

OPPOSITE: *Buffalo in Arusha National Park.*
BELOW: *Ngurdoto Crater, best visited by morning.*

of the park; by keeping to the right at the fork you will reach the Ngurdoto Gate. With the latter option, the grassland plains are left behind and are replaced with dense forest and cool air. Once at the gate, find out if the Ngurdoto Crater rim road has been completed; this will enable you to drive along the entire rim without retracing your route. It is always a good idea to ask about road conditions and any recent road changes within the park. At the Ngurdoto Gate is a small museum, worth a few minutes of your time as it houses several interesting specimens of insects, birds and bones. As you pass through the gate, the road on your left leads to the Momela lakes, while to your right the road ascends to the Ngurdoto Crater rim. The road will eventually come to a Y-junction; by taking the right fork you arrive at the crater rim.

As the park's elevation changes, so the wildlife inhabiting those areas also varies. In the forest it is important to keep looking towards the canopy as this may be your best opportunity to view the exquisite black-and-white colobus monkeys. They live in troops, and their long bushy white tails are often spotted first. The monkeys' calls echo

through the canopy as they move gracefully through the trees, seldom leaving the security of the branches.

Many plant and trees species are evident in the crater rim forest, among the most obvious the wild (strangler) fig *(Ficus thonningii)*, the wild olive *(Olea hochstetteri)* and the wild mango *(Tabernaemontana usambarensis)*.

The best time to visit the crater is in the morning when cool clear air prevails. Animals are most active at this time, and you may spot bushbuck, common in the montane forest, both here and at Meru, or the shy red duiker as it moves quietly through the trees. Also pleasing are the playful antics of the olive baboons and the inquisitive tree-dwelling blue monkeys. Birdlife is abundant and the forest is seldom silent for long. As you make your way to the right along the rim, there are several opportunities to view the crater floor below and its 3-km (2 miles) extent to the opposite rim. Visitors to the park are not allowed to descend to the crater floor, but designated picnic and observation areas are well placed and offer a bird's-eye view of the crater. Buffalo are often seen on the floor as there is ample water and grazing. Seldom seen but often heard is the Silverycheeked hornbill, which has an impressive casque, thought to amplify its loud call, which echoes through the forest while it gracefully glides through the canopy. In the forest you may catch sight of the regal Crowned eagle, which can be identified by its crest and short wings. Due to its size and strength, this large bird preys mostly on monkeys. Verreaux's eagle may very occasionally be sighted around the crater rim.

The left fork of the Y-junction below the crater rim takes you towards Leitong, the highest point on Ngurdoto Crater at 1,853 m (6,080 ft). This road is a little steeper, but, at the top, a brief moderate walk will take you to the expansive panorama of crater, Momela lakes and, on a clear day, Kilimanjaro.

Momela Lakes

If the road around the crater rim has not yet been completed, it will be necessary for you to retrace your tracks to the main road that approaches Ngurdoto Gate. Here you can pick up the road that heads to the Momela

BLUE MONKEYS

Although these monkeys appear black out of the sunlight, they are in fact a dark, bluish-grey; the fur around their face is longer and lighter than the rest of the body. Blue monkeys live in family troops of four to six, but a group may consist of up to 12 members.

Males weigh between 3.5 and 7 kg (7.5–15 lb). Feeding time for blue monkeys takes place high up in the trees in the morning and late afternoon; their diet is made up of leaves, flowers, fruits, berries and bark, as well as young birds, eggs and insects. During the day the monkeys come down to the lower tiers of the forest. They mark their territories with sharp cries in the very early morning and early evening. Enemies of the blue monkey are leopards, Crowned eagles and pythons.

Blue monkeys occur in forested areas.

lakes, approximately 9 km (6 miles) away. As you travel along this road, Mount Meru rises majestically on your left, forming an imposing backdrop to herds of elephant and a wide variety of plains game. Continuing on this road you pass the Senato Pools, Lake Jembamba, Lake Longil and Lokie Swamp. More often than not, these pools are dry, but when there is water they host much activity. Each area has an observation/picnic site, and it may be worth a quick check – even during the dry season – to see if any animals or birdlife are present. Lokie Swamp on the left and Lake Longil on the right tend to have more water throughout the year. Around Lake Longil you are likely to hear the characteristic cry of Africa – that of the Fish eagle – as the lake contains tilapia, the bird's major source of food. Early morning and late afternoon are the best times here as animals come to drink. The scenery of tall reeds and papyrus is calming and the birdlife can be thrilling.

Upon reaching the lakes you are advised to drive anti-clockwise around the circuit. There are seven lakes in all: El Kekhotoito, Kusare, Small Momela, Rishateni, Big Momela, Tulusia and Lekandiro. You will notice that each lakes is not only different in appearance, but also in its birdlife. This is the result of different chemical compounds in each lake, which produces dissimilar algal growth. Fed by underground springs, some of the lakes are less alkaline than others, as is the case with Small Momela Lake. Here lower alkaline levels can accommodate communities of hippo. Several species of waterfowl can be seen in

TOP: *Big Momela Lake, Arusha National Park.*
ABOVE: *The Fish eagle, with its haunting cry of Africa, may be seen at Lake Longil.*

the lake district throughout the year, and during the months of October to April numbers soar because of migrants from the northern hemisphere. The Egyptian goose, the Little grebe, and various herons and egrets are plentiful; fluctuating in number but usually present are Greater and Lesser flamingos.

It is estimated that almost 400 species of birds have been spotted in the park. As well as waterfowl, forest dwellers and grassland inhabitants are all to be found all year. The distinctive Olive pigeons are often seen in the higher and lower montane forests feeding on the wild olives and juniper berries.

Mount Meru

Heading west from the lake region for approximately 1,500 m (1,640 yd), you reach Momela Gate. From here it is possible to go south back to the Arusha–Moshi road, go north on the Ngare Nanyuki road towards Momella Lodge or cross the main road and the Ngare Nanyuki River into the Meru section of the park. Look for elephant as the vegetation opens up, and Maasai giraffe browsing on the acacias.

Standing is Tululusia Hill (the word Tululusia means 'sentinel'). At the foot of the hill, the swamp is skirted by lovely yellow fever trees *(Acacia xanthophloea)*, where herds of buffalo, waterbuck and warthog are often seen grazing. A waterfall in the area is lovely to visit, though sometimes the road is washed away after heavy rains. The walk to the waterfall can be delightful, but you must be accompanied by an armed ranger.

After passing the campsite markers, the main road gradually ascends through lower montane forest. It is a peaceful drive and in among the stately old African olives *(Olea hochstetteri)* and wild, or strangler, figs *(Ficus thonningii)*, it is possible to observe the shy bushbuck, and even Maasai giraffe. Elephant droppings can often be seen, but the animal is usually only encountered at higher altitudes. Birdsong fills the air while the ground may be covered with an array of flowering shrubs and creepers. Continuing along the road, you will come to the fantastic Fig Tree Arch. This is a splendid example of the amazing survival tactics of the wild fig. Seeds dropped by birds can take root in the crook of a host tree. As the seed germinates, it puts out aerial roots that reach downward and eventually touch the ground. As the wild fig grows and strengthens, it entwines and eventually strangles the host tree.

From here the road becomes steeper. With the rise in elevation – approximately 2,300 m (7,546 ft) – you enter the higher montane

---

CLIMBING MOUNT MERU

If you plan to climb to the Meru summit – at 4,566 m (14,980 ft) – it is best to allow for at least three days (climbing Mount Meru has been done in a day, but is usually tackled in three). It is necessary to obtain advance permission from the park warden at Momela Gate and a fee is payable. Mount Meru is usually climbed from Olkokola, on the western side of the crater. The best time of year for climbing is between October and February; it sometimes rains during November. You cannot walk without a park ranger as an escort, as the many buffalo can pose a threat. Mountain boots are recommended for the relatively steep sections of the climb, although during the dry season hiking boots should suffice. Climbers are urged to supply their own climbing gear – some equipment can be hired but the supply is limited. Two huts are available for climbers, with firewood provided. These are Miriakamba Hut which accommodates 48 people and Saddle Hut, further up, accommodating 24 people. The three-day climb consists of the following routine: on day one hikers walk

from Momela Gate to Miriakamba Hut, then explore Meru Crater. Day two is the climb to Saddle Hut, and then up to Little Meru and back. On day three, hikers ascend Meru's summit, after which they return to Miriakamba Hut, or carry on back to Momela Gate. Certificates are only issued to climbers who begin and end their journey at Momela Gate.

Mount Meru rises above coffee plantations.

ATMOSPHERIC LODGES

MOUNT MERU GAME SANCTUARY AND LODGE
This log cabin-styled hotel is set in peaceful gardens, tucked away off the Moshi road. The 17 en-suite rooms are spacious although somewhat dark and in need of some updating. A large enclosed area contains eland, waterbuck, ostrich, pelicans, egrets and peacocks. A cosy outside fireplace in an alcove separates each room. The bar and dining room also overlook the gardens and sanctuary. Mount Meru Lodge is in close proximity to Arusha National Park.
MOUNTAIN VILLAGE LODGE This quaint lodge, located on a working coffee estate on the Moshi road, has exceptional gardens with a breathtaking view. The dining room, lounge and office are accommodated in a renovated old colonial house. The gardens provide a wonderful haven to indulge in afternoon tea and catch up on notes, write postcards or just revel in the surroundings. Lake Duluti lies below and clear days can reveal both Kilimanjaro and Mount Meru. The lodge's 42 thatched-roof rondavels, with en-suite facilities, are set among the winding paths of the colourful gardens. Activities include walks and horseback riding through the coffee estate and around Lake Duluti. For keen bird-watchers, the birdlife is prolific.

forest, evidenced by the changing vegetation. African pencil cedar *(Juniperus procera)* and podo, or East African yellowwood *(Podocarpus gracilior)*, are now predominant species. Orchids, ferns and mosses hang from most branches and it is also possible to see vibrant flashes of colour from the Hartlaub's turaco and the Narina's trogon. About 2 km (1 mile) up from the Fig Tree Arch is a wonderful little picnic site, Jekukumia, off to the left-hand side. The small waterfall and secluded glade is a perfect place to rest and stretch your legs. From here you can walk to where the salty waters of the Jekukumia River and the sweet waters of the Ngare Nanyuki join. Take care while walking, however, as buffalo are plentiful, and stinging nettle *(Urtica masaicus)* can penetrate your clothing.

Travelling further up the road for approximately 2.5 km (1.5 miles) you arrive at Kitoto observation and picnic site. On a clear day wonderful scenic views of Mount Meru and the park below can be enjoyed from here. You can carry on driving up to the Meru Crater and Miriakamba Hut. This stretch of road is quite steep and a four-wheel-drive vehicle is necessary. If you are moderately fit it is also possible to walk to the crater – it is about an hour's trip via the Jekukumia River. Though steep in some sections, this is a delightful way to appreciate the beauty of

Fig Tree Arch on the Mount Meru crater road.

Mount Meru. If you arrive after the rains, it can be muddy and slushy, but there is a profusion of wildflowers. The crater suddenly unfolds before you; the magnitude of the ash cone and the cliff face falling away below are quite spectacular.

MOSHI

Located 60 km (37 miles) east of Arusha on the Arusha–Moshi road, this is the largest city in northeastern Tanzania. It is a good place for travellers to stock up on basics. There are many tree-lined streets, and the city centre bustles with activity. Several shops and kiosks in the town should meet most supply requirements, and banking and postal needs can be attended to. Fuel is readily available.

Lying east of Moshi, off the Taveta road (on the Kenyan border), are two secluded lakes that are seldom visited from the Tanzanian side. Northernmost of these is Lake Chala, one of the finest examples of Kilimanjaro's many parasitic cone lakes. Bordering on Kenya, the lake's sparkling waters are fished and swum in regularly, and the site

A fruit and vegetable market in Moshi.

offers truly panoramic views. The lake rarely receives visitors, making it a delightful secluded hideaway. Take care when descending to the water's edge as the paths are steep in certain areas.

To the south of Lake Chala, also resting on the border with Kenya, is the much larger and slightly saline Lake Jipe. The area is peaceful, little visited, and a sheer delight for those seeking total wilderness. Make sure you are fully equipped and have all the necessary supplies when visiting the area. Check with locals in Taveta, Himo (near Kilimanjaro) or Moshi for current road conditions.

KILIMANJARO NATIONAL PARK

The tallest mountain on the African continent, lying northeast of Arusha, rests quietly at the edge of the plains with its incredibly beautiful snow-capped peaks. Rising above the Kenyan border it stands in Tanzania, 330 km (205 miles) south of the equator. Gazetted fairly recently, in 1973, the Kilimanjaro National Park was officially opened in 1977, and only includes the land above 2,700 m (8,860 ft). This comprises the moorland and highland zones, the Shira Plateau at 3,962 m (13,000 ft), and the peaks of Kibo

and Mawenzi at 5,895 m (19,340 ft) and 5,149 m (16,894 ft) respectively. Below the park is an area designated as a forest and game reserve, gazetted in 1921.

The meaning of the name 'Kilimanjaro' is under some dispute, but whether one examines the roots of the Chagga name, the Maasai, or even the coastal interpretations, the underlying theme generally revolves around the mountain's size, its spiritual significance or the snow and the cold.

Formation of Mount Kilimanjaro

Over a million years ago, the plains were immensely unstable, buckling and cracking from the powerful force of movements deep within the earth. The Kilimanjaro Depression was created as a result of this violent activity and with it molten rock forced up to the surface formed the volcanoes Ol Molog, Kibongoto and Kilema along a 100-km-long (60 miles) ridge that reached 3,000 m (9,843 ft) in height.

The formation of Kilimanjaro started 750,000 years ago, when it consisted of three large vents: Shira, Kibo and Mawenzi. Over thousands of years Shira eventually collapsed, becoming extinct; Mawenzi remained active a while longer but eventually also became extinct and began to erode; Kibo continued with massive eruptions around 360,000 years ago that released black lava over the Shira caldera, creating the area known today as the Saddle, at the base of Mawenzi. The lava also spread far to the north and south. This particular lava is known as rhomb porphyry lava (igneous rock composed of large rhomboid crystals embedded in a mass of smaller crystals), distinct because of its dark colour and its crystalline shape.

Though eruptions continued to occur, and Kibo reached a height of almost 5,900 m (19,358 ft), the mountain's growth had ceased about 450,000 years ago and the volcano in fact began to sink. Erosion helped create the tall jagged peaks of Mawenzi and Shira's plateau. Kibo meanwhile levelled out and was covered during the ages with ice and glaciers. The Kibo barranco (a steep-walled ravine) was formed 100,000 years ago by a tremendous landslide. Kilimanjaro's southeastern and northwestern reaches are speckled with numerous parasitic vents that erupted during the slow tapering off of volcanic activity in the area. In Kibo's final burst of fury, the Ash Pit, the Inner Crater and the present, perfectly formed caldera were created and are now permanent features of this magnificent free-standing mountain.

Humans have lived near the mountain for centuries, and, though there have been no major archaeological discoveries, rings and bowls made from obsidian flakes (dark glassy volcanic rock formed from hardened lava) were found on the western slopes. Among the earliest references to Kilimanjaro was the Greek Ptolemy's description 18 centuries ago. Six to seven centuries ago Chinese accounts referred to a great mountain west of Zanzibar. Johannes Rebmann, a German missionary, was the first European to see the snowy peak in 1848. His sighting was reported in the *Church Missionary Intelligencer* in 1849 but was greeted with much scepticism from the Western world. Kilimanjaro's summit was not physically reached until 1889 by geographer Hans Ludwig Meyer.

Today, the slopes of Kilimanjaro are traversed by a great many people. Some visitors choose to keep to the lower regions, while others forge ahead on one of the six designated routes, laden with woollies, and porters and packs in tow.

Vegetation on Kilimanjaro

There are five types of vegetation zone on the mountain. Each zone rises approximately 1,000 m (3,280 ft) higher than the previous one, and each zone is progressively colder and drier, with a noticeably diminishing animal population.

LOWER SLOPES From 800 to 1,800 m (2,625–5,905 ft), the lower slopes receive ample water from rainfall higher up the mountain, and, together with rich volcanic soils, have been heavily cultivated and extensively cleared for livestock. On the northern and eastern slopes it is possible to see the original vegetation (scrub, bushland and lowland forest) as the area is somewhat drier and poor for crop growing. Wildflowers such as the pinkish *Clematis hirsuta* and the blue morning glory grow in this area, as does the purple Vernonia and the strongly smelling Lippia and Lantana. Wild animals are not often sighted in this zone, but the clicks and screams of the greater galago (or bushbaby) and the tree hyrax are a common night-time sound. Birds are plentiful as their food sources are varied and there is an abundance of nesting sites. The most commonly seen bird species are the Whitebrowed robin chat, Common bulbul, the Tropical boubou and the Speckled mousebird.

MONTANE FOREST The forest begins at 1,800 m (5,905 ft) and is the most fertile and luxuriant of all the mountain zones; in fact, 96% of the water on the mountain originates in this montane forest. The heavy moisture results in cloud which traps the sun's heat, making this region extremely humid.

Clear nights can be quite cold, while daytime temperatures average 15 °C (59 °F). The most common tree of this region is the *Macaranga kilimandscharica*, with its large heart-shaped leaves; the tall *Podocarpus milanjianus* with its long curling leaves is also numerous. Unlike most mountain forest zones, there is no bamboo forest on Kilimanjaro; it appears only in small patches. Higher in this zone the giant heath tree (*Philippia excelsa*), with tiny leaves and small white flowers, becomes a regular sight, and near the upper edge of the forest the endemic *Senecio johnstonii* begins to show in wetter areas. Forest dwellers are quiet and generally stay in and around the trees for protection. It is not uncommon to see the blue monkey and the exquisite black-and-white colobus monkey. Lots of squirrels scurry around and attentive eyes may spot a bush duiker, the Abbot's duiker or the small red duiker. Leopards are known to live in this region, but are seldom seen. The birds of this zone can often be found near the large fig

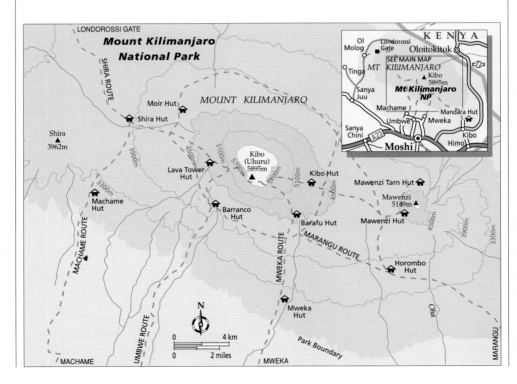

trees, feasting on the sweet fruit. Commonly seen are the brilliant green Hartlaub's turaco and the Silverycheeked hornbill.

LOW ALPINE ZONE The 2,800-m (9,187 ft) line marks the beginning of the low alpine zone, which has two distinct environments: the heath area, marked by heathlike shrubs and heather such as the giant *Erica arborea*, and the moorland of the higher regions, with clusters of lobelia and senecio (or groundsel). Giant lobelias can grow to 3 m (10 ft), while the groundsels reach heights of 9 m (30 ft). The alpine zone is cool, the air usually crystal clear. Above 3,000 m (9,843 ft) frost is common, yet the sun is quite intense. There are many flowers in the tussocky grasslands, the most common of which are the everlastings *Helichrysum argyranthum* and *H. meyeri-johannis*. Also present is the unusual pine-cone-shaped *Protea kilimandscharica*. Eland are seen from time to time as are duikers, buffalo and elephant; rocky areas may host klip-springers. The four-striped grass mouse is a common small rodent, sometimes seen dashing between the grass tussocks. Birds do not occur in great numbers in the moorland, but the Alpine chat is common and the Streaky seedeater is often sighted near the Horombo Hut. The Augur buzzard and Mountain buzzard may be seen overhead, while the clever Whitenecked raven keeps a watchful eye for

ABOVE: *Kilimanjaro towers over the Arusha area.*
BELOW: *The beautiful Kilimanjaro protea.*

food, whether it be rodents or scraps left by walkers. The Alpine swift is also quite common, as is the attractive Scarlettufted malachite sunbird, usually seen feeding on nectar from the flowers of the giant lobelia.

ALPINE ZONE At 4,000 m (13,124 ft) the alpine zone begins where, it is said, 'it is summer every day, and winter every night'. Daytime temperatures can reach 40 °C (104 °F) while, during the night, the mercury drops below 0 °C (32 °F). Vegetation needs to be hardy to survive here, and there are only around 55 species in the area. Most common are slow-growing lichens. Everlastings occur, as well as the tussock grass *Pentaschistis minor*. Birds of prey and ravens are occasionally seen, but they do not live in this zone. The vegetation of the higher zones becomes extremely sparse, but at these heights the views are breathtaking. Kibo's glaciers and Mawenzi's dykes (jagged fingers of igneous rock) are exceptional, while the Saddle looks rather like a moonscape.

ABOVE 5,000 M (16,405 FT) TO THE SUMMIT Arctic conditions – hot sun during the day and freezing temperatures at night – prevail above 5,000 m (16,405 ft), discouraging plant life. However, a flowering plant, *Helichrysum newii* – the highest recorded at 5,670 m (18,603 ft) – uses the warmth given off by Kibo's small vents in order to survive in these hostile conditions. Once you have achieved this height, there is a spectacular 'view of the world'. Snow lies all around, and you can see Kibo's Inner Crater with its 15- to 20-m-high (49–66 ft) walls, the Ash Cone in the caldera and, inside the cone, the Ash Pit, which is 120 m (394 ft) deep and composed of shale and boulders that have tumbled into it. The Great Northern Glacier cloaks the northern summit of Kilimanjaro and is a combination of terraces with the edges fluted into pillars.

Climbing Mount Kilimanjaro

MARANGU ROUTE This is the most frequently used corridor and the round trip generally takes six days. It begins at the Marangu Gate,

Klipspringer may occur in the Low Alpine zone.

and is clearly marked, but climbers should carry a map on all routes. Main highlights of this particular path are the lush forest, the scenery and the wildflowers at Maundi Crater, as well as the fabulous views of the Kibo and Mawenzi peaks.

MWEKA ROUTE This is the fastest and most direct passage to the summit (around five days), but it is also the steepest. The route begins near Moshi at the College of Wildlife Management. Highlights of this journey are the wonderful views of Kibo, the views over the vast expanse of open plains, and the Southern Glaciers.

UMBWE ROUTE This corridor begins near the Umbwe Mission, just northwest of Moshi. It is scenic, but is considered to be relatively short and steep (around 5 days up and down). It is more often used as a descent trail (around 2 days) from Mweka and Machame. Highlights include views of Kibo, the Great Western Breach and the Kibo barranco.

MACHAME ROUTE This trail (around five to six days) begins further northwest of Moshi in the village of Machame. Vehicles can be left at the school or hotel. Main highlights are the distinct, beautiful vegetation zones.

Marangu route traverses many different habitats.

SHIRA ROUTE The Shira Plateau is described as being one of the most fascinating areas of the mountain. The road to Shira requires a four-wheel-drive vehicle and should be taken slowly for better acclimatization. Heading north from Boma la Ng'ombe, the drive is about 78 km (48 miles). The rest of the way is completed on foot – about half an hour's walk. From the Shira Hut walking options range from one to four hours; these are not full circuits. Highlights include exceptional views while driving, the parasitic cones of the Shira zone and the wonderful changes in vegetation. The Shira Plateau consists of grassland, heath and moorland where the extraordinarily large senecios can reach up to 10 m (13 ft) in height. You will also see the Shira Cone, which rises 200 m (656 ft) above the plateau, and the Shira Ridge, which has sheer cliffs 400 m (1312 ft) high.

GREAT WESTERN BREACH ROUTE TO KIBO CRATER The Lava Tower Hut, which is the base from which the ascent on this side is made, can be reached from the Shira, Machame or Umbwe routes. The Great Western Breach route is extremely steep and is recommended only for climbers who are fit and capable. An ice-axe can be a useful item of equipment on this climb. Main highlights are the breathtaking views of the Western Breach and access to Kibo Crater, which includes the Terrace, Northern Glaciers, Inner Cone and the Ash Pit.

SUMMIT CIRCUIT, MAWENZI AND SADDLE There is a circuit that winds around the base of Kibo and varies in altitude from 3,700 to 4,600 m (12,140–15,093 ft). The southern side has several points where climbers can join or leave the circuit, but, once on the north side, there are no deviations.

The Saddle between Mawenzi and Kibo can be reached from the Marangu or Summit Circuit routes. Climbers heading up Mawenzi actually begin from the Saddle, but this climb should only be attempted by experienced rock climbers. Routes to the Saddle and Mawenzi peak also begin at the Mawenzi Hut or the Mawenzi Tarn Hut.

Planning your climb

PROCEDURES All climbers must check in with the rangers and give details of planned routes; this is essential in the event that someone needs to be rescued. It is mandatory to hire a guide and it is recommended that you only use authorized guides and porters. Children under 10 years of age are not permitted above 3,000 m (9,843 ft). Book huts well in advance. All visitors are urged to dispose of their garbage properly, ensuring a clean, unspoiled climb for future travellers.

Climbing can be undertaken all year, but the best months are January and February with warm clear days and September with its cool clear days. July, August, November and December can also be good, with passing thunderstorms in the later months. The heaviest rainfall is from March to June.

PREPLANNING If you are hoping to reach the summit, you should be in good physical condition, that is, you should be able to jog for 30 minutes without shortness of breath. Do not attempt to climb higher than 3,000 m (9,843 ft) if you have a sore throat, a common

The last water point on Mount Kilimanjaro.

cold or any type of breathing impairment. People with heart and lung ailments are advised not to climb at all. An attitude of 'mind over matter' is important, though the climb should be taken at your own pace and not rushed beyond your personal limits.

A good supply of fluids is essential when climbing. It is recommended that you drink at least 4–5 litres (7–9 pt) of water or fruit juice per day, and that you keep a bottle with you at all times. Above 4,000 m (13,124 ft) it is best to breathe through the nose because the air is so dry. Sweating must be controlled and is best regulated by starting off the climb wearing layers of clothing which can be removed or added as required. Change clothing immediately if it becomes wet. Appetite usually tapers off above 4,000 m (13,124 ft), so food supplies should be especially appealing for this part of the climb. Light foods high in carbohydrates are recommended, such as bread, cereals and rice (dehydrated foods are unappealing at high altitudes). Citrus fruits and bananas reduce alkaline levels

in the blood caused by the climb. Start your climb with two pairs of shoes that have been 'broken in': a light pair for walking and using around the huts, and a second pair for mud, rain, snow and ice. Clothing should include a sweater, windproof jacket, rain gear, long underwear, hat and lightweight cap, mittens/gloves, shoes, socks (cotton or wool), scarf, sunglasses, sunblock, first-aid kit, toilet paper, medicines, sweets/nuts, fruit, water bottle, torch with spare batteries, and money should you wish to purchase drinks at Mandara Hut (climbers can also purchase bottled water each day thus avoiding the extra weight of carrying your entire trip's supply). Limited items such as a sleeping bag can be rented from authorized climbing companies.

EMERGENCIES If you have opted for the Marangu Route a rescue team is on call throughout Kilimanjaro National Park. However, all other routes require that you contact park headquarters in an emergency;

they will send for rangers and/or experts. Moshi has a large hospital which can deal with such emergencies.

For further information and tips about climbing and hiring authorized guides contact: Kilimanjaro Mountain Club, PO Box 66, Moshi. An alternative when looking for guides and porters is the YMCA in Moshi.

MKOMAZI GAME RESERVE

This reserve located to the southeast of Mount Kilimanjaro on the border between Tanzania and Kenya, and lying directly alongside Kenya's Tsavo National Park, was gazetted in 1951. Since then, however, neglect and abuse in the form of poaching, overgrazing and burning have had drastic long-term repercussions; by 1987, 87% of the wildlife had been slaughtered. The future of the Mkomazi Game Reserve did not look promising until the joint intervention in 1988 of the George Adamson Wildlife Preservation Trusts, directed by Tony Fitzjohn and the Tanzanian Department of Wildlife.

The reserve covers 3,276 km^2 (1,260 sq. miles) and not only has breathtaking landscapes, but is also shadowed by the silhouettes of the Usambara and Pare mountain ranges. Covering 70% of the area is acacia-commiphora bushland, although there are areas of baobab and flat-topped acacia (*Acacia tortilis*). The hills and valleys of the reserve provide a perfect backdrop for the more than 450 bird species that have been recorded, among them the uncommon Threestreaked tchagra, the Blacknecked weaver and Rosy-patched shrike.

The first five years of rehabilitation have proved successful as wildlife populations are returning to the reserve and are continuously growing in number. Animals are best seen around the springs, waterholes and dams. The area around Dindira Dam in the northwest section of the reserve is exceptionally good; here Coke's hartebeest (kongoni), impala, buffalo, elephant, Grant's gazelle, zebra and Maasai giraffe are commonly seen. Present also, though less commonly seen, are kudu, eland, oryx and gerenuk. Predators occur

in the reserve too, though the extensive numbers of kopjes and often dense scrub can prove to be excellent camouflage.

The current development programme for the reserve includes a rhino sanctuary which, it is hoped, will be operational by 1996, and a wild dog project. The establishment of a semipermanent tented camp and two small mobile camps is in the planning stages, as well as the introduction of walking safaris with armed rangers, and night game drives.

An outreach programme that is looking at the issues and problems facing the local communities is well under way and is making some headway with answers and solutions, while also helping the residents of the area to understand the needs of the reserve and the importance of conservation. Animal numbers are not staggering, but the game reserve's exciting plans for the future and the sheer beauty of the area afford visitors a wonderful bush experience in a little visited reserve.

TARANGIRE NATIONAL PARK

Lying southwest of Arusha National Park, Tarangire, with its rolling hills, riverine forests, acacia woodlands and ancient baobabs, covers 2,600 km^2 (1,000 sq. miles). The dry season attracts high concentrations of wildlife to the area as the park provides the only permanent water in southern Maasailand by way of the Tarangire River.

The standard of roads within the northern section of the park is acceptable, though visitors should approach areas consisting of black cotton soil with caution during the rains, as many roads become impassable. This soil is arid throughout the dry season, even cracking at times, but come the rains it becomes a black sticky mess that can delay game drives for hours. Visitors to the park generally keep to the northern and middle sections, as the southern section is currently served by a minimal road system, much of which is for the use of park authorities only.

Entrance into the park is prohibited before 06:00 and guests are required to return to their lodges or campsites by 19:00. Bollards occur throughout the park, but it is a good idea to have a map as some roads are not marked. Visitors can get out of their vehicles in open areas provided they do not approach the animals or take unnecessary risks. Activities centre on game drives which, combined with the dramatic landscapes and views, ensure that guests enjoy their stay. There can be no better way to watch life on the African plains than to have a picnic in the shade of a giant baobab or on the bank of a river.

Fauna and flora in the park

Tarangire National Park forms part of an ecosystem that includes Lake Manyara National Park to the northwest and five surrounding game controlled areas (the most northerly being Lake Natron). This ecosystem is based around patterns of annual migration, and plays an important role in the preservation of wildlife, particularly as the ever-increasing problem of human encroachment becomes a serious threat. Although the park contains wildlife all year, the vast majority of plains game moves off with the arrival of the short rains in October and November. The long rains generally begin in March and it is not until June that the plains and forests of Tarangire once again brim with wildlife. The wetter seasons can be worth a journey, however, especially for bird-watchers.

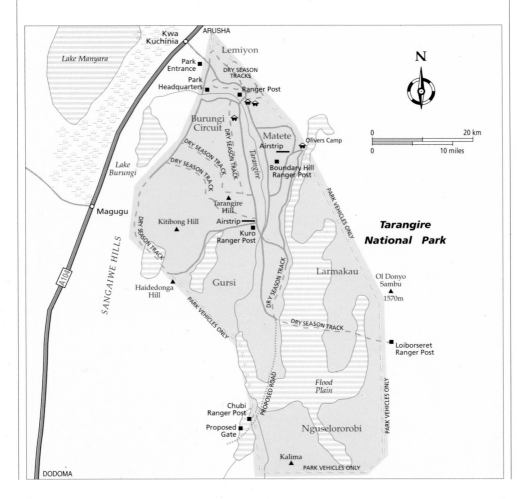

As is the case with many ecosystems, the plant and tree life dictates the species of wildlife existing in particular areas. Changes in ecosystems are occurring all the time, but recent years have seen a dramatic alteration in the vegetation along the river: damage to acacias caused by elephant action and fire are slowly transforming the area from riverine forest to open expanses.

One inhabitant of the park you're not likely to miss is the tsetse fly. This pest has had a major influence on livestock rearing by the locals and the choice of suitable grazing throughout Tanzania as it can carry a form of sleeping sickness called trypanosomiasis. For this reason, the Maasai people have avoided this area with their cattle in the past, but, as attempts to eliminate tsetse fly from the region are becoming more successful, encroachment on the wildlife is likely. (Wild animals over the years have become immune to its bite, but domestic stock is still susceptible.) Though 'tryps' is not often found in the tsetse of Tarangire, it is advisable to keep your legs and arms well covered and protected. Bites can produce soreness and swelling, but this usually dissipates quickly.

Lemiyon, the most northerly triangle of the park, is the first section encountered on entering the gate. It is defined by the western

YE OLDE TIME-KEEPER

A prominent indigenous tree is the baobab (*Adansonia digitata*). Distinct in appearance and believed to survive for several centuries, some of these quiet giants have been shown by recent carbon dating to be close to 3,000 years old. Usually found growing in low-lying arid and semi-arid regions, the baobab stands tall and robust, with a bole circumference of up to 10 m (33 ft). The tree's stubby, unruly branches give it an air of having been uprooted and deposited head-first in the soil. Its branches are bereft of leaves most of the year, while the tree's white blossoms are lovely to look at but carry a most unpleasant bouquet. Practically every part of the baobab can be consumed and is used by both man and beast. Leaves, fruit, flowers, seeds and roots are all used for medicinal purposes, particularly for fever and vitamin C deficiencies. The baobab's hollow trunk is used by hornbills as a nesting rook, by the locals to bury their dead, and even as a water reservoir; some trees have been known to have a capacity of 140,000 litres (30,800 gal)!

The baobab's wood is spongy and so is clearly not suitable for building material, firewood or charcoal. However, its fibrous bark has a multitude of uses, from ropes, mats and cloth to the creation of musical instruments. The baobab is an extremely adaptable tree, and is able even to survive fires. Once its outer

skin has been stripped away, it is capable – if left to recover undisturbed – of regenerating new bark. These attributes help to prolong the life of the amazing baobab despite both man-made and natural adversities.

A baobab in Lake Manyara National Park.

and eastern park boundaries and the Tarangire River to the south. The terrain is a mix of grassland plain and acacia-combretum woodland in between; rich black cotton soils also occur. Wildlife is often found in high numbers throughout this region, and majestic baobabs are everywhere. Seen throughout most of the year without any leaves, the tree's enormous size and stature plays an important role in the Tarangire ecosystem. The semi-hollow bole of the baobab serves as a refuge for nesting birds, particularly hornbills, and the tree is amazingly tolerant to damage caused by bark-stripping elephants. Also throughout the northern section of the park is the toothbrush tree *(Salvadora persica)*, the twigs of which are, in fact, used as toothbrushes by some of the local people. The park headquarters and airstrip are in the Lemiyon area as are some of the public campsites.

Beyond Lemiyon, the park is divided lengthwise into Matete (named after the tall elephant grass and reeds that grow on the riverbanks) to the east and the Lake Burungi Circuit to the west. Matete is the best area to watch game at the river. This is a unique phenomenon, as the waters of the river are saline and usually shunned by game. But the wild animals seem to have developed a tolerance for it. Birdlife is prolific; birds are commonly found nesting in the thorny, gnarled and twisted branches of the umbrella acacias' *(Acacia tortilis)* flat-topped canopy.

RIGHT: *Mashado Luxury Tented Safaris, Tarangire.*
BELOW: *Tarangire Safari Lodge.*

Zebra and giraffe on the Tarangire River.

The Lake Burungi Circuit on the western edge is a lovely drive, approximately 80 km (50 miles) in total, which meanders through acacia and combretum woodland. Burungi, and Kitibong to the south, feature doum palms *(Hyphaene compressa)*, as well as the candelabra tree *(Euphorbia candelabrum)*. The latter is one of the few trees not used in traditional medicine as it produces a milky substance that is highly toxic, causing blindness and ulcerations if it comes into contact with the skin. A viewpoint located roughly 8 km (5 miles) from the park's western border looks over the alkaline lakes, Burungi and Manyara, and the peaks of Milima Mitatu (Three Hills) – an impressive sight.

Further to the south are the Kitibong Hill and Gursi sections of the park, and, on the east side, the seasonal swamp Larmakau. The Gursi area has black cotton soils near Haidedonga Hill on the western border and acacia-commiphora woodland edging the river. The arrival of the rains sees a dramatic change come over the Larmakau area. The soil rapidly absorbs the rainwater and becomes sticky, turning into swamps. Hippos love this muddy marshland – in fact, the name Larmaukau derives from the Maasai word for hippopotamus, *ol lakau.*

The Nguselororobi and Mkungunero areas, a combination of open plains, marshy areas and freshwater pools, are difficult to access unless under extremely dry conditions. Viewing of wildlife can be good but limited, and waterfowl is plentiful but can be seen elsewhere in the park in more accessible areas.

Tarangire's wildlife

During the dry season, which lasts from June to September, Tarangire's landscape teems with wildlife: plains game and predators alike are present in great numbers. The early morning and late afternoon is the best time for game-viewing as the coolness promotes activity among most of the wild animals. Ungulates ranging from the tallest – the Maasai giraffe – to the smallest – the dik-dik – browse on treetops and low-lying bushes. Around rocky terrain and kopjes, rock hyrax and shy klipspringers are often seen. Spotted and striped hyenas occur throughout the park, and their whoop is a common sound at night. It is possible to encounter large herds of buffalo, especially in the Kitibong Hill region. The exquisitely marked fringe-eared oryx is common to the Matete area, and the massive, shy eland can be seen along the Burungi Circuit. Baboons and vervet monkeys occur throughout the park but are usually seen moving in troops in the Matete area. Spending most of the day foraging, preening and keeping track of their territories, they commonly move to the safety of trees at night to avoid becoming the prey of leopards and Martial eagles.

The large predators, such as lion, leopard and cheetah, can be seen throughout the park as well as some of the less sought-after hunters – civets, jackals and rare hunting dogs. If you keep an eye on termite mounds, you may catch the curious, playful antics of a mongoose troop or spot the lazy lines of a monitor lizard basking in the sun. Don't ignore the branches above, as in Tarangire particularly pythons are known to rest in the trees along the river.

With the dry season comes the return of Tarangire's most famous animal herds, elephant. These gentle giants can be found close to the river as well as throughout the park. Travelling in bachelor groups or family herds

THE AFRICAN ELEPHANT

The largest land mammal, the African elephant (*Loxodonta africana*) is much larger than its Asian counterpart and begins life weighing around 113 kg (250 lb), is half a metre (2 ft) at the shoulder and will continue to grow throughout its life. Females grow to 2.5 m (8 ft) and weigh 2,720 kg (6,000 lb), while males range from 3 to 3.5 m (10–12 ft) and weigh close to 5,440 kg (12,000 lb).

The elephant's massive skull is relatively light to compensate for the enormous tusks it carries. The animal uses a technique of flapping its impressive ears gently back and forth to move the blood around, which in turn cools the body; an elephant's ears will stand straight out in aggression, or while charging. Its trunk has two prehensile protrusions which enable it to pick up items as delicate as a feather or, to the other extreme, push over an entire tree. However, this skill is not an instinctive one and must be learnt; youngsters are often seen wiggling their trunks around, sometimes even stepping on or tripping over them! By the age of 6 months, they will have come close to mastering the use of their trunk, drinking water and consuming adequate amounts of vegetation. Adults eat roughly 5% of their body weight daily and, at one drinking session, will suck up 100–200 litres (22–44 gal) of water before squirting it into their mouth.

Females become sexually mature at around 11 years, and produce their first calf by about 13. Generally a female will become pregnant again soon after the birth of a baby, allowing the calf to suckle until the birth of the next one in 22 months. This cycle continues throughout the female's lifespan.

The African elephant is an extremely social animal. In a casual greeting ceremony, it will place the tip of its trunk in another's mouth, or, in a more formal ceremony, will flap and raise its ears, sound off a greeting rumble or touch others' trunks. Elephants are encountered either singly, in a natal group led by a matriarch and consisting of females, babies and adolescents, or in bachelor herds consisting of males who have attained sexual maturity at 10–15 years and have left the family group. Elephants spend most of their day eating and drinking; they are constantly engaged in the search for food. In the heat of the day they take refuge in forested areas, emerging onto the open plains once the relentless sun has given way to evening.

composed of females and their young, they spend their days moving through the park in search of food, water and shade. Herds average in size between 20 and 30 members, though a few have as many as 100 to 200 individuals. In the dry season, the elephant population can reach as high as 3,000.

Over 300 species of birds have been recorded in Tarangire, and breeding records show some of the highest numbers in the world. It is possible to view waterbirds, game birds, weavers and even ostriches. On the open plains, look for the Rednecked spurfowl, as well as the Kori bustard – the heaviest flying bird (12 kg; 26 lb). During mating season, the male Kori bustard puts on an impressive display, puffing out the white plumage around its neck and tail. The Bateleur eagle, named after the French word for 'tumbler', is breathtaking when displaying its acrobatic manoeuvres, and can be identified by its rich black-and-white plumage and stark red beak. Though the Ground hornbill roosts in trees at night, it is usually seen on the ground feeding on grubs, insects and small reptiles. The hornbill is the size of a turkey, but has striking black feathers and is bright red around its face. Long eyelashes give these hornbills a distinct character, as does their haunting, melancholy call heard in the early morning and late evening. Flashes of striking colour are provided by rollers and bee-eaters. Birds of prey are abundant, among them many species of vulture and the Martial eagle.

LAKE MANYARA NATIONAL PARK

Resting in the Great Rift Valley, this park covers only 330 km² (120 sq. miles) of which the lake takes up 230 km² (86 sq. miles). Lake Manyara lies at the foot of the dramatic escarpment formed by the western wall of the Rift's eastern arm. Noticeably here, there is no eastern wall to the Rift; rather the landscape gently eases into a depression. As a result, some of the area's most spectacular scenery occurs here. The name *manyara* is the Maasai word for the pencil plant (*Euphorbia tirucalli*) which is often planted to form thick barricades that serve as livestock bomas.

TOP: *The olive baboon.*
ABOVE: *The Kori bustard is found in Tarangire.*

75

The size of the park makes it a perfect destination for day trips, but bird enthusiasts may want to visit for a longer period. Picnic sites have been designated throughout the park and offer panoramic views, shade and latrines. There is a small museum inside the gate office which offers information on the formation of the lake and Rift Valley, and what can be seen in the park. The museum has several bird and animal specimens on display, but unfortunately the passage of time is taking its toll on these exhibits. Visitors can drive in the park from 06:30 to 19:00. Note that the late afternoon/early evening light is spectacular along the lake shore. The long dry season is from June to September with less hazy days occurring in June; a short dry season during January and February is also superb for game-viewing.

The habitats that exist throughout the park are determined by the geological structure of the region. Porous volcanic rock in the

LION: PRIDE OF THE PREDATORS

Lion are the largest of Africa's cats. In contrast to the cat family's more solitary members, such as the leopard and cheetah, lion are the only true social cats as they live in prides, complex social groupings made up of a core of females with one or two or more males, who will mate with any of the females within the pride. Males may join together and will sometimes compete with single males in an existing pride in an effort to take control of it. Cubs from various females are born around the same time and mothers will share their milk with the different cubs, adopting them if a mother dies. Females are responsible for hunting and rearing the young, while males defend the territory. Since they don't always have speed on their side when stalking more agile prey, females often work together to trap their victims. Lions generally sleep during the day (often resting for 18–20 hours) and can hunt at night, but it is possible to witness a lion kill in daylight, either during the early morning or late evening. At Manyara, favourite lion prey is buffalo, wildebeest, zebra and antelope.

A pride of lion in the Ngorongoro Crater. Lion may be seen throughout this area.

Mto-wa-Mbu near Lake Manyara National Park.

northern section allows for good drainage at the base of the Rift wall and the rivers and streams flowing out support the dense tropical vegetation of the ground-water forest. Around the Msasa River and further south is nonporous, hard crystalline rock; here there are conspicuously fewer watercourses and less forest-like vegetation. Areas of acacia woodland occur south of the river, with open grassland plains around the edges of the lake.

Hippo Pools

The hippo pools on the Simba River in the north of the park are an important part of a visit to Lake Manyara. As you make your way to the lake from the seclusion of the forest, the vegetation changes dramatically, opening out to grassy plains with wild mangos *(Tabernaemontana usambarensis)* and the doum *(Hyphaene ventricosa)* and wild date *(Phoenix reclinata)* palms. It is possible to get out of your vehicle at the hippo pools and view the abundant birdlife that gravitates to the marsh as well as the several pods of hippo

that rise and submerge in their murky abodes. Hippos weigh between 2,000 and 3,000 kg (4,400–6,600 lb). Their skin is extremely sensitive to the harsh sun and they therefore submerge themselves in water for much of the day; the reddish colour on their skin is produced by a mucous gland secretion which protects the skin from drying out. Hippos can remain underwater for three to five minutes, sometimes longer if necessary, before resurfacing, which allows them to breed, give birth and suckle while submerged. They leave the water in the late evening, when it's cooler, to feed off the vegetation of the land, consuming up to 60 kg (130 lb) during one feeding session – at Manyara they often graze on the sedge growing close to the lake shores.

On land, one should always avoid coming between a hippo and its path to or from the water as it can become very aggressive – and is extremely dangerous. Generally placid, hippos can become engaged in fierce battles over territory – evident by scars on the backs of some hippos – when they display an impressive array of tusks in yawn-like gestures and employ ferocious biting tactics.

Waterbirds are abundant at the hippo pools. Look for Sacred ibis, Knob-billed ducks, African jacanas, Greater cormorants, Water dikkops and Blacksmith's plovers. January to May sees the arrival and nesting of European wood storks, while in July Yellow-billed storks, White pelicans and Pinkbacked pelicans arrive by the thousands. Flamingos also make a showing at Manyara throughout the year, sometimes shrouding the lake in pink. Throughout East Africa, both the Lesser and Greater flamingos migrate regularly between the various soda lakes, so their presence at Lake Manyara is unpredictable from one year to the next. This is a most pleasant spot, and can be visited several times during the day with new discoveries at each visit.

Manyara's wildlife

The forested sections between the escarpment wall and the lake are full of wildlife and birds that can be fully appreciated by following the tracks that weave in and out of palm thickets, acacia woodland, and the baobab

Hippo pools, Lake Manyara National Park.

and sausage trees (the latter, *Kigelia africana*, has been given its common name because of its large, elongated fruit). The shade provided by the trees is a relief from the gruelling sun for both visitors and resident wildlife populations. Bird-watching in the ground-water forest may prove difficult as the common trees such as *Bridella micrantha*, *Ficus sycamorus* (wild fig) and *Antiaris toxicaria* reach massive heights. But one bird that is usually heard is the Silverycheeked hornbill.

In the southern half of the park are two easily accessible hot springs, Maji Moto Ndogo ('little hot water') and, in the extreme south, the hotter Maji Moto (the temperature can reach 60 °C/140 °F). The heated water emerges from fractures in the rock originating very deep within the earth, caused by the faulting of the Rift Valley. At Maji Moto, look carefully at the rocks near the escarpment for the shy, elusive klipspringer. These small antelope have narrow, cylindrical-type hooves that enable them to leap agilely over rocks. Both males and females carry horns.

Blue monkeys and vervets are commonly seen within the safety of the trees, while baboons can be encountered moving throughout the park while searching for food. Elephant are regular inhabitants during the drier seasons and are often seen in the shade of trees or heading for the lake shore.

Buffalo too are present, though they tend to stay hidden. Maasai giraffe and impala are residents all year round.

Probably the animal that visitors come to see most is the famous tree-climbing lion. The acacia woodland south of the Msasa River in the northern section of the park consists primarily of umbrella trees (*Acacia tortilis*), whose curving branches and shade-providing canopies are an ideal spot to retreat to in the heat of day. Often from beneath the treetops, a lazy tail or careless paw can be seen dangling as a lion indulges in one of the things it does best ... sleep.

As many as 380 bird species have been recorded in the park; worth noting are the Wattled, Glossy and Ashy starlings, Cliff chats, Rufous crowned rollers, Fantailed widowbirds, Red and Yellow barbets and the Giant kingfisher.

MTO-WA-MBU

The town of Mto-wa-Mbu (meaning 'mosquito creek') is on the edge of Lake Manyara National Park, just before the road ascends the escarpment of the Rift Valley's eastern arm. There are several *dukas* (small shops) in which to purchase refreshments and minimal supplies, and fuel is available along with some budget camping facilities.

Once you're on your way to the Ngorongoro Conservation Area, you will climb the escarpment, where a couple of viewpoints offer panoramic vistas of the Rift floor and Lake Manyara. The wind can be quite strong, but it is definitely worth a few pictures. The road twists and winds through extremely diverse countryside. There is a concentration of agricultural fields and herds of cattle.

About 25 km (16 miles) after leaving Lake Manyara, the next landmark is the town of Karatu. Time permitting, a stopover at the secluded Gibb's Farm in the Ngorongoro highlands, 4 km (2.5 miles) from Karatu, provides a pleasant break, even if you only stop for lunch. Over the next 40 km (25 miles), you may start to feel the temperature change as you gradually climb to higher elevations.

TOP: *Vervet monkey, Ngorongoro Crater.*
ABOVE: *Sausage tree,* Kigelia africana.

The coffee plantations and fields of vegetable crops slowly give way to the denser vegetation of the crater highlands. After checking in at the Lodware Gate, you enter the paradise of the Ngorongoro Conservation Area and begin your ascent to the crater rim.

NGORONGORO CONSERVATION AREA

Spanning roughly 8,300 km² (3,192 sq. miles), the Ngorongoro Conservation Area (NCA) is a perfect microcosm of East Africa: it combines breathtaking vistas and valuable archaeological sites with mountains, forests, grassland plains, extinct volcanoes, and a staggering profusion of wildlife. The goal of the area, administered by the Ngorongoro Conservation Area Authority (NCAA), is to accommodate the needs of the wild animals and the local Maasai people and their domestic stock, at the same time protecting the natural habitat. The Ngorongoro Crater, which was declared a World Heritage Site in 1978, is

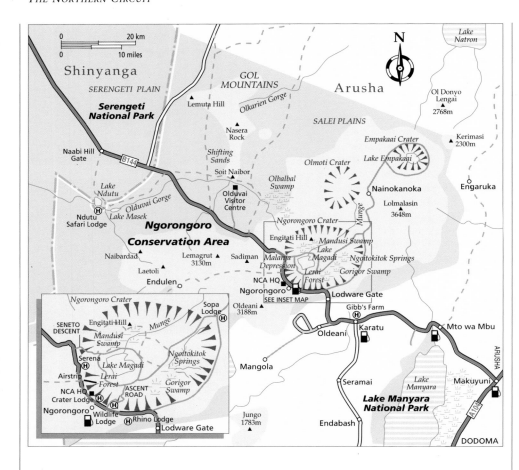

GIBB'S FARM

This is a delightful lodge with lovely gardens and a peaceful setting overlooking panoramic vistas. The food is delicious and the staff warm and accommodating. With an ideal location, between Lake Manyara and the Ngorongoro Conservation Area, Gibb's Farm is set amid coffee plantations and rolling hillsides. Originally built by a German in the 1930s, the farm was later purchased in 1948 by James Gibb. In 1972 Gibb's Farm was converted to a lodge, but continues to exude an old-world charm today. Dinner is served in the inviting old farmhouse, and most appealing are the home-grown vegetables and freshly ground coffee produced on the farm. Accommodation is offered in the form of 15 double rooms in cottages built along a garden path. There are walks to nearby caves and a waterfall, and a safari service is offered through Gibb's Farm Safaris. Telephone and fax facilities are both available. Gibb's Farm's sister lodge is the Ndutu Safari Lodge, which is located in the Ngorongoro Conservation Area adjacent to Serengeti National Park.

relatively small in proportion to the whole area – that is, 260 km² (100 sq miles) or 3% of the conservation area.

The NCA's grassland plains are also home to the famous archaeological sites of Laetoli and Olduvai Gorge where traces can be seen of man's ancient ancestors, who walked, used tools and hunted in this area.

Wildlife populations move freely in and out of the NCA depending on the water resources and time of year. The grassland plains, part of the Serengeti ecosystem, become the temporary residence after the 'short' rains of millions of white-bearded wildebeest, or gnu, on their annual migratory trek. When the plains dry up at the end of the 'long' rains in May/June, they begin their journey west and north to the grasslands of Serengeti and Masai Mara.

The conservation area is subject to two climatic seasons, dry and wet, which vary according to geographic location. For example, during the wet season, usually from November to May, the plains resting at the foot of the western face of the surrounding mountains are considerably drier and the area is known as the 'rain shadow'. The eastern and southern highland zones are moister as they catch the westward winds from the

Indian Ocean. The first few months of the dry season – June and July – can be quite cool to cold at night, so visitors to the area should ensure they have a sweater or jacket. The cold causes condensation of moisture in the air and the crater rim may be cloaked in mist, but the crater floor below is clear and bright. Grass fires later in the dry season create a haze, spoiling the panoramic views, but the warmer month of October and the onset of rain in November quickly clears the skies.

Highlights of the NCA

During a stay at the crater rim, you will no doubt spend a day exploring the floor below, observing the varied wildlife. Breakfast or a picnic lunch at any of the designated sites is an excellent way to escape the sun's rays. The Ngorongoro Conservation Area is world renowned for the diversity and vast numbers of its wildlife; notably, there are some species that are common throughout East Africa and in the conservation area but are absent in the crater itself. The lack of giraffe is obvious, presumably due to the absence of trees to browse on. Also not present are impala, though the reason for this is not clear.

The entrance to Ngorongoro National Park.

A day trip to the Olmoti or Empakaai crater is a wonderful way to explore the highlands and volcanic landscapes, but a Conservation Area ranger must accompany all travellers heading into these areas. The roads in this area are rough, so, if you are equipped for it, a better option would be to camp at the edge of either crater rim. Walking and camping are permitted as long as a ranger is present.

Olduvai Gorge is also worth a day trip during a stay in the Conservation Area, but many visitors opt to spend time at the gorge on their way to or from Serengeti National Park. At the Olduvai site, you will need to pay a nominal fee, which permits access to the area and to the museum filled with both authentic and reproductions of artefacts. Also included is a brief lecture on the site, its finds and the work carried out by the Leakeys. If you are travelling in a four-wheel-drive vehicle, it is possible to go down into the gorge to see specific dig sites, including where Mary Leakey found the skull of *Zinjanthropus* (now classified as *Australopithecus boisei*). Visitors are welcome to enjoy their lunch under a temporary shelter at the rim of the gorge, which serves to block the heat of the sun and breaks the wind that is always present.

Lakes Ndutu and Masek – as well as the open plains – are the most dramatic in the wet season, from November to May, when they teem with wildlife. Although it is difficult to pinpoint the exact whereabouts of the wildlife as it moves into the area, it usually doesn't take long before visitors are trailing numerous species of herbivores and predators across the plains.

Formation of the NCA

The geographical activity that created the geological structure of the Ngorongoro Conservation Area actually began over 500 million years ago. Movement in the earth's crust forced the underlying rock up to the surface where it was exposed to the elements of rain, wind and sun over millions of years. Evidence of harder rock withstanding these erosive forces is still apparent in the gneiss and

quartzite Gol mountains and Lemuta Hill in the far northwest sector of the Conservation Area, and the granite and gneiss kopjes of the Serengeti plains; once ancient hills, they are now gradually eroding away.

The African continent has maintained its present shape for roughly 70 million years. The giant crack that developed 20 million years ago, tearing the earth's crust apart and allowing the land to sink in between, is today known as the Great Rift Valley. With the subsidence of the land, increased intense heat caused melting of the rock, resulting in hot lava forcing itself through rifts and fissures. Thus began the slow formation of the Ngorongoro Conservation Area's volcanoes. The rifting activity and subsequent build-up of layers of basalt and ash from lava flows over millions of years gives an indication of the age of the volcanic cones. It is believed that some of the oldest are Lemagrut, Oldeani and Sadiman – whose eruption 3.6 million years ago preserved the famous Laetoli archaeological find: fossilized footprints made by early upright-walking hominids, *Australopithecus afarensis*.

As a volcano, Ngorongoro slowly built up in size; it is, in fact, thought to have rivalled Kilimanjaro in size about 2.5 million years ago. Ngorongoro's vents starting filling with dense rock, however, inhibiting the molten lava's progress and forcing it to take other paths. The structural weaknesses that occurred with the retreating lava caused Ngorongoro's peak to collapse inward, forming the modern world's largest perfect caldera. This process occurred many times in the area, and small hills and cones formed by escaping molten lava can be seen throughout the region today. Ancient rifted walls are also still visible, a good example being the 1,000 m (3,280 ft) granite Eyasi escarpment that runs past the lake of the same name.

Volcanic activity gradually subsided and by about 2 million years ago the basic formation of the area had reached its peak. With the onslaught of the elements, helped by the erosive action of rocks and soils carried along by the rain, the land was shaped and moulded.

Elephant are among the wildlife in the crater.

The rains contributed to the opening up of canyons and in time enormous lakes formed in the valleys with the constant inflow of water. At one time the area around Olduvai contained an enormous lake (which no longer exists today). Rivers originating from the top of escarpments carried with them minerals which were eventually deposited into the lakes. This gradual build-up resulted in alkaline waters which left behind deep soda pans as the lakes dried up.

The fertile soils of the Salei and Serengeti plains in the north of the NCA are a result of Kerimasi's (to the northeast) last eruption in which lime-rich ash was carried west with the prevailing winds, settling on top of the existing lava beds and over the Gol mountains. Olduvai was still taking form, but the great lakes of the valley floor were beginning to reduce and subside. Ol Donyo Lengai, or 'mountain of God' in the Maa language, began to form and eventually built into a massive cone. Lengai still produces steam, and sometimes even ash, from vents in its crater. It erupted as recently as 1983.

On the Conservation Area's plains are the amazing Shifting Sands, a moving 9-m-high (30 ft) barchan (or crescent-shaped) dune formed from the black ash spewed out by the dormant Lengai (*see* panel on page 84).

Vegetation within the NCA
The dense and beautiful vegetation of the highlands and forests changes with elevation. The lower reaches feature heavy concentrations of indigenous crotons. The broad-leaved species *Croton macrostachyus* is a large deciduous tree with fuzzy, heart-shaped leaves and soft yellow flowers. *Croton megalcarpus*, whose name refers to its large seeds which tend to sprout wherever they fall, is fast-growing and has large elliptical leaves with silvery undersides that aid water retention. Just after the rains, spikes of pale yellow flowers occur, though they are short-lived. Squirrels and birds eat the nuts which are rich in protein and oil, while some African communities ingest the oil and bark to kill

intestinal worms. The flat-topped red thorn (*Acacia lahai*) and the enormous *Albizia gummifera*, which plays an important role in soil stabilization, are also present here.

On the higher slopes, the *Nuxia congesta*, recognized by its distorted bole and, during the rains, its clusters of white flowers, and the strangler fig *(Ficus thonningii)* are the most prolific trees. Mosses, ferns and orchids are conspicuous in the moister areas, as is the lichen, old man's beard (*Usnea*), draped eerily in tangled tufts from tree branches. Along the roadside you are likely to see the yellow blossoms of the shrubs *Psiadia punctulata*

SHIFTING SANDS

Located just north of Olduvai is a fascinating natural phenomenon, a barchan (crescent-shaped) dune known as the Shifting Sands, composed of ash blown west after one of Ol Donyo Lengai's eruptions roughly 30,000 years ago. There are several other dunes created in the same manner, though they are further away and not as large. The 100-m-long, 9-m-high (109 yd, 30 ft) Shifting Sands can by no means be compared to the giants found in Namibia, but its unique location, set as it is in the grassland plains, and its continual westward movement make it an interesting stop on your safari. The dune moves only during the dry season, covering an average of 17 m (18 yd) per year as indicated by the concrete markers first set up in 1969. The dune's shape is formed by the westward winds which continuously blow the sand up the windward side, forcing it to crest over the peak and tumble down the leeward side. Many granules roll to the sides of the dune, forming the tight curves. The wind swirling around the dune aids in keeping its shape as it slowly moves across the open savanna. As you walk around the dune you will see the iridescent colours of many dead dung beetles. One theory is based on the fact that female beetles create a ball of dung which they dig into the ground in order to lay an egg in it, after which the developing larva eventually eats away its protective dung sphere to emerge as a beetle. But often the young beetle finds that the dune has moved over the area in which its dung ball was originally buried. Unable to dig itself out of the sand, the beetle dies. As the dune moves slowly across the plains, the dead beetles are uncovered.

The Maasai people believe the Shifting Sands is sacred. Maasai women perform ceremonial dances there to ensure fertility, good rainfall and good health for their children.

Shifting Sands can be reached by crossing through Olduvai Gorge. The track heads west with the Soit Naibor hill rising on the right; Shifting Sands lies a few kilometres ahead. A four-wheel-drive vehicle is required and visitors must be accompanied by a guide from the Visitors Centre at Olduvai.

The NCA's intriguing Shifting Sands.

with shiny tapered leaves, and the *Conyza newii* with serrated tapered leaves and bright yellow button clusters. You may also see the tall, erect *Hibiscus vitifolius*, displaying pale yellow petals with a deep maroon centre. Although many of the flowers in the area appear yellow, they contrast with the deep blue of the spreading herb, elephant ears *(Commelina bengalensis)*, and the common shrub *Vernonia auriculifera*, which has large pale-pink to pale-violet flower heads. Another lovely flower is the *Crinum macaowanii* with its trumpet-shaped pink and white flower; there is an even rarer albino species.

The road down to the crater is one of the best places to view the tall euphorbias, *Euphorbia bussei* and *E. candelabrum*. At first glance they appear very similar, but on closer inspection you may notice that the branches of *E. candelabrum* are long and straight, lacking the ripple effect of the more numerous *E. bussei*. The most prolific shrubs, all related species, are *Lantana trifolia* with mauve and slightly yellow flowers, *Lippia javanica* and *Lippia ukambensis*, both of which have white and yellow clusters.

The most extensive vegetation type on the crater floor is grassland. The long grasses are usually a combination of red oat grass *(Themeda triandra)*, Rhodes grass *(Chloris gayana)*, which thrives in alkaline soils, and bamboo grass *(Pennisetum mezianum)*, distinguished by its tufted spikes and found in many types of soil, although it often occurs in black cotton soils. The short grasses, more palatable to wildlife, are predominantly made up of finger grasses *(Digitaria)*, common star grasses *(Cynodon dactylon)* and drop seed grasses *(Sporobolus ioclados)*.

Flowers emerge with the rain. Throughout the crater floor and along the rim you will notice the bright orange petals of the tall lion's mane *(Leonotis sp.)*, which can be seen all year round, and after a little rain, the white semiparasitic wastepaper flower *(Cycnium tubulosum)*. Plentiful too are the deep-purple flowers and yellow fruit of the Sodom apple *(Solanum incanum)*. This weed is related to the potato and tomato, and the fruit is not

Euphorbia bussei *on a descent road to the crater.*

only eaten by rhino, elephant and Grant's gazelle, but is also used by local communities as a treatment for warts.

Yellow fever trees *(Acacia xanthophloea)* occur in the forests of the crater floor. On your ascent from the crater look for wild bananas *(Ensete ventricosum)*, which don't produce edible fruit but have attractive leaves that sport a bright rib through their centre, and the exceptional Cape chestnut *(Calodendrum capense)* with its lovely pink flowers and spiky fruit. The rare *Delphinium leroyi* has superb delicate white flowers.

The vegetation of the crater plains is very similar to that of the open plains of Serengeti and Salei. The lack of trees is evident – their roots cannot penetrate the layer of lime that has formed a crust below the surface of the lime-rich soil. Where erosion has occurred because of waterholes and streams, and around kopjes whose ancient rock formations trap water to promote the growth of certain plant life, you are more likely to see the hardier umbrella tree *(Acacia tortilis)*, figs and *Commiphora* sp. Look for flowers such as the pink *Ipomoea jageri*, the yellow *Commelina africana*, the blue *Pentanisia ouranogyne*, and the striking yet deadly poisonous red-and-yellow leopard lily *(Gloriosa superba)*.

Crater Highlands

Your journey to the Ngorongoro Conservation Area will probably start off from Arusha and go through the lowland areas of Lake Manyara, taking you up the fertile escarpment, past the town of Karatu and finally to the even higher crater highland forests at the southern border of the NCA, where entry is through the Lodware Gate. The road twists and turns on its way to the crater rim. Thick vegetation is all around, and you may catch a glimpse of flowers in bloom or be stopped temporarily by a troop of baboons crossing the road. Along your journey you will be compelled to stop and enjoy the exquisite views and expansive landscapes, which may include Oldeani, lying away to the left. Upon reaching the crater rim you will no doubt stop at the viewpoint, marked by a memorial to the many individuals who lost their lives in the protection and conservation of wildlife. On a clear day, views of the crater expanse and floor below are memorable.

In these forested highland areas, you move into a world of tall canopies, mosses, lichens and the soft filtering light of the sun through the montane forest, different from tropical forest as a result of its higher elevation and the fact that it receives less annual rainfall. The forest is vital to life in and around the area, providing water for the vast farmland communities to the south, the people and their cattle, and the wildlife in the NCA.

Ngorongoro's great variety of animals are not always seen, especially nocturnal species such as porcupines, bushbabies and bats, and the even more elusive genets and civets. Most obvious is the olive baboon (blue monkeys are often heard but seldom seen as they live high in the canopy), and larger mammals moving through the forest, such as elephant and buffalo. Antelope are also present, the most common being duiker and bushbuck.

Buffalo can be seen at Lake Manyara, as well as the Ngorongoro highland forests.

Even the large predators are known to exist in the shadows of the forest. Lion are periodically sighted, and leopard, though exquisitely camouflaged, may sometimes be seen moving through the dense vegetation or casually perched in a branch of a tree. While watching the trees, visitors may glimpse the endearing tree hyrax, although this little creature's blood-curdling, high-pitched territorial call may not be so enchanting!

In the crater highlands, birds are more easily heard and seen than the wildlife. You will most often encounter a variety of weavers, Anteater chats, Schalow's wheatears, Common bulbuls, Fiscal shrikes, Boubou shrikes and Speckled mousebirds. Game birds are plentiful and include the Helmeted and Crested guineafowl and Hildebrandt's francolin. Melodic variations of cooing from Tambourine and Redeyed doves add to the peace of the forest. Higher in the trees you may observe the Silverycheeked hornbill, whose off-white casque and loud grunting call are unmistakable. Also lending vibrant flashes of colour to the highlands are the Yellow bishop, dazzling Narina's trogon and the bright green Livingstone's turaco, whose call is synonymous with the forest. Sunbirds like the Bronze (a metallic bronze-green) and Tacazze (a metallic violet) are frequent visitors to the lodges as they, too, enjoy the beautiful gardens. Look out for the Eastern doublecollared sunbird which is metallic green except for a red and yellow breast.

Birds of prey such as the Augur buzzard with its conspicuous red tail and the incredible Verreaux's eagle can often be seen soaring high over the crater rim in search of prey. Common around the lodges are the persistent African black kites and the disreputable-looking Marabou storks.

Looking carefully at the crater floor some 610 m (2,000 ft) below, you can spot the different types of habitat present in the 18-km (11 miles) diameter of the crater. Grassland, marsh, lakes, a riverine zone, forest and rolling hill-slopes unite to create a unique and self-sufficient environment. The crater rim is roughly 2,200 m (7,218 ft) above sea

The Blacksmith plover (TOP) *and the Crested guineafowl* (ABOVE) *are found in the highlands.*

level. To the north, the rim and slopes are dry, while to the southeast and east the dense forests produce moisture and often a shroud of mist. In the crater, you can often see, with the help of binoculars, herds of grazing buffalo or elephant.

As no accommodation is available on the crater floor, you will have many more opportunities to gaze down onto the spectacle below from your lodge or campsite, most of which are situated on the southern and western edges of the crater, though there is one lodge in the far northeast section. From the viewpoint, the rim road heading west will lead you to the lodges and Ngorongoro village some 12 km (7.5 miles) away. Just beyond the first lodge, on your right, you will pass the main ascent road, as well as another important marker: the memorial marking the graves of zoologists Dr Bernhard Grzimek and his son Michael. These two men played an important role in the struggle to understand the ecological issues of the area and they were pioneers in undertaking the first ecological surveys in the 1950s. In 1959, during the filming of *Serengeti Shall Not Die*, Michael was tragically killed when a vulture flew into his plane. His father continued their important work right up until his death in 1987. Both men are buried atop the Ngorongoro Crater and remain a constant reminder of the importance of conservation and wildlife issues.

The crater has many roads, although some may become impassable during the wet season. Visitors are urged to stay on the main roads as driving irresponsibly disturbs the wildlife's habitat. You may also endanger both your own lives and those of the wild animals. Generally, there are sufficient formal tracks and roads to allow guests to get

---

THE SMALLER PREDATORS

Two small, unique predators, the genet and civet (as well as several species of mongoose), all belong to the Viverridae family. They differ from other cats in that they have shorter legs and longer muzzles which can accommodate 36–40 teeth, and all members of this family have nonretractable claws.

SMALL OR COMMON GENET *(Genetta genetta)* This creature is strictly nocturnal, living a primarily solitary life, although at times family units are seen. It has a long, slender body, short legs and a long tail – almost the length of its head and body – which is ringed and usually ends with a whitish mark (occasionally the tip is dark). Along the cat's body, round and elongated spots run in five rows on either side of a dark spinal stripe. The genet has enormous eyes with white spots above and below, and a long pointed nose. Sleeping by day, it becomes active at late dusk until around midnight. It is an adept climber, has excellent eyesight and a good sense of hearing. Genets prey on rats and mice, small birds, eggs, snakes, frogs, fish and insects. The best opportunity of seeing this mammal is near tented camps and lodges, where it is well habituated to the constant activity.

AFRICAN CIVET *(Civettictis civetta)* Also encountered singly, this nocturnal animal is often seen moving about regularly used pathways. It is much larger than a genet, weighing 9–15 kg (20–33 lb), and is roughly the size of a small to medium dog; its back legs are noticeably longer than its front legs. The civet's grey-to-brown hair is spotted with long to roundish dark markings and it has rings on its shorter, bushy tail. The animal has smallish eyes surrounded by dark rings, a pointed muzzle and white ear tips. Civets mark their territory – in a fixed home range – by scenting the area using their anal glands (the secretion is known as 'civet' and is sometimes used by the cosmetics industry as a fixative for high-quality perfumes). These cats feed mainly on hare-sized mammals, smallish birds, reptiles, fallen fruit and amphibians.

SERVAL *(Felis serval)* This cat is predominantly nocturnal, but it is not uncommon to see them in reed beds and tall bushland in the cooler early mornings and late evenings. They are generally seen singly, although hunting pairs or females with their young can sometimes be spotted. The serval is marked with elongated spots, has rings on an unusually short tail and has enlarged black-tipped ears, which are useful when listening for approaching prey. The cat's agile leaps are achieved with its long legs, enabling it to catch birds on the wing. Its diet is made up mainly of birds and small mammals.

Game-viewing at the Ngorongoro Crater.

close to the game without having to resort to destruction of the habitat. The animals are well habituated to vehicles, making observation of game that much more enjoyable.

Ngorongoro Crater

There are three main roads that are used to gain access in and out of the Ngorongoro Crater. The main descent road is located on the west side, north of the lodges, approximately 13 km (8 miles) from the village of Ngorongoro. After passing the airstrip and Serena Lodge, you will see the grassy Malanja Depression to the left and the volcanoes of Lemagrut and Sadiman further to the west. Continuing along the rim road, you will come to an opening in the rim. This is Windy Gap and the start of the main descent road. Caution should be taken whenever driving along this steep descent, especially in the colder weather when it may be shrouded in mist or in the wet season when it can be slick and muddy. This descent road comes out at the Seneto Springs, to the west of Lake Magadi. Expanses of short grass surround the springs and wildlife that typically inhabits the grassland plains is often found here, along with predators and elephant. Birdlife is also prolific and it is well worth spending some time scanning the area. The springs are also the only area on the crater floor where the Maasai may water their livestock (cattle and goats). The animals graze around the Malanja Depression, and you can often see groups of Maasai herding their cattle. If you want to photograph them, you usually have to negotiate a fee.

The crater itself generally has a wide variety of birds. From November to May, many migratory species are present, the most common being Abdim's storks and European wood storks; the Black stork and European shoveller have also been recorded. A large bird often seen walking across the plains is the Kori bustard, sometimes putting on its regal courting display. Other species on the open grassland expanses are the Rosybreasted longclaw, Blacksmith's and Crowned plovers, Blackbellied bustard, the large flightless ostrich and – usually seen in pairs – the exquisite Crowned crane. Look for both Red and Yellow oxpeckers precariously perched on buffalo, zebra, rhino and many other mammals as they peck on the move.

The main ascent road is located on the southern wall and can be picked up east of the Lerai Forest. As it cuts back and forth, magnificent views are revealed, as are the unusual plants and foliage of the rising crater wall. As the road continues up it cuts into an amazing forested canyon before finally reaching the top. Another road at the northeast corner of the crater is used predominantly by guests staying at the Ngorongoro Sopa Lodge, for both the descent and ascent of the crater.

Lake Magadi, Lerai Forest and Seneto Springs

In the west of the crater floor lies Lake Magadi. In Swahili *Magadi* refers to the lake's alkaline or soda composition, while in the Maa language, the lake is referred to as *Makat*. The lake varies in size throughout the year, but consistently remains fairly shallow. During the dry season a white crusty layer is left behind bearing traces of the wet season's activity in the form of impressive spoors from ungulates and predators alike. Several roads wind around the lake, connecting it with other areas of the crater floor.

Below the lake, slightly to the west, is the Lerai Forest, which provides a unique habitat for many species of animals as well as birds. The Maasai name *Lerai* refers to the yellow colour of the acacias, or fever trees (*Acacia xanthophloea*), in the area. Animals large and small retreat to the protection of the forest and make use of its vegetation and water courses. You are likely to find elephant, bushbuck, eland and waterbuck both in the forest and around the swampy areas. The shade and cool of the forest is quite different from the conditions of the open plains, and the tracks through the area are well laid out to ensure that visitors have a pleasant and fulfilling drive. Nestled in the forest is the Lerai picnic site for some rest and relaxation. The site has a water tap and pit latrines.

Additionally, two campsites no longer in use, Fig Tree and Acacia, are located northwest of the forest and also make delightful picnic sites. It is said that some of Fig Tree camp's old figs – a sacred tree to many ethnic groups – were planted around 1840 by the Datoga people at the grave of one of their leaders who died in battle against the Maasai.

In the Lerai Forest you are likely to see smaller birds such as the flashy bee-eater, African hoopoe, shrikes and weavers, as well as guineafowls and francolins. The most obvious bird around Lake Magadi's shores is the Lesser flamingo, with fewer numbers of the Greater flamingo. This ribbon of pink moves from the crater at night, preferring the waters of Lake Natron further north for breeding. At the lake also look out for the Blackwinged stilt and Curlew sandpiper.

Ngorongoro's Marshlands

North of the lake is Engitati Hill, Munge Stream and the Mandusi-Swamp. The road between the Seneto Springs and Engitati passes a handful of small pools in among the swamps known as Goose Ponds. This is another area worth taking a look around as the elusive serval cat is a regular here; so are numerous waterbirds and wildlife seeking out water. The Munge Stream flows from rainwater that has collected in the shallow crater of Olmoti to the north; the waters are routed down Olmoti's southern slopes into the Ngorongoro Crater via the Mandusi Swamp and finally emerge to feed Lake Magadi. A circular track climbs Engitati Hill, to the north of the Mandusi Swamp, and in the dry season it is possible to cut across the marsh to where the Munge Stream enters the lake. Several roads around the swamp area offer good game-viewing and pleasant scenery, but again it should be noted that during the wet season these tracks can become impassable.

To the east of Lake Magadi, the Silalei and Rumbe hills are seen. Silalei, with its gravel-pit top, is near the eastern slope road that leads to Sopa Lodge. Though quite windy at the top of the hill, the steep road on the east side is worth the effort as it is an ideal spot to look for wildlife and enjoy the scenery.

Nearby, a stream cuts along the roadside before it heads down towards to the Ngoitokitok Springs at the eastern foot of the crater. A year-round water supply in this swampy area promotes high concentrations of game, and around June it is common to see the white-bearded wildebeest in their rutting season. It is thought that numbers within the crater can reach 10,000 during the migration.

The small lake and springs of Ngoitokitok provide a superb setting for watching waterbirds and hippo. An old fig tree marks the perfect spot, which is often used by picnickers because of its peaceful setting and the inviting landscape that surrounds it. As a result of the increasing use of the area, African black kites make quite a nuisance of themselves by swooping down and grabbing food directly out of visitors' hands. Caution must be taken if you decide to eat outside your vehicle. An alternate idea for picnicking may be to choose one of the special sites in the Lerai Forest, although it must be noted that the vervet monkeys here are quite sneaky, and precautions need to be taken with the storage of food.

The Ngoitokitok Springs feed the Gorigor Swamp to the southeast. This is an area favoured by the black rhino (the white rhino species doesn't occur in Tanzania) and, though it is rather tempting to deviate from the main tracks, it is best to stay on them as the local terrain can be very wet and it is easy to get bogged down in the mire. The black rhino is undoubtedly one of the greatest sights of the crater. Though its numbers have

The base of the Ngorongoro Crater.

GREATER AND LESSER FLAMINGOS

A brilliant wash of pink at some of the Rift Valley's alkaline lakes indicates that Lesser flamingos and, to a smaller degree, Greater flamingos, are present – sometimes in their millions. Excellent fliers as well as swimmers, flamingos belong to the oldest bird family still in existence: *Phoenicopteriformes*. Fossil remains prove that they existed in the Tertiary period of the Cenozoic era – seven to 70 million years ago. Flamingos actually lose their pink colour when deprived of their natural planktonic diet. Their unusual eating habits and their specially designed bills allow both the Lesser and Greater flamingo to coexist in areas where little else can survive.

LESSER FLAMINGO *(Phoenicopterus minor)* The plumage of this species is dark pink, and its curved bill is carmine-red. Lesser flamingos generally appear in highly gregarious flocks of a hundred to thousands; they are 100 times more numerous in Tanzania than the greater flamingo. Both species have curved bills that contain a unique filtration system – by turning their heads upside down, food and water are pushed in and filtered by the tongue, which forces out the brackish water, leaving the food that is ingested almost completely dry. A deep keel in the lower mandible of the Lesser flamingo's bill acts as a float while the entire surface of the inside of the bill is covered with fine lamellae; this allows the bird to feed on smaller organisms – blue-green algae *(Spirulina platensis)* and diatoms – in the surface waters of the lake. When water is drawn into the bill, the lamellae lie flat, but as it is pumped out by the tongue, the lamellae stand erect, holding back the spirulina. The daily food intake of a million flamingos is around 180 tonnes! Nesting can occur in large numbers – over half a million at one time. Nests are cone-shaped and made of mud; a single egg is laid, which will incubate for 28–30 days. The young are able to swim in 10 days and are fully fledged after 65–75 days.

GREATER FLAMINGO *(Phoenicopterus ruber)* The larger of the two species, this bird's plumage is white, washed with a dusty pink, while its bill is light pink and tipped in black. The Greater flamingo is also highly gregarious. The bill of this species lacks the refined filtration system of the Lesser flamingo: it has a shallow keel in the upper mandible and the inside of its bill is only partially covered with lamellae, as it ingests larger foods such as molluscs and crustaceans, which it finds in a somewhat limited area near the bottom of the lake.

A flock of Lesser flamingo (Phoenicopterus minor) *at Lake Magadi.*

dwindled as a result of poaching, the crater floor is unique in that, in 1995, it harboured a population of about 14. A browser, the black rhino is a solitary animal; however, a male and female pair are sometimes seen during the breeding season, and a mother and her calf will stay together until the calf is approximately three or four years old.

From the main bridge west to the Lerai Forest, the swamp is more open and it is somewhat easier to view wildlife and birds. It is here, just at the forest edge, where you can pick up the ascending road to the crater rim. The open areas of the crater floor comprise mainly grassland plains and soda pans. Wildlife here is abundant and the area is criss-crossed with roads enabling visitors to move about the crater floor with relative ease. The open expanses and waterholes (especially during the dry season) attract plains game: you will see Burchell's (or common) zebra, wildebeest, Coke's hartebeest (kongoni), Thomson's and Grant's gazelle, and also warthog, which was not present in the crater until the mid-1970s. Elephant (predominantly males as females and their young move out of the crater in search of better nutrition) are visible across the crater floor in the open plains, although they are often found in the Lerai Forest too. At Mandusi Swamp and Ngoitokitok Springs, hippo are always entertaining, whether splashing about or slowly rising and submerging in the waters. Patience proves productive for the photographically inclined traveller.

Low-lying areas are perfect spots to look for predators, who ensure the balance of nature. The most common are lion, spotted hyena, the blackbacked jackal and the golden jackal. Occasionally sighted is the cheetah, leopard, bat-eared fox (usually in groups of three to six) and the serval.

The wetter swamp areas such as Gorigor, Mandusi, and the Ngoitokitok and Seneto springs host a multitude of waterbirds, including the Glossy and Sacred ibis, African jacana, Hamerkop, Saddlebilled stork, Yellow-billed stork, African spoonbill, Spurwinged goose, Egyptian goose, and the Redbilled and

The Martial eagle may be spotted at swamps.

Hottentot teal. Herons – Blackheaded, Grey, Squacco and Night – are plentiful. Several species of egret are visible too. Predators are plentiful: look for the Fish eagle among the treetops along watercourses. You may also spot the Augur buzzard, Tawny and Martial eagles and the Blackbreasted snake eagle. Scavengers of the crater are abundant and include the Egyptian vulture, and the more common Lappetfaced, Whiteheaded, Hooded and Whitebacked species, as well as the Ruppell's Griffon vulture.

THE GREAT SERENGETI AND SALEI PLAINS

To the north and west of Ngorongoro Crater, the vast Serengeti and Salei plains sustain great numbers of wildlife specific to open grassland all year round, including Maasai giraffe and topi (which are missing from the crater). However, seasonal changes have a marked effect on the actual numbers – which range from several thousand in the dry season to a few million in the wet. During February and March it is extremely exciting to visit the plains as the wildebeest herds are generally present and annual calving takes place. It is at this time that an estimated 400,000 wildebeest calves are born within a six-week period. This mass birthing phenomenon takes place when water and fresh grazing are plentiful, which helps to reduce infant mortality from predation.

The increased numbers of herbivores also see an increase in predators: the natural food chain maintains its course, ensuring that wildlife numbers are kept under control. Whether death occurs through natural causes or predation, the plains are kept clean with the arrival of nature's rubbish collectors: vultures, Marabou storks, hyenas and jackals.

Little creatures also play an important role in the plains life cycle. Banded mongoose are often seen scurrying across the grasslands, stopping and standing sentry momentarily as they go. Watching these curious and playful characters is time well spent. Another small resident of the plains is the impressive agama lizard, often found on rocks and kopjes. These remarkable creatures are very active and seemingly always on the move. The female's colour is very similar to the rock she inhabits but the brightly coloured male has a turquoise body and striking head of orange or pink. The male is most often seen displaying its unique habit of marking its territory – that is, bobbing its head up and down. These fascinating creatures are also extremely photogenic for the keen photographer.

On the Serengeti and Salei plains the birdlife is similar to that of the crater plains, though seen more often are Yellowthroated sandgrouse, ostrich, Secretary bird, Crowned plover and Kori bustard.

NASERA ROCK, OLKARIEN GORGE AND GOL MOUNTAINS

If you are heading to Olduvai Gorge from the crater, you will follow the crater rim road westwards, once again passing the Malanja Depression, and instead of descending into the crater you should continue on the main road which turns towards the west. The terrain begins to change dramatically into the dry, arid expanse of the open plains. This all-weather road is not difficult to navigate if it has recently been graded, but generally the road is roughly corrugated and very dusty. Though other vehicles may whiz past you, it is recommended that you drive slowly and carefully in order to protect the wildlife in the area, yourself and your vehicle. The plains only receive about 600 mm (24 in) of rainfall each year, but caution should be taken during the wet season as flash floods may occur. If you take it easy, you can enjoy the rugged yet captivating scenery, and you are guaranteed to see a variety of wildlife and also a number of Maasai en'kangs (villages). After travelling for approximately 21 km (13 miles), you reach a signposted road on the right for Olduvai Gorge.

Again, this road should be taken slowly. After 6 km (4 miles), you arrive at the museum site of Olduvai Gorge. The gorge is located in the Serengeti plains, the southern portion of which forms part of the Ngorongoro Conservation Area while the northern portion falls within the Serengeti National Park. The name 'Serengeti' stems from the Maasai word *siringet*, meaning a vast area. The soil of the plains is rich in nutrients provided by centuries of volcanic activity, and, although they are dry for most of the year, grass grows well during the wet season and the plains are transformed by massive congregations of wildlife. Further north of the gorge lie Nasera Rock, Olkarien Gorge and the Gol mountains and, lying to the east of these, the Salei plains. This is an extremely remote area with superb views and landscapes. However, due to its remoteness and rugged terrain, travelling through here requires extensive planning, a great deal of cross-country driving and a lot of patience.

NASERA ROCK This is a massive rock formation close to 100 m (328 ft) in height. Both man and beast have sheltered here for thousands of years. Nasera can be climbed by the energetic and, though a bit steep in spots and fairly blustery at the top, the view of the plains is worth the effort. From November to May is the best time to visit Nasera as the wildlife on the plains – which includes the migrating wildebeest – is overwhelming.

OLKARIEN GORGE Located at the eastern edge of the Gol mountains, the gorge can be reached via the Malambo road (track), which cuts into the main road at the foothills of the Ngorongoro highlands. Distances and road conditions dictate a slow passage through this area and making arrangements to camp may be the best solution to enjoy it to the full. The road passes the Olbalbal Swamp (east of the Olduvai Visitor Centre), then continues north across the plains, with the Gol mountains always rising to the left. Eventually the road enters woodland habitat where a trough runs west and east: this is Olkarien Gorge, whose scenic beauty is truly inspiring. Driving west to the mouth of the gorge, a superb setting encourages walking in and around the cliffs. From March to April Olkarien Gorge is transformed into a natural nursery for the massive Ruppell's Griffon vulture as the cliffs and rock faces are their primary nesting ground.

OLDUVAI GORGE AND LAETOLI

Olduvai Gorge drains the southern Serengeti plains and the mountain ranges of the area. It originates just west of Lake Ndutu, lying on the Serengeti National Park boundary, and runs east, embracing both Ndutu and Lake Masek, then continues its rocky passage into the Olbalbal Swamp, at the northern base of the Ngorongoro Crater.

BANDED AND DWARF MONGOOSES

BANDED MONGOOSE (*Mungos mungo*) The most commonly seen mongooses are the banded and dwarf species (although there are many related species). These animals are often seen scurrying around termite mounds and across the open plains. The banded mongoose, so-named for the transverse bands that run across its body from the shoulder to the tip of its thickset tail, is a delightful character that moves about – as much as 10 km (6 miles) a day – in search of food. Diurnal animals, they live in troops of up to 30 members and generally can be found sleeping in termite mounds, but they are also often seen basking in the sun in the early mornings. Having an excellent sense of sight, smell and sound, mongooses communicate with a constant bird-like twittering, especially when foraging. Members of a troop will vigorously defend each other if under attack by larger predators. Their main diet consists of reptiles, mice, eggs and insects; prey that emits a distasteful secretion such as millipedes and frogs is often rolled or rubbed in the soil prior to eating.

EASTERN DWARF MONGOOSE (*Helogale undulata*) This small species, weighing 200–350 g (half a pound), has a reddish-yellow coloration and a thickset tail. These animals live in gregarious troops of 20–30 members, with an alpha female and male. They are known to forage together with hornbills, who feed on the insects missed by the mongoose troop and also aid in spotting enemies such as goshawks. The troop appoints a sentry which stands guard, changing its strategic position as the rest continue to forage. Eastern dwarf mongooses unite against their enemies, placing the oldest and strongest in the front line of defence. Unless there is a new litter or a troop member is injured or sick, the mongooses move to a new refuge each day. Their diet consists mainly of small rodents, insects and, like many mongoose species, eggs, which they open by rolling them through their legs, allowing them to hit a tree or rock.

A dwarf mongoose in the Tarangire.

DISCOVERY OF EARLY MAN

Evidence shows that two different hominid species were present in the earliest or deepest levels of the gorge – Beds I and II (that is, archaeological excavations have resulted in the labelling, or identifying, of excavated sections as Beds I to IV). The hominid finds were both descendants of *Australopithecus afarensis*, discovered at Laetoli, but had larger brains and more known skills. *Australopithecus boisei* (also known as robustus) had a brain size of about 500 cc, was of stocky build and because of his large tooth structure was most likely vegetarian. (*Australopithecus* means a 'southern apelike man', while *boisei*, meaning 'of Boise', refers to one of the first men who showed an interest in the Leakeys' work by helping to fund it.) *Homo habilis*, or 'handy man', was smaller in stature but had a slightly larger brain (600 cc). It is believed that he made use of simple tools, scavenged off predators' kills as well as hunting smaller animals, and still ate a vegetarian diet – typical of today's hunter-gatherer habits.

BED I (APPROXIMATELY 1.9 TO 1.7 MILLION YEARS AGO) The fossil remains excavated at this level include many types of antelope, an enormous giraffe with sweeping horns named Sivatherium, a sabre-toothed cat, hyena, jackal, hippo, crocodile, white rhino, two types of elephant, and even flamingos and pelicans.

UPPER BED II (1.7 TO 1.1 MILLION YEARS AGO) A change occurred 1.5 million years ago when faulting of the earth's crust drained the lake, leaving only a river. Upper Bed II revealed animals of the time to be more typical of those habituated to riverine forest and open plains. They were also larger than the modern-day species. Stone tools also discovered prove the presence of hominids. 'Handy man' (*H. habilis*) had been phased out after having evolved into 'upright man' (*Homo erectus*), who was capable of making more refined stone tools and hand axes (his brain capacity had increased to 950 cc). *A. boisei* was still present but with the steady evolution of *H. erectus* he soon disappeared from the fossil beds.

BED III (1.2 MILLION TO 900,000 YEARS AGO) This level has revealed very little fossilization: the climate of that period – about 1.2 million years ago – had become increasingly dry and hot. Red soil strata indicative of this in Bed III of the gorge are clearly defined.

BED IV (900,000 TO 400,000 YEARS AGO) Conditions of the area obviously improved around 800,000 years ago as this level shows the continued presence of *Homo erectus* and his improved tools. Signs of rivers and the resultant presence of wildlife are reinforced by the fascinating discovery of a large hippo skeleton surrounded by stone tools, which points to the hunting abilities of *Homo erectus*.

NDUTU (24,000 YEARS AGO) AND NAISIUSIU (24,000 TO 0 YEARS AGO) Superimposed on the Masek Bed, which was the result of layers of ash from eruptions by Kerimasi, 400,000 to 100,000 years ago, are the Ndutu and the most recent Naisiusiu beds, formed by Ol Donyo Lengai's subsequent eruptions. The Naisiusiu Bed has yielded a hominid skeleton estimated at 17,000 years old; this is *Homo sapiens*, or 'modern man', with the largest brain yet (1,400 cc).

Visitors to Ngorongoro's Olduvai Museum will see fascinating archaeological artefacts.

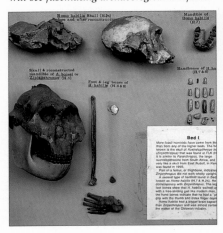

The name Olduvai is a mispronunciation of the Maasai word *Oldupai* for the wild sisal (*Sansevieria ehrenbergiana*), a plant that is common throughout the area. Here in a 50-km (31 miles) stretch that is sometimes 90 m (295 ft) deep, a gorge cut in the earth reveals distinct layers of rock harbouring a wealth of historical information.

Three and a half million years ago Sadiman, to the west of Ngorongoro Crater, puffed and spewed out masses of grey ash, covering a good portion of the plains. Subsequent rain settled the ash, which in turn played a natural record-keeping role by preserving the animal spoors that existed at the time. Some of the animals that roamed the plains then were very different from what they are today. For example, there are traces left by the Hipparion, a horse-like animal with three toes. However, similar modern-day species also existed then, as records show that giraffe and guineafowl were plentiful.

Through the discoveries at Laetoli, a site to the south of Olduvai, by world-renowned archaeologist/palaeontologist Mary Leakey in 1976 and 1978, we know that at least three hominids also walked across the plains. Known today as *Australopithecus afarensis*, they probably resembled ape more than man; the height of this early ancestor was believed to average 1.5 m (5 ft), while its brain (measured in cubic centimetres) was small at only 400 cc – today man's brain averages 1,400 cc. However the fact remains that this ancient hominid walked on two legs, leaving his hands free, possibly to carry tools or weapons, and to hunt and defend himself.

Olmoti, directly to the north of Ngorongoro Crater, erupted almost two million years ago, depositing a thick layer of lava over the plains and the site at Olduvai (a layer of black basalt is visible today at the bottom of the gorge). With the formation of an alkaline lake (no longer in existence), similar to that of Manyara though not as large, animals were drawn to its waters. The repeated cycle of volcanic debris being deposited in the lake pan formed the basis of the archaeologically excavated Beds I and II at Olduvai (*see* panel).

Looking east over Olduvai Gorge.

The gorge was formed in the two periods that followed the formation of Beds I through IV, that is, beginning 400,000 years ago. The Masek Bed overlying Bed IV was built up from the volcanic matter erupting from Kerimasi, at the extreme northeastern edge of the NCA. Here, meticulously fashioned tools of quartzite were found. Faulting began to occur around 100,000 years ago and the Olbalbal depression formed further east of where the original lake existed at the base of Ngorongoro. Run-off water that collected on the plains during the wet season was channelled to the newly formed Olbalbal, cutting the deep scar which was to become Olduvai Gorge. Thus the evolution of early man revealed itself to archaeologists in the multilayered walls of the gorge, right down to the very base of the ancient lava beds.

The success of early archaeologists

The archaeological riches at Olduvai were first discovered in 1911 by Professor Kattwinkel, a German entomologist. He had come in search of butterflies, but overwhelmed by the huge amount of fossilized matter around him, he collected samples which he sent to Berlin to be identified. Backed by the Kaiser, Professor Hans Reck visited the site in 1913 to collect and identify additional specimens. The outbreak of World War I prevented further excavation at the gorge. Dr Louis Leakey, an archaeologist from Kenya, saw the Olduvai finds some years later in a Berlin museum. Excited by the prospect of what the gorge could reveal on human evolution, he and Reck returned to Olduvai in 1931 to continue exploration of the area. Reck later ceded the site's scientific excavation rights to Leakey. Although funding for the dig was not forthcoming, Louis Leakey and his wife Mary persisted in their quest to reveal what lay embedded in the earth. Years of digging unearthed numerous animal skeletal remains and man-made tools, but it was not until 1959, 28 years later, that the discovery of a humanlike bone was made by Mary Leakey: it was the jawbone of earliest man, originally named *Zinjanthropus* but reclassified as *Australopithecus boisei*. After the discovery of *A. boisei*, substantial funding was provided by the National Geographic Society, enabling the Leakeys to continue their archaeological diggings. *Homo habilis* was discovered in 1960, and *H. erectus* in 1963. Sadly, Louis Leakey died in 1972, but Mary continued their work, and in 1976 made her discovery of the preserved footprints at Laetoli. Mary Leakey retired from field work in 1984 and currently resides in Kenya.

Lakes Ndutu and Masek

Located within the Olduvai Gorge, these two alkaline lakes offer quite a change from the vast open plains. Lake Ndutu rests on the Serengeti National Park boundary; both lakes therefore attract the wildlife and the Maasai water their domestic stock at Ndutu throughout the year. During a visit to Lake Ndutu, visitors generally pass back and forth between the Serengeti National Park and the Ngorongoro Conservation Area; it is therefore necessary to obtain the required permits for each area, which can be arranged via the rangers at Ndutu Lodge or at Naabi Hill gate.

If you are starting from the conservation area, 6 km (4 miles) north of the main Olduvai Gorge crossing – on the main road between Serengeti and NCA – a signposted track leads in a southwesterly direction, crossing the open plains parallel to the gorge for about 20 km (12 miles). It then enters the acacia woodland zone, descending into the Ndutu/Masek valley (Lake Ndutu comes into view after roughly 5 km, or 3 miles). If you begin from Serengeti, a track off the main road – about 4 km (2.5 miles) south of Naabi Hill – heads southwards to the Ndutu/Masek valley. In the acacia woodland you will spot wildlife in the shade of the trees.

When driving around the lakes, be sure not to drive too close to the edge. Though the ground may appear solid and dry it is easy to get stuck in the soft mud and the weight of the vehicle causes it to become quickly bogged down.

During the dry season, from June to November, the lake region is usually heavily populated with elephant and birds, and there is always plenty of resident plains game. Lake Ndutu may dry out leaving a bowl of white cracked earth from the soda, while Lake Masek retains its water throughout the year. A few resident hippo can be seen at Masek, and the marshes and waterhole west of Ndutu are easily navigated, with enjoyable scenery and a variety wildlife.

The wet season (from late November to end May) brings an increase in the numerous wildlife herds (wildebeest, Burchell's zebra, eland and gazelle) that return to the plains around the lake region to graze during the rains. The wildebeest herds in particular, while trekking across the plains in their constant search for grass and water, will cross the lakes rather than deviate from their chosen path, no matter how short the deviation. If the crossing goes calmly, all is well, but at times panic breaks out when larger groups try to cross at once and in the resulting pandemonium, many lose their lives – either from trampling or exhaustion. Adding to this is the presence of calves (born during February and March), which often get lost or drown in the confusion. Sadly, they will die if they are not reunited with their mothers, as wildebeest do not suckle or care for another's calf. Scavengers and predators such as lion, hyena and vultures are often seen combing the lakes at this time.

The lake area is a superb place to camp, and there are several designated sites that can be booked through the rangers at Ndutu Lodge. The supply of drinking water is a year-round problem due to its alkalinity. Campers should not expect to get their water supply from Ndutu Lodge, whose wells and boiled rainwater are not for public consumption. Make sure, therefore, that you have enough drinking water and supplies with you.

Off the Beaten Track:
Empakaai Crater

If you ascend the Ngorongoro Crater's eastern rim via the Lemala road, you will come to a Y-junction. The right fork leads you to

Empakaai Crater, Ngorongoro Conservation Area.

the Sopa Lodge, the left to Empakaai Crater. Driving time to the Empakaai Crater from the junction is two hours over roughly 39 km (24 miles), which will take you to the first opening at the crater. Road conditions vary over the rough, corrugated and dusty terrain. Fuel supplies are only available at Ngorongoro Crater. If you plan to stay the night in the area, there are only campsites at Empakaai Crater; otherwise you can arrange to stay in one of the lodges or at a campsite at Ngorongoro.

The trip to the crater passes through the breathtaking scenery of the NCA's crater highlands; occasionally, you will see plains game and ostrich. The Maasai people live in the amazing depressions and bowls of the highland slopes, and their villages seem to blend gracefully into surroundings that appear quite prehistoric. Near Empakaai Crater, people are infrequent, though they are certainly present. Flowers can always be seen in the highlands, but during and just after the rains the rolling expanses and ridges

become multicoloured blankets featuring thousands of red-hot pokers (*Kniphofia*) in brilliant yellows, oranges and reds, with everlastings, Impatiens and Cycnium on the lower reaches, and Crinums and Leonotis gently swaying in the breeze. Goldenwinged and Amethyst sunbirds gracefully dance from one flower to the next.

The crater rim looks down onto a stunning lake with forest all around. The crater measures roughly 6 km (4 miles) in diameter, and its relatively deep lake contains both fresh and alkaline water. Flamingos can sometimes be seen hovering close to the lake shore, and Lengai rises to the north, while all around

is serenity and peace. The open area at the crater rim can be used as a campsite, although there are other options further along the track, which has some steep sections. About 6 km (4 miles) ahead, there is another small opening in the rim where it is possible to set up a smaller camp, and also to descend on foot to the lake. The spectacular walk, which takes roughly three hours there and back, has some very steep sections.

Nights at Empakaai can be extremely cold, especially during June and July. Wildlife such as bushbuck, buffalo and leopard is occasionally seen; for this reason, a ranger must escort visitors on their journey to the area.

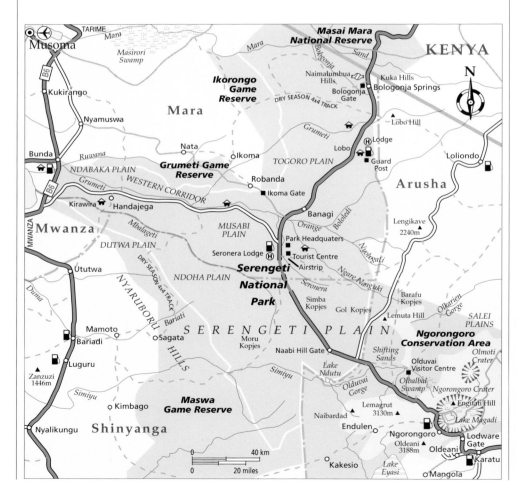

SERENGETI NATIONAL PARK

Wildlife is the focus of activity in the Serengeti National Park. The beauty and richness of the park can be enjoyed throughout the year, although travel can be slowed considerably during the wet season. Game concentrations vary dramatically with the ebb and flow of the wildebeest migration, but the variety of habitat and sheer size of Serengeti ensure that wildlife is seen year-round. For visitors with limited time, the Seronera Valley area may be the best option for game-viewing, especially leopard and lion. A picnic breakfast or lunch at a kopje or along a river is an excellent way to heighten your safari experience. Another option is to gain a bird's-eye view of the wildlife from a hot-air balloon. An early morning departure, gentle lift-off, the lush rolling expanse of the Serengeti plains below, and a champagne brunch complete this very special experience.

The Serengeti ecosystem comprises seven controlled regions, whose establishment was based on the annual migratory pattern of the wildebeest. To the north lies the Masai Mara Game Reserve in Kenya, to the northeast Loliondo Game Controlled Area, to the south and southeast Ngorongoro Conservation Area, to the southwest Maswa Game Reserve, and in the northwest the Grumeti and Ikorongo controlled areas. Fences do not exist, so the wildlife roams freely throughout this ecosystem, depending on the time of year and available vegetation and water.

The name Serengeti evolved from the Maasai word *siringet*, meaning 'vast, or boundless, plains'. The predominant feature of Serengeti, Tanzania's largest national park

LEFT: *The colourful agama lizard.*
BELOW: *Wildebeest migration in the Serengeti.*

at 14,763 km² (5,625 sq. miles), is, in fact, its plains: long- and short-grass expanses, islands of rock known as inselbergs or kopjes, acacia woodland, scrubby thicket and watercourses that support riverine forest.

Professional hunters began to enter the area in the 1920s, bringing safari-goers and trophy-seekers. However, the resulting reduction in wildlife during the next 30 years in the Serengeti led to a slow programme of conservation awareness. By 1951 the open plains – including the Ngorongoro Highlands – were established as a national park. By the mid-1950s relations between the Maasai and the park authorities had begun to deteriorate because the Maasai, the area's original inhabitants, were being prevented from grazing and watering their cattle there. By 1959 the park boundaries were altered. The Ngorongoro Conservation Area was established as a separate area, incorporating a section of the Serengeti plains, the highlands and the crater itself, in order to accommodate the Maasai and their herds. The extension of the Serengeti's southern and northern perimeters was due in great part to the conservation efforts and survey strategies of Bernhard and Michael Grzimek.

As with any ecosystem, the habitat of the Serengeti is delicate and can easily be destroyed. Visitors are permitted to drive off the roads in the park, but should do so only when absolutely necessary. However, due to the higher concentrations of vehicles in the Seronera region, off-road driving is strictly prohibited within a 16-km (10 miles) radius of the area. Travelling through the park is not allowed before 06:00 or after 19:00. Remember to allow plenty of time to complete your planned circular route or to reach your final destination for the day, especially in the rainy season.

From time to time roads and tracks within the park boundaries are closed to give certain areas a break; at the same time, new tracks can be cut through the environs. It is always wise to check with the rangers at the gates for current road conditions and the need to make any appropriate changes.

Hot-air ballooning over the Serengeti.

Serengeti Plains, Seronera Valley and Western Corridor

The short grassland plains extend from the foothills of Ngorongoro to just inside Serengeti National Park's southeast boundary. These plains are a hive of activity during the rains from November through May. The grass is sweet and new, and the animals take advantage of the short-term spurt of growth. With their continuous quest for grazing and water keeping them on the move, the short-grass plains will be quickly depleted with the onset of the dry season as no permanent water source exists here.

Entering the park from the southeast corner via the Naabi Hill Gate, you quickly ease into the long-grass expanses. Observing the vast plains is similar to watching wheat billow in a breeze. The rolling landscape appears endless and is broken only by the occasional kopje or sporadically situated watercourses. Conspicuously missing from the open plains are trees. The hard pan soil inhibits their growth, except where water or heavy animal traffic has broken the ground.

Throughout the Serengeti, kopjes occur in various shapes and sizes. The rock formations and surrounding vegetation provide shelter and food for many types of wildlife. The smooth, round edges of these spectacular inselbergs have been formed through erosion not only from the elements, but also from high and low temperature changes that have occurred since time immemorial. Wild sisal is sometimes seen around the kopjes. Spending

AFRICA'S BEAUTIFUL CATS

When you are looking for predators, watch the wildlife of the open plains, such as topi, Thomson's gazelle, wildebeest and impala. These animals are the first to recognize danger and will focus alertly on the direction from which they can sense any tension.

CHEETAH The cheetah, which can be recognized by the black tear marks below its eyes, is the specialist hunter of the plains: this cat has foregone strength for speed (it is the fastest land animal on earth), and with its sleek lines and low body fat, it is capable of achieving speeds of up to 100 km/h (60 mph) over short distances. It also has blunt, nonretractable claws to ensure better traction. Cheetah hunt singly, in the morning and evening, and also at midday when the heat is high, a time when other predators such as lion and leopard are forced to rest. Cheetah can often be seen sitting atop a termite mound, scanning the plains for prey. Their favourite quarry is the Thomson's gazelle. Cheetah occur as solitary animals or they form groups – either mothers with their cubs or two to three males. Cubs are born with a silver streak on their backs, which is thought to aid in camouflage on the plains.

If visitors do come upon a cheetah, they should approach with care as vehicles that get too close to the animal often disturb the cheetah's daytime attempts to catch prey.

LEOPARD A shy and solitary creature, the leopard is a night-time hunter. Its beautiful spotted coat blends well with the shade of trees, allowing the creature to remain well camouflaged for much of the time. Leopard occur in woodland and forest as well as in bushland or rocky habitats. When looking for this predator, pay special attention to kopjes and rocky crevices, but also look to the trees for a straight, vertical line – it may be a leopard's tail as this predator often lies in the crook of a tree branch.

Leopard kill their prey by suffocation; their main source of food is the impala. These cats demonstrate their strength by dragging their prey – which can weigh twice their body weight – high into a tree, away from poaching predators and scavengers. Leopard are highly adaptable creatures and seem to survive even in the suburbs of certain African cities; they can endure long periods with very little water. A leopard should be approached slowly, and if possible in an indirect fashion.

A cheetah mother with cubs.

A leopard in the branches of an acacia tree.

some time driving around these areas proves not only rewarding for game-viewing, but also affords visitors the opportunity to enjoy a unique feature of the Serengeti plains. When visiting the Moru kopjes, be sure to take a look at the Maasai rock paintings.

The Seronera Valley is located in the southern-central region of the park. Wildlife viewing is generally very good, and is made easier with fairly good roads and tracks. There are several kopjes and many watercourses and rivers that are worth visiting. Along the rivers you are likely to see the wild, or strangler, fig *(Ficus thonningii)*, fever trees *(Acacia xanthophloea)* and umbrella trees *(Acacia tortilis)*. The valley is also a good place to look for the sausage tree *(Kigelia africana)* and the *Balanites aegyptiaca*, both favoured by leopard. The riverine forest along the Seronera River is rich in wildlife and offers excellent opportunities to view hippo wallowing in the waters right from the main road.

North of Seronera the landscape changes as you drive through the Banagi area towards Lobo Wildlife Lodge and Lobo Hill, which

Thomson's gazelles abound in the Serengeti.

is situated on the extreme northeastern boundary of the park. The vast expanses of grassland plains dramatically disappear as woodland, forest and thick scrub take over. The watercourses of this northern area are lined with wild figs and mahoganies. The wildlife changes too; it is in this section of the park that visitors are most likely to see elephant. The great herds of the annual migration are found here roughly from August until November, when the short rains begin. Worth a stop is the hippo pool on the Orangi River, about 6 km (4 miles) north of Banagi, and the Olemangi salt lick, northwest of Lobo Wildlife Lodge.

The Western Corridor is again different from the vegetation of the northern section. Leave Seronera via the main road and turn west after about 5 km (3 miles). The Grumeti River follows the road on the right-hand side, then the central mountain range rises to the left and ahead, and Lake Victoria lies just beyond the Ndabaka Gate. Candelabra trees *(Euphorbia candelabrum)* are widely dispersed in the area around the gate. The land here is composed of black cotton soil and, although beautiful with its wildflowers after the rains,

driving is difficult and it can become quite an arduous task to navigate the area; a four-wheel-drive is essential in the rainy season, while standard vehicles do pass in the dry season. Throughout the Serengeti flowers such as hibiscus and Cycnium appear after the rains; the flowers of the aloes and the bright orange blossoms of the lion's mane (*Leonotis nepetifolia*) are beautiful to look at, and also attract the spectacular sunbirds.

The wildebeest migration moves into the Western Corridor during the dry season, from June to October, as there is more permanent water here.

ANTELOPES OF THE PLAINS

COKE'S HARTEBEEST Also known by its Swahili name, *kongoni*, Coke's hartebeest is a sturdy, yellowish-brown antelope with a long, narrow forehead. Both males and females have twisted, 'S'-shaped horns. The animal has preorbital and foot glands; it has a good sense of sight, sound and smell and is most active in the early morning and late evening. Hartebeest are commonly seen on the open plains in herds that average 10–15 members in size. They drink daily if water is available, but can go for long periods without water. Coke's hartebeest are usually preyed upon by lion, and younger animals by leopard.

THOMSON'S GAZELLE Often referred to as 'tommies', these small antelope occur most commonly on the grassland plains. They can be recognized by a white stripe that runs over the eye from horn to muzzle. Their body colour is mainly fawn, with a wide lateral black stripe extending from the foreleg to the rear. The gazelle's underside and inner legs are white, the tail short and black. Horns occur on both sexes (although they are smaller on the female) and have a weak 'S' shape, although strongly ringed. Herds comprising females, their young and a dominant male average 30 members. Tommies are more active in the early morning and late evening. They are preyed upon by cheetah, but are also taken by lion, leopard, hyena and python, with younger gazelles falling victim to jackal, serval and baboon.

GRANT'S GAZELLE Considerably larger than Thomson's gazelle, Grant's gazelle are often seen together with tommies on the open plains. Their overall colour is pale fawn with white undersides but, unlike tommies, their rump is white with black edges. Horns, having a lyre shape, occur on males and females but are stronger and more pronounced on the male. There are usually 20–30 members to a herd, and the herds can be seen foraging during the early morning and late evening periods. Like Coke's hartebeest, Grant's gazelle can go for long periods without water, but the animal prefers to drink daily if water supplies are available. Similarly to tommies, their main enemies are lion, leopard and cheetah, with the younger gazelles being preyed upon most often by jackal, serval, caracal, python and birds of prey.

A group of Grant's gazelles.

105

Serengeti's wildlife

Few game reserves can compare with the vast numbers and variety of wildlife found in Serengeti National Park. The best game-viewing times are in the early morning and late evening when cooler temperatures encourage more activity. Plains game such as Burchell's zebra, wildebeest, Thomson's and Grant's gazelle, topi and Coke's hartebeest (kongoni) occur in great profusion. Also rarely seen in the vicinity of the Gol kopjes in the southeast of the park is the exquisite fringe-eared oryx. Klipspringers (in the north) and rock hyrax – both adapted to rock climbing – feature prominently around the kopjes. Buffalo and impala occur throughout the park; elephant generally in the central to northern reaches; the Maasai giraffe among the acacias; and the long-haired Defassa waterbuck in the wetter areas. Around Lobo Hill look for the shy mountain reedbuck, oribi and the grey bush duiker, while the Western Corridor is the best area for roan antelope and eland. Black rhino are known to occur in the park, but their solitary existence and small numbers make them extremely difficult to spot.

Lion and cheetah are often spotted; the Gol kopjes is particularly good for cheetah. Leopard are not uncommon, especially in the trees of the Seronera Valley. The bat-eared fox, hyena and black-backed jackal are seen regularly, but hunting dogs are a rare sight.

You are sure to see troops of baboons and vervet monkeys, especially around the lodges and camps, but keep your eyes trained on the treetops in the western and northern areas for the black-and-white colobus monkeys. Hippos are always enjoyable to watch and abound in the Seronera and Orangi rivers.

Reptiles include many crocodiles in the rivers; the Grumeti River boasts some of Africa's largest specimens, reaching 5.5 m (17–18 ft). The agama lizard, with its dazzling colours, is usually found around the kopjes, while tortoises, skinks, monitor lizards and even snakes are present though seldom seen.

Birds commonly seen on the open plains are the Kori bustard, Yellowthroated sandgrouse, ostrich, Secretary bird – and the superb flash of colour from the Lilacbreasted roller. The Seronera Valley has a rich assortment of birds; visitors can enjoy the fluid movements of bee-eaters, the cackling calls and erratic flight patterns of the Helmeted guineafowl and Greybreasted spurfowl, and the iridescent ambers and blues of the Superb and Hildebrandt's starlings. The dazzling blue-violet of the Ruppell's longtailed starling is also sure to impress.

Occurring throughout the park are Marabou storks and six species of vulture: Ruppell's Griffon, Whiteheaded, Whitebacked, Hooded, Egyptian and Lappetfaced. Birds of prey are ever present, as are nightjars and sunbirds, especially when the aloes are in bloom.

The great migration

The annual movement of the wildebeest follows the rains. As the land starts to dry up in early April, an estimated one million wildebeest and another half a million ungulates – zebra, eland and Thomson's gazelles – begin moving away from the short-grass plains of the Ngorongoro Conservation Area – which they have now exhausted – westwards to the long-grass plains and woodlands of the Serengeti Plain's Western Corridor, almost to Lake Victoria. They then cross the Mara River north into Kenya's Masai Mara National Reserve. An individual may trek 3,000 km (1,864 miles) in total. The crossing of the turbulent Mara River is often characterized by panic as groups of nervous wildebeest try to jump into the water at once, sometimes causing a stampede with the animals trampling each other, sliding down muddy banks and, through sheer exhaustion, eventually falling prey to the waiting crocodiles. Wildebeest carcasses can often be seen strewn along the riverbank. From August to October the wildebeest reach the Mara plains, where they remain until the end of October. November finds them trekking back to Tanzania as the rains return to Ngorongoro, generating new growth of sweet grass on its plains. With the return of the wildebeest herd to Tanzania, the migratory cycle will begin once again after the passing of the rains.

The breeding season, or rutting, takes place in May and June, with much lowing and territorial bullying by the male wildebeest. Birthing occurs from late January to mid-March, in the Ngorongoro Crater and the conservation area's short-grass Serengeti plains. Family units generally comprise 20–30 females and their calves, guarded by a single territorial bull.

Often characterized as 'clowns' or 'fools' because of their strange appearance, the wildebeest has adapted well to its environment, and has turned survival into an art. An important factor in the animal's amazing ability to survive is their sheer numbers (the sudden surplus of newborns at a certain time of year means that predators have little impact on these numbers).

A symbiotic relationship exists too in the Serengeti-Mara ecosystem between the many types of browsers and the grasses of the

Helmeted guineafowl occur in the Serengeti.

plains that support the migratory animals. Successive grazing allows large numbers of these browsers to live harmoniously together: the coarser portion of the grass is eaten by zebra, whose upper and lower teeth can accommodate the tougher sections; topi, Coke's hartebeest (kongoni), Grant's gazelle and wildebeest shave the grass down further, leaving the stubs and freshly grown shoots

River crossing during annual migration.

for the lighter grazers such as Thomson's gazelle. An important grass for the migrating animals – and one that is widely spread – is red oat grass *(Themeda triandra)*, which re-seeds well after fires. Others are *Digitaria macroblephara* (finger grasses) and *Sporobolus marginatus* (drop seed grasses).

Off the Beaten Track: Lake Natron

The driving time from Klein's Gate in the northeast of the Serengeti National Park to Lake Natron to the east of the park is approximately five-and-a-half hours over a distance of 145 km (90 miles); from Lake Natron to Mto-wa-Mbu the time is approximately four hours over a distance of 101 km (63 miles). The condition of the roads is mostly fair, although some sections are composed of deep sand and can be extremely dusty. A four-wheel-drive vehicle is essential. Accommodation is available at campsites at Lake Natron and Engaruka. Note that there is no fuel available between Serengeti and Mto-wa-Mbu, so plan carefully.

Lake Natron Camp is a beautiful site at the base of the escarpment wall, with lots of shady trees. Bandas are available, but reservations need to be made in Arusha. Otherwise, the 'Saimon Kamakia', Ol Donyo Lengai Waterfalls Camping Area is a wonderful site on the banks of the Ngare Sero River. The tranquil sound of the water is very calming and clear mountain water is close at hand. There are pit latrines on the site. The walk to the waterfalls begins here, and the Maasai villages are not far away.

The journey to Lake Natron offers wildlife, rugged countryside, unquestionable beauty and fascinating glimpses of traditional Maasai life. This safari should not be undertaken in the wet season, and would probably be most suited to vehicles travelling in convoy. The roads are extremely remote and infrequently travelled. Several small tracks venture into the bush, but the main road – which is fairly well marked – should be adhered to unless otherwise indicated. You will travel through open tracts and sections of game-controlled areas.

A Maasai woman in the Lake Natron area.

On leaving the Serengeti boundary, the scenery changes little. Acacia scrub prevails with hills looming in the distance. After 12.5 km (8 miles) the track passes a maize field, after which is a small village. Look out for a building on the right with a flag. You will occasionally pass Maasai people wearing their striking purple *shukas* (robes).

At 22.5 km (14 miles) there is another small village, whose landmark this time is the euphorbia, which grows well in the area. At 32 km (20 miles) the landscape changes to a huge open plain; Maasai en'kangs (villages) can be seen in the distance. Local people are encountered with more regularity here. The village of Wasso is reached after 48.3 km (30 miles). Passing a large building on your left, turn right at the junction just beyond; a school should be on the right-hand side. Passing through the village and a dry riverbed, the road at 51 km (32 miles) comes to a gentle Y-junction; head to the left. The terrain has opened up to become rolling plains. At roughly 65.3 km (40.5 miles) the road hits a Y-junction; once again head left. The road meanders through rocky landscape till it reaches another Y-junction at 85.3 km

(53 miles), where you head to the right. The track becomes quite rocky and has some steep sections. You will probably see hornbills in the area, moving between the scrubby landscape and the struggling crops. After 93 km (58 miles) you pass some grey buildings on the left. Once more, massive euphorbias seem to grow everywhere. Ol Donyo Lengai comes into view ahead and is then on the right-hand side. The road and the landscape have flattened out; there are no longer dry rivercourses and plains game is common.

After travelling for 119 km (74 miles), the road reaches the edge of the Rift Valley escarpment. The views are extraordinary, with the Great Rift stretching from left to right, Lake Natron in the distance and Lengai keeping an ever-watchful guard over it all. The escarpment road down to the valley can be quite steep and includes a few hairpin bends. The boulders alongside the road are decorated with the bright pink desert rose and the delicate *Delonix elata*. On reaching

the bottom, your speedometer should read about 126 km (78 miles). Unrelenting hills and crags show signs of ancient watercourses, though it is obvious that now there is little moisture. The Maasai can sometimes be seen digging in the sandy riverbed in search of water. Queleas, hornbills and barbets can be seen, but most wildlife remains concealed during the high daytime temperatures. At 131 km (81 miles), near a passable rivercourse, yet another Y-junction is encountered. The two forks lead to the same destination, but the choice is up to the driver. To the left is sand and dust, in some places quite deep; to the right the road becomes a bone-jarring, rocky adventure. Whichever path is taken, the obstacles only last for a few kilometres. Lake Natron is not far from here, and at 136.4 km (85 miles) is a wonderful lookout point with impressive views of the

The road to Lake Natron leads through ruggedly beautiful countryside.

lake and Ol Donyo Lengai directly ahead. Continuing along the main road, you will reach the village of Ngare Sero at 145 km (90 miles). Access to the lake and the campsites is beyond the village, though this is a good place to stop for refreshments and a rest. Heading out of town, the road splits into a Y; cross the river to the left for the lakeshore area and waterfall campsite, to the right for the campsite at the escarpment base.

LAKE NATRON When driving near the lake, take care that the ground is not wet or your vehicle may flounder; it is more advisable to walk. Flamingo are very seasonal and can be seen at the lake at various times of the year. Most often seen are the Lesser flamingo, which come to feed on the algal growth in the saline waters. When flamingo are present in large numbers, the lake appears to be covered in shimmering pink lace. Cattle often graze and drink in the marshy areas along the lake's edge, and they also make a dramatic picture as the Maasai herd them across the dry salt pans left by the lake's receded waters.

The dormant volcano, Ol Donyo Lengai appears to be covered with snow, but this is in fact a cloak of volcanic ash. You can climb the mountain, accompanied by a local porter and guide. Comfortable, sturdy shoes are recommended, along with long trousers, as there are plenty of nettles. Dress in layers as temperatures vary with the changes in elevation, as well as during the course of the day. Most climbs start at about 02:00 or 03:00 in order to benefit from the coolness; because the scree slopes are harder during the cool hours, they are easier to climb. The hike up and down takes between six and eight hours. This climb could be rated as difficult, as there are a few fairly long steep areas.

The Ngare Sero River runs down from the Rift's escarpment wall, and the water is clear and fresh. There are two waterfalls in the area, and it is well worth the journey upriver to see them. Guides are readily available at the campsites; it is strongly suggested you take one as they know where to cross the river. The water is relatively warm and, at the falls, inviting pools beckon for a refreshing

Oldonyo Lengai looms over the Lake Natron area.

dip. The walk takes about 35–40 minutes and requires some careful footwork along the river. Vultures are often seen overhead, as well as the delightful Redwinged starlings and Whitethroated bee-eaters.

Maasai en'kangs are dotted throughout the area, and it is possible to arrange a visit from any of the campsites for a small fee. The children are adorable, and are curious about visitors. The women may sing, bring out jewellery, guide you through a house, or simply go about their chores. The young warriors generally remain in the background, with one of them taking charge. The Maasai live with herds of cattle and goats, so visitors should be prepared for flies. These can be quite bothersome upon arrival at the en'kang, but can usually be ignored after a while. Many visitors wish to trade for jewellery and Maasai artefacts and so often bring T-shirts, pens and cheap watches, clocks or radios. Unfortunately, when any of these items stop working or the batteries run down, they are tossed into the bush. More sensible trading items may be lead pencils, red or dark blue scarves or bandannas, small metal boxes that carry boiled sweets or throat lozenges, and old beaded jewellery.

When leaving Lake Natron, head around to the left of Lengai and ask the locals for the Arusha. The journey will cross ancient lands and many dry riverbeds. Keep to the main track with Lengai staying on your right. After 26.7 km (16.5 miles) the track comes to a Y-junction. By heading to the right, you will come abruptly to a fantastic depression, or crater. If at the junction you head to the left, you continue on the main track. Plains game is often seen now, moving across the open grassland. At 27.9 km (17 miles) the road crosses a dry riverbed and then through massive rugged expanses with distant mountain ranges. Go to the right at the Y-junction that appears at 36 km (22 miles). Dust and sand are predominant now, and around 40 km (25 miles) the road descends a hill, with Maasai en'kangs at the bottom. The road splits, and the choice is up to the driver as both tracks head to the left, towards the village of Engaruka. Dust and sand conditions prevail and will be your determining factors. On reaching 49.7 km (31 miles) you should have arrived at Engaruka. There is a small campsite here and some old irrigation ruins believed to have been built three to six centuries ago. The stone walls that resembled those at the Great Zimbabwe ruins (although nowhere near as large) have been destroyed as many of the local people have excavated here, looking for hidden treasures. Passing through Engaruka, the road crosses two small streams and bears to the left. Baobabs are interspersed with thorn trees. You will meet another village at 79.6 km (49 miles) and a Y-junction, where you should head to the right. Euphorbias appear on your left in large numbers. A Y-junction at 99.7 km (62 miles) leads you to Mto-wa-Mbu if you turn right, and towards Arusha by turning left. The left fork comes to a T-junction on the main all-weather road. A signpost on the left indicates: Act Belgium Seed Farm. By turning left you will head back to Arusha; turn right to Mto-wa-Mbu, Lake Manyara and the crater highlands.

Maasai elders near Lake Natron.

ADVISORY: THE NORTHERN CIRCUIT

CLIMATE
Most of this region has two rainy seasons: the short rains from October to the start of December, and the long rains from March to June. Daytime temperatures average 25–30 °C (77–86 °F); in June and July jackets may be required in the evening and morning, especially at the Ngorongoro Crater.

BEST TIMES TO VISIT
June to October are dry and most people visit then. June has the least haze and dust. During July and August, pelicans and Yellowbilled storks gather at Lake Manyara. In January and February migratory wildebeest reach the Ngorongoro Conservation Area; European wood storks roost at Lake Manyara and Eurasian migrants begin to arrive. The long rains in March to May can make travel slow and animals are widely dispersed, but birdlife is prolific.

MAIN ATTRACTIONS
The scenery, wildlife and local people are all of interest. Nowhere else do such numbers and varieties of game appear as on the plains and crater highlands. Migratory birds flock to Rift Valley lakes such as Manyara, and the Ngorongoro Crater is awe inspiring. Kilimanjaro, Mount Meru and Ol Donyo Lengai stand guard over this beautiful, diverse land.

TRAVEL IN THE NORTHERN CIRCUIT
The tarmac road between Arusha and Moshi is good, as is the south-bound Arusha–Dodoma road until the Tarangire National Park turning beyond the Makuyuni junction, just northeast of Tarangire and due east of Lake Manyara. The road off the main thoroughfare at Makuyuni, heading towards Lake Manyara, Ngorongoro Conservation Area and Serengeti, is an all-weather road, but may be slow due to bumps and corrugations or standing water.

HEALTH HAZARDS
Take precautions against malaria. Wear long sleeves and trousers to reduce the risk of bites from tsetse flies. Beware of dangerous animals. If planning to climb Mount Kilimanjaro and Meru, stock up with recommended medical and other supplies.

INTERESTING EXCURSIONS
Camel Safaris Camels Only, The Adventure Centre; tel. (255) 57-7111, fax 8997. PO Box 12095, Arusha.
Climbing Kilimanjaro Kilimanjaro can be climbed all year. January and February have warm days with the odd rainshower. March to June are wettest, with snow clouds at higher altitudes (there is always snow at the summit). July is cold, but fairly clear.

August and September are cool with clear days, but there often is cloud cover. In October to December thunderstorms leave nights and mornings clear. Kilimanjaro Mountain Club, PO Box 66, Moshi. Try the YMCA in Moshi for guides and porters.

TRAVEL TO ARUSHA TOWN
By air Arusha is 45 minutes from Kilimanjaro International Airport. Arusha Airport handles local, charter and private flights. Transport arrangements must be made from the airport to the destination.
By land From Nairobi the journey to Arusha takes some 4 hours, with a border crossing at Namanga. There are several daily shuttle and bus services into town. The road is good with patches of broken tarmac. From Dar the best route is via Moshi 60 km (37 miles) east of Arusha. The journey takes roughly 8 hours over 650 km (404 miles) on good tarmac roads. The road from Dodoma is dismal and slow.

ACCOMMODATION
City and surrounds
Eland Motel On the Arusha–Nairobi road, this is a small hotel with clean, basic accommodation. Traffic can be noisy. PO Box 7226, Arusha.
Hotel Equator In city centre, simple accommodation overlooking river. Tel. (255) 57-8410, telex (255) 42034. PO Box 3002, Arusha, or Bushtrekker Hotels, tel. (255) 51-31957, telex (255) 4-1178. PO Box 5350, Dar es Salaam.
Impala Hotel 1 km (half a mile) from city centre. 63 rooms en suite. Bar, dining room. Safaris organised at hotel. The fastest Bureau de Change in Arusha! Tel. (255) 57-8448/84451, fax 8220/8680, telex 42132 TOURS TZ. PO Box 7302, Arusha.
Manor Hotel Near city centre, reasonable rates, comfortable rooms. P O Box 1706, Arusha.
New Arusha Hotel Moderate rooms, two bars, a dining room and swimming pool. Tel. (255) 57-8541, telex 42034. PO Box 88, Arusha, or Bushtrekker Hotels, tel. (255) 51-31957, telex 41178.
Novotel (Mount Meru) 168 rooms. Restaurants, bars. The Nairobi/Arusha shuttles stop here, safaris begin and end their journey here. Tel. (255) 57-8502, fax 8502. PO Box 877, Arusha.
Outpost Bed & Breakfast One room en suite, five double rooms. Tea and light meals. Tel. (255) 57-8405. PO Box 11520, Arusha.
Victoria House There are 15 en-suite rooms, bar, dining room. Safaris organized at hotel. Tel. (255) 57-2422, fax 8218, telex 42114 LAITOR TZ. PO Box 7319, Arusha.

Camping
Arusha Vision Just behind the Hotel Equator is this enclosed campsite on the banks of the Themi River. It has tents for hire, meals provided by staff, hot water and a laundry service. PO Box 12330, Arusha.

Masai Camp Situated off the old Moshi road near the city centre, bar and restaurant with a fireplace. Hot showers, fenced. Tel./fax (255) 57-8299. PO Box 6130, Arusha.
Meserani Snake Park On the Arusha–Dodoma road; snake exhibits and a bar. PO Box 13669, Arusha.

WHERE TO EAT
Chick King, Goliondoi Road. Quick and easy.
Hotel Impala, 1 km (half a mile) east of the clock tower. Menu offering local and international fare.
Johnny's Ravalia Restaurant, Sokoine Road. Has wonderful vegetable samosas for vegetarians!
K's Patisserie, India Street. Delicious pies.
Mambo Café, Goliondoi Road. King-size sandwiches and tasty salads; also gift shops on the premises.
Mandarin Chinese, Serengeti Road. Good food.
McMoody's, Sokoine Road. Serves hamburgers.
Mezza Luna, Moshi Road. Good Italian food.
Naaz Hotel, Sokoine Road. Affordable Indian food.
Piita Pizzeria, Sokoine Road. Good Italian food.
Shanghai, Sokoine Road. Reputed to offer the 'best Chinese food in Arusha'; secure parking.
Soweto Bar, off the main Nairobi–Moshi road. Excellent local fare and grilled meats.
21 Casino, Old Moshi Road.
When We, Sokoine Road. Nice pub.

TRAVEL TO ARUSHA NATIONAL PARK
By air The closest airstrip is in Arusha, 25 km (16 miles) away.
By road From Arusha, head east on Arusha–Moshi road towards Moshi. Cross Usa River, turn left onto dirt road signposted for Momella Lodge. Road fair to good. At Y-junction; if you turn left, you enter the park, heading for Momela Gate. If you turn right here, you enter the park via Ngurdoto Gate, approximately 3 km (2 miles) away.

ACCOMMODATION
There are five lodges in the vicinity of the park, and four campsites within the park boundaries. Walk-in guests are welcome, but it is advisable to make reservations before arrival, especially during the high season.

Safari lodges
Dik Dik Ltd Off Arusha–Moshi road just before Usa River. Dining room, terrace, swimming pool. Bunga-lows en-suite with fireplaces. Tel./fax (255) 57-8110/8498. PO Box 1499, Arusha.
Momella Lodge North of Momela Gate. Cottages and rondavels. Dining room and bar, swimming pool. Camping facilities. Tel. (255) 57-6423/6426, fax 8264, telex 42119 LIONS. PO Box 999, Arusha.
Mount Meru Game Sanctuary and Lodge Cabin-style accommodation. Tel. (255) 57-3303, fax 8268. Conservation Corporation, PO Box 751, Arusha.

Mountain Village Lodge This hotel has exceptional gardens and spectacular views of Lake Duluti. Tel. (255) 57-2699, fax 8205. PO Box 376, Arusha.
Ngare Sero Mountain Lodge Some 1,500 m (1,640 yd) up the same road as Dik Dik. Cottages have spacious rooms, and the cuisine and service are excellent. Tel. (255) 57-3629, fax 8690, telex 42047 MM ARS T, ARUSHA. PO Box 425, Arusha.

Rest house, hostel, huts and campsites
A rest house for five near Momela Gate and a hostel for 78 can be booked through warden. Four campsites: just inside Ngurdoto Gate and at foot of Tulu-lusia Hill. Firewood provided on request. Campsites have water tap and pit latrines. Park Warden, Arusha National Park, PO Box 3134, Arusha.

Moshi
Lutheran Uhuru Hostel (65 rooms, four suites) in three buildings. All en suite, mosquito nets, screens. Local fare; no alcohol. Conference facilities. Tel. (255) 55-54084/55868. PO Box 195, Moshi.
Moshi Hotel 60 rooms, dining room and bar, disco on Saturdays. Some rooms en suite. Tel. (255) 55-55212. PO Box 1819, Moshi.

TRAVEL TO KILIMANJARO NATIONAL PARK
By air Kilimanjaro International Airport, 56 km (35 miles) west of Moshi, is the closest air field.
By road Moshi approximately 60 km (37 miles) from Arusha, joined by good tarmac road. From Moshi next landmark is Himo, 27 km (17 miles) on. Turn north and Marangu Gate is 16 km (10 miles) ahead.
By rail Moshi can be reached by train from Dar es Salaam. However, inevitable delays and postponements can make this mode of travel unreliable.

ACCOMMODATION
Babylon Lodge Basic accommodation. Experienced guides and porters PO Box 227, Marangu.
Kibo Hotel 5 km (3 miles) from Marangu Gate, moderate accommodation can arrange guides and porters for climbers. PO Box 102, Marangu.
Marangu Hotel 37 km (23 miles) from Moshi. 28 rooms en suite, bar, dining room, pool. Camping possible. Guides and porters arranged. Tel. (255) 55-51307, fax 50639. PO Box 40, Moshi.

Hostels, huts and camping
Kilimanjaro Mountain Lodge Just inside Marangu Gate, bunk beds. Enquire at gate.
Camping Sites designated by park warden in Kilimanjaro National Park. Coffee Tree Campsite is an enclosed area near gate. Sitting room, electric outlets, fireplace. Flush toilets and water, no hot water. Alpine Tours Tanzania, PO Box 835, Marangu.
Hostels There are two hostels near the park gate, both of which are set up as large dormitories.
Huts Most huts on mountain should be booked with the park warden. For the above, contact the Warden, Kilimanjaro National Park, PO Box 96, Marangu.

TRAVEL TO MKOMAZI GAME RESERVE

By air Several airstrips for air charter services; arrange ground transportation before arrival.

By road Located in the northeast corner of Tanzania, 5 km (3 miles) east of Same on the Moshi–Tanga road. The road network in the reserve's northwest section is better maintained than in other areas in the reserve.

ACCOMMODATION IN THE RESERVE

Two basic bandas at Ibaya in northwest corner. Camping possible, no ablution facilities and a ranger must accompany all campers. Moshi, under 100 km (60 miles) away, offers standard accommodation.

TRAVEL TO TARANGIRE NATIONAL PARK

By air Two airstrips in park for private and charter flights. Larger one in Matete region near Tarangire Safari Lodge and park headquarters. Smaller strip near Kuro Ranger Post area may close during rainy season. Transfers to and from airstrip must be pre-booked. Make sure pilot does not to take off until transport has arrived.

By road Only one entry gate at Lemiyon, extreme northern sector. Arusha–Dodoma road tarmac for 106 km (66 miles), turn left on dirt track for 10 km (6 miles) to the main gate.

ACCOMMODATION
Safari lodges and luxury tented camps

Oliver's Camp Just outside park in Lokisale Game Control Area. Six double tents; hot showers. Library-cum-bar tent. Bird-watching and game-viewing. Day trips and night game drives in Land-Rovers. Mobile camps arranged. Closed during April and May. Tel./fax (255) 57-8548/3108. PO Box 425, Arusha.

Tarangire Safari Lodge Manyara tents or bandas, en-suite. Patio, bar and dining room have spectacular views. Swimming pool. Tel./fax (255) 57-7182. Serengeti Select Safaris Ltd, PO Box 2703, Arusha.

Tarangire Sopa Lodge Multi-level decks, dining areas with views. Suites spaced apart. Swimming pool; television and video. Diesel available. Tel. (255) 57-6886, fax 8245. PO Box 1823, Arusha.

Mashado Luxury Tented Safaris, Tarangire Fully inclusive rates for everything from game drives, laundry service, liquor to air transfers. Accommodation is in spacious Manyara tents with en-suite facilities. Bar, library, dining tent. PO Box 14823, Arusha.

Campsites

Special campsites in park arranged; pre-book in dry season with warden. Sites do not have water, and only one site has a pit latrine. Park Warden, Tarangire National Park, PO Box 3134, Arusha.

Kigongoni Campsite This campsite in an enclosed compound, 5 km (3 miles) outside the park gate, has basic ablution facilities. PO Box 2533, Arusha.

TRAVEL TO LAKE MANYARA

By air An airfield at the top of the Rift Valley escarpment is available for charter service.

By land Gate 120 km (75 miles) north of Arusha. First 75 km (47 miles) good tarmac, then bumpy stretch to Mto-wa-Mbu, outside gate. 4x4 necessary in the rains. Fuel/light shopping in Mto-wa-Mbu.

ACCOMMODATION
Hotels and luxury tented camps

Kirurumu Tented Lodge Ten tents with wooden decks, en-suite; hot water. Bar. Guided walks to Kirurumu Gorge arranged. Tel. (255) 57-7011/7541, fax 8226, telex 42103 AFTA. Hoopoe Adventure Tours Tanzania, PO Box 2047, Arusha.

Lake Manyara Hotel 100 rooms en suite, bar, gift shop, pool. Wildlife videos nightly. Petrol and diesel for sale. Tel. (255) 57-8502/2711, fax 8221.

Lake Manyara Serena Lodge On Mto-wa-Mbu rift wall. 66 en-suite rooms and a suite. Tel. (255) 57-8175, fax 8282. Serena Lodges and Hotels, PO Box 2551, Arusha.

Maji Moto Camp 10 tents, flush toilets, bar, dining. Tel. (255) 57-3303, fax 8268. Conservation Corporation, PO Box 751, Arusha.

Hostel, bandas and camping

Hostel The hostel for 48 is located at park headquarters, just outside the gate.

Bandas Ten clean, basic bandas can be booked, but there is no running water.

Camping Near the park entrance are two campsites with pit latrines and water taps. Special campsites can be arranged through the park warden.

Write to the Park Warden, Lake Manyara National Park, PO Box 12, Mto-wa-Mbu, or write to Tanzania National Parks, PO Box 3134, Arusha.

TRAVEL TO NGORONGORO
CONSERVATION AREA

By air Airstrip on crater rim west of Ngorongoro village; Lake Manyara has small airfield 2 hours from crater rim; Ndutu Lodge has an airstrip within the conservation area. Four-wheel-drive vehicle hire and transfers to lodge or camps must be pre-arranged.

By road Head south from Arusha on the tarmac for 75 km (47 miles) to turnoff at Makuyuni. Turn right onto all-weather road and head west across Maasailand; NCA headquarters some 100 km (60 miles) on. Although this journey can be fairly bumpy and dusty (or muddy and slippery, depending on the time of year), there are plenty of places to rest.

ACCOMMODATION
Safari lodges

Gibb's Farm This lodge in the Karatu area has excellent staff and offers delicious cooking. Tel. (255) 57-6702/8930, fax 8310, telex 42041 PANKER TZ. PO Box 6084, Arusha.

Ngorongoro Wildlife Lodge Perched on rim of crater. Spacious bar and dining area with a large fireplace. There are 75 rooms; central heating, television and video. Tel. (255) 57-8502/2711, fax 8221.
Ngorongoro Crater Lodge Dining room, bar and glassed-in area with views of crater. Tel. (255) 57-3303, fax 8268. Conservation Corporation, PO Box 751, Arusha, or tel. (254) 2-750298/750780, fax 746826. PO Box 74957, Nairobi.
Ngorongoro Sopa Lodge Northeast corner of crater rim. Fireplaces in main building, 92 rooms. Television and video, swimming pool. Tel. (255) 57-6886, fax 8245. PO Box 1823, Arusha.
Ngorongoro Serena Lodge Building hidden from the crater floor. All rooms have en-suite facilities. Tel. (255) 57-8175, fax 8282. PO Box 2551, Arusha.
Ndutu Safari Lodge 32 double rooms and 6 double tents. Airstrip nearby. Tel. (255) 57-6702/8930, fax 8310, telex 42041 PANKER TZ. PO Box 6084, Arusha.

Camping

Simba Camp On crater rim, 1 km (half a mile) past NCA headquarters turnoff (no camping on crater floor). Nights cool. Limited facilities; basic ablutions and water. Supplies can be obtained in the village, recommended you arrive fully stocked.
Designated campsites Olmoti, Empakaai (see Off the Beaten Track p. 99), Olduvai Gorge and Lake Ndutu. Permission to be obtained from NCA Authority and fees paid before using sites. PO Box 1, Ngorongoro or PO Box 776, Arusha. Campsites just outside Karatu.

TRAVEL TO SERENGETI NATIONAL PARK

By air Airstrips at Seronera and Lobo for air charter services, Mashado use an airstrip to the southwest of the park.
By road Main entry into Serengeti National Park at Naabi Hill Gate via road from Arusha, 320 km (199 miles). Gate to Seronera Lodge 45 km (28 miles), Seronera to Lobo Lodge , 75 km (47 miles).

Visitors from Lake Natron should use Kleins Gate northeast of park, 20 km (12 miles) from Lobo Wildlife Lodge. Bologonja Gate, linking Tanzania and Kenya is restricted to residents or travellers with special permission. West, on a dry-weather road, is Ndabaka Gate: access to routes that connect up with Musoma and Mwanza on the shores of Lake Victoria.

SPECIAL EXCURSIONS

Hot-air Ballooning Contact Tanzania Serengeti Balloon Safaris, tel. (255) 57-7111, fax 8997, or The Adventure Centre, PO Box 12095, Arusha.

ACCOMMODATION
Safari lodges and luxury tented camps

Grumeti River Camp Ten tents en suite. Birds, wildlife abundant. Tel. (255) 57-3303, fax 8268. Conservation Corporation, PO Box 751, Arusha.

Mashado Luxury Tented Safaris, Serengeti South Manyara tents en-suite, dining room and bar. A maximum of 16 guests can be accommodated. Airstrip nearby. Tel. (255) 57-8434/8917, fax 8435. PO Box 2782, Arusha.
Klein's Camp Bar, dining room, 8 cottages, swimming pool. Game-viewing, bird-watching, nature walks, night drives. Tel. (255) 57-3303, fax 8268. Conservation Corporation, PO Box 751, Arusha.
Lobo Wildlife Lodge 75 km (47 miles) from Seronera. 75 rooms, one suite, a large bar and dining area, and a swimming pool. An airstrip is nearby. Tel. (255) 57-8502/2711, fax 8221.
Migration Camp Attendant for each of 16 tents, electric lights. Bar, dining tent. Swimming pool. Tel. (255) 57-7111, fax 8997. The Adventure Centre, PO Box 12095, Arusha.
Serena Kirawira Camp Tents with private bathrooms. Tented dining room, bar and reception area. Tel. (255) 57-8175, fax 8282. PO Box 2551, Arusha.
Serengeti Serena Lodge 30 minutes west of Seronera Valley. 66 double rooms. Tel. (255) 57-8175, fax 8282. PO Box 2551, Arusha.
Serengeti Sopa Lodge Rooms with en-suite facilities, bar and conference room with satellite television. Boutique and coffee shop. Tel. (255) 57-6886, fax 8245. PO Box 1823, Arusha.
Seronera Wildlife Lodge 75 rooms and a suite, outside terrace. Booking desk, departure point for Tanzania Serengeti Balloon Safaris. Workshop, petrol and diesel for sale park and an airstrip nearby. Tel. (255) 57-8502/2711, fax 8221.

Camping, guest-houses and hostel

Public campsites Naabi Hill arranged at gate, Moru and Seronera through warden at Seronera, Kirawira and Lobo through wardens. Make arrangements for **special and wilderness sites** with park authorities before arrival. Sites unfenced, take safety precautions against dangerous animals. Firewood and water at designated sites. Check locations and procedures with the park authorities.

There are two guest-houses for visitors, and one hostel for school children. The Warden, Serengeti National Park, PO Box 3134, Arusha.

General services

There are dispensaries, garage facilities and fuel (when available) at Seronera's park headquarters/Visitors' Centre and Lobo Wildlife Lodge.

ACCOMMODATION IN LAKE NATRON

Lake Natron Camp Situated on the Rift Valley escarpment wall. Bandas are available. Contact The Safari Company, PO Box 207, Arusha; (255) 57-8060; fax 8059.
Saimon Kamakia, Ol Donyo Lengai Waterfalls Camping Area Located on the Ngera Sero River, this is a peaceful spot with lovely views. PO Box 34, Loliondo.

THE SOUTHERN CIRCUIT

Distances throughout the Southern Circuit are vast, and therefore are most often tackled by air. Road conditions vary from excellent tarmac surfaces to the uncompromising and fiendishly slow stretches containing potholes – or worse, patches of broken tarmac. However, what can become part of the experience is an appreciation of the massive wilderness expanses where few tourists venture – the reality of Africa, untamed and pristine.

If you are travelling through the southern region by road, cities and towns play an important role, providing the necessary basics such as fuel, food, water and communication. This also forms an important part of the preparation process while you are planning your route through the south.

DODOMA

Dodoma is situated in the semiarid centre of the country, 242 km (150 miles) from the town of Morogoro to the southeast, which many tourists use as a stopover before driving to Mikumi or the Selous Reserve. To the southwest of Dodoma is Ruaha National Park (although the distance between them is vast), while Mikumi National Park and Selous Game Reserve are to the southeast. The city is experiencing constant albeit slow progress. Before the arrival of the colonials, the area was a settlement for the semipastoralist Wagogo people. The caravan routes passed through this early settlement but it was not until 1910, when the Central Railway line finally reached Dodoma, that the city truly developed. Also with the arrival of the railway came commerce, the development of light industry and human settlement. During German colonization in the early 1900s, the intention was to use Dodoma as their administrative capital, but the outbreak of World War I changed their plans. The city became a supply station and transfer depot for the

Selous Game Reserve's hot springs.

army troops. However, misappropriation of local grain supplies and cattle stocks by first the Germans and later the British quickly pushed the city into decline as thousands of people died in the Mutanya and Kaputula famines. The meaning of 'mutanya' – scramble – implies perhaps the desperation of the local people at the time when food was temporarily made available, while 'kaputula' was the term given by the locals to the shorts worn by the British, who, they felt, had precipitated the famine. The railroad proved to be an advantage to the people of the area as limited supplies could be brought in, but this mode of transport required fuel; the resultant deforestation that occurred in order to provide this fuel subsequently played a key role in the massive erosion that has since taken place throughout the area.

During the 1930s, Dodoma was used as a stopover for the newly established Cape-to-Cairo flights. During the 1970s it was chosen as the site for the Pan-African Telecommunications Network, which opened up radio communication to 11 African countries.

There is some discussion that Tanzania's capital might one day be moved to Dodoma, but the tremendous costs involved in such a transfer are prohibitive. Today, light industries and religious organizations feature prominently in the city. Another industry of significance is the wine industry. Grapes were first successfully introduced in 1938 by the Holy Ghost Fathers, and later, in 1957, by Father Irioneo Maggioni, a Passionist Father at the Bihawana Mission. Vineyards can be seen throughout the surrounding areas and guided tours can be arranged through the Dodoma Wine Company.

Kondoa region rock paintings
Halfway between Dodoma and Arusha (to the north) lies the quiet village of Kolo. Nestled in the hillsides around Kolo are several sites that are ancient visual reminders of the past. The region has many rock shelters with cave paintings, but the Kolo paintings are by far the best examples and are more easily accessible.

Thought to be created by Khoisan-speaking people, the style corresponds with the Aurignacian paintings (believed to belong to a flint culture that existed during the palaeolithic period in Europe) found in France. Dating back to 3400 BC, these extraordinary rock paintings depict the animals and customs of the people at the time; they represent fashion, dancing ceremonies, wildlife and hunting scenes. Unfortunately, the natural elements are having an adverse effect on many of the paintings; however, they retain an incredible charm and are an important insight into the past.

It is necessary to visit the site with an escort, which can be arranged through the Department of Antiquities office in Kolo, before you head down the 7-km (4 miles) dirt (murram) track to the site. A four-wheel-drive vehicle is recommended. At the site there are three separate rock shelters with paintings. The walks are not long (graded easy to moderate), although there are a couple of slightly steep sections. There is a campsite in the area; fees are paid to the Department of Antiquities officer on duty. Fuel is available most of the time in the nearby village of Kondoa.

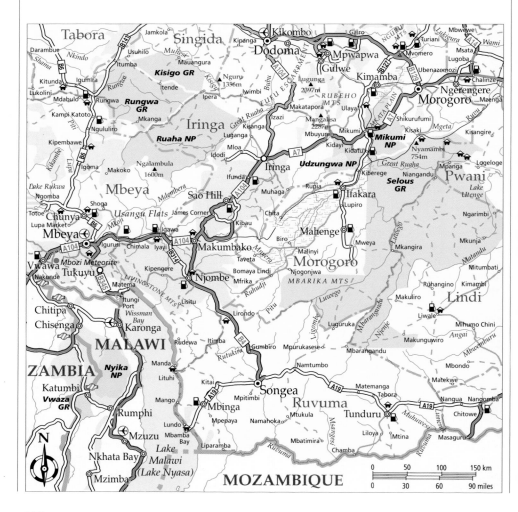

The rock paintings at Kolo, north of Dodoma.

MOROGORO

Located approximately 195 km (121 miles) – or 3 hours – west of Dar es Salaam and 90 km (56 miles) east of Mikumi National Park, Morogoro is tucked into the foothills of the Uluguru Mountains. The town bustles with activity and trade and is often used by visitors to obtain foreign exchange (a slow process), to restock with supplies and to refuel, especially if they are travelling to or from the wilds of the Selous Game Reserve, eight hours away. The fertile soil of the area produces fruits and vegetables which are sold locally and displayed in a fanfare of colour at the city market. All along the main road into the city centre, mattresses and pillows are on display, stuffed with sisal or kapok and painted in bright shades of pink, blue and yellow. Across the road is a tannery and further down, a kiosk that sells only bicycle seats.

MIKUMI NATIONAL PARK

Mikumi is Tanzania's third-largest national park. Gazetted in 1964, in 1975 its boundaries were extended to its current size of 3,230 km² (1,225 sq. miles). Its location is unusual – running through the park for about 50 km (31 miles) is the TANZAM Highway, connecting Tanzania and Zambia. However, it is a delightful park, with lovely views across its various habitats. Of special note is the park's location in the Mkata flood plain, where plains game and birdlife are prolific, depending on migratory patterns. The plain is surrounded by mountain ranges: to the east is the Uluguru range while to the southwest lie the Lumango Mountains; moving steadily west and northwards from here, the heights of Mbesera, Madizini and Mazunyungu not only paint a dramatic picture but also harbour animal species not found in the open savanna. As the edges of the plain rise up to the mountain slopes, they are clothed in 'miombo' woodland. The Selous Game Reserve borders Mikumi to the south; it is the largest reserve in Africa and together with Mikumi forms an enormous ecosystem that nurtures and supports the migratory habits of zebra, buffalo and elephant.

Mikumi is ideal for visitors to Tanzania with limited time for the true 'wilderness' experience. The park's proximity to Dar es Salaam and its variety of wildlife are a great advantage. The best time to visit is during the dry season, from June to February; the short rains in November and December can make travel in the park difficult. Long grass in June and July can obstruct game-viewing but is generally not a deterrent.

Mikumi is stunning in the early morning and late afternoon when its panoramic views are enhanced by the light and its wildlife is at its most active; this is the best time to be in your vehicle, moving around. Excursions along the Kisingura Circuit, around the Hippo Pools and the Vuma Hill Drive can prove to be most rewarding. There are several picnic and observation points throughout Mikumi. Travel within park boundaries is permitted between 06:00 and 19:00; close attention should be paid to map indicators of main roads and dry season tracks, especially if visitors are in the park during wet periods.

Vegetation within the park

Mikumi's habitats range from low-lying grassland plains in the centre of the park (around the Mkata flood plain), with patches of black cotton soil, to the rising foothills of nearby mountain ranges where wooded grassland gives way to thick miombo woodland, made up mainly of *Brachystegia* trees. Within the plains are hardpan ridges with virtually no tree growth except occasional hardy acacia and tamarind trees. Trees that do occur in the area and are not to be missed are the majestic baobabs *(Adansonia digitata)* – especially one in the southern extension of the park that is said to be the largest in the area – *Hyphaene* palms with their wavy trunks dotted sparsely here and there, and the regal borassus palms *(Borassus flabellifer)* with distinctive spindle-shaped trunks. At one time the latter occurred in great numbers, a fact that led to the naming of the park and nearby village at its western border after the palm (Mikumi is the Swahili word for the borassus palm). Another tree of the plains is the deciduous *Sclerocarya caffra*, whose small green fruit is much favoured by elephant.

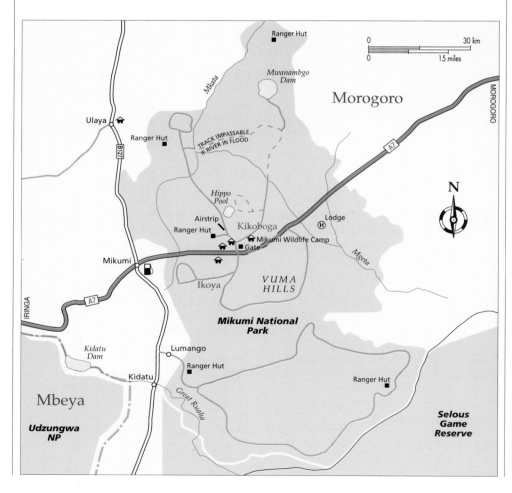

Mikumi's wildlife

Numbers of wildlife in the park boundaries ebb and flow through the year but visitors are seldom disappointed, with normally good sightings of elephant, buffalo and Maasai giraffe. Plains game, including eland and Lichtenstein's hartebeest, with their predators (lion and leopard) are usually also seen – you need to keep close to waterholes in the dry season. A different species of wildebeest from that found in northern Tanzania – the blue wildebeest, or brindled gnu – also occurs. African hunting dogs live in the park but are rarely seen. The miombo woodlands can yield sightings of sable antelope, greater kudu and the black-and-white colobus monkey. Although tsetse fly occurs throughout the park, it is much more common in miombo woodland. There are hippo in the pools, and many waterbirds.

Over 300 bird species have been recorded in Mikumi. Eurasian migrants flock to the park from October to April to join the park's resident inhabitants. Commonly seen on the plains are Lilacbreasted rollers, Blackbellied bustards, hornbills, ostrich, guineafowl, and francolins. Cattle egrets, Hamerkops, Saddle-billed storks, and Red and Yellow bishops are generally found in the marshy areas and at the Hippo Pool, along with waterfowl. Soaring high above, the Bateleur eagle does his aeronautics while the Tawny eagle keeps a watchful eye from aloft.

SELOUS GAME RESERVE

Declared a World Heritage Site in 1982, the 50,000-km² (19,293 sq. miles) Selous (pronounced 'Se-loo') is Africa's largest reserve. Its ecosystem comprises the reserve, surrounding unpopulated land, the Mikumi National Park in the north and the Kilombero

LEFT: *Mikumi Wildlife Camp.*
BELOW: *The distinctive Maasai giraffe.*

Game Controlled Area in the west. These combined regions form roughly 75,000 km² (28,900 sq. miles) of protected land.

The Selous has been the centre of several historical events, beginning with the find of stone implements belonging to prehistoric man; there is also tangible evidence of the caravan routes that were established through the interior for the transportation of slaves and ivory to Kilwa on the coast. And then there is the famous 'magic' water used in the Maji Maji Rebellion of 1905, which is said to have come from an area near the lakes that are linked to the Rufiji River.

During World War I, the German cruiser *Königsberg* sheltered in the Rufiji Delta east of Mtemere. She was sunk in 1915 by the British. The Germans adapted many of her shells to use as land-mines, and removed her 4.1-inch guns, carrying them overland to continue their campaign. One of these guns

The Saddlebilled stork occurs in Mikumi NP.

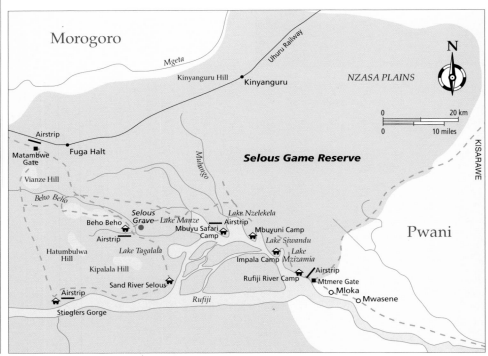

now rests in the National Museum in Dar es Salaam, while another is said still to be lying veiled in earth and brush near the Rufiji River at Kidai. Another wartime remnant in Selous is an old German steam engine lying derelict in the far south of the reserve.

Undoubtedly one of the most important historical encounters in the reserve was that in January 1917, near the Beho Beho area, between the British and the German forces led by General Paul von Lettow-Vorbeck. It was in this conflict that the explorer Frederick Courteney Selous, DSO, died at the age of 66. While the British regiment, the Legion of Frontiersmen, was attempting to surround the Germans, Selous was struck by the bullet of a German sniper. Both sides mourned the death of the distinguished Selous, revered as the greatest white hunter of them all, and it is said that a letter of condolence was issued by the retreating von Lettow-Vorbeck. As a tribute, the reserve was named after the naturalist and explorer, and today a simple stone in the Beho Beho area marks his grave.

The area designated for safaris is in the northern sector of the park, including the Rufiji River and five interconnecting lakes. There are hunting concessions to the north and south of this designated zone. Reputed to have some of the largest elephant herds remaining in the wild, the Selous embodies the rugged, suspense-filled beauty of true Africa. Its secluded vastness and wilderness keeps the annual tourist numbers extremely low, and it is the ideal destination for travellers wanting to 'get away from it all'.

TOP: *The lovely Sand Rivers Selous Lodge.*
ABOVE: *The Rufiji River, Selous Game Reserve.*

Vegetation

Dominant throughout the reserve is miombo woodland, mainly *Brachystegia*, *Combretum* and *Julbernardia globiflora* tree species. The woodland is dry and harsh and can be difficult to photograph; although it may appear uninviting, patient observation reveals the natural beauty of the area. Grassy woodland areas are also interspersed wherever the spiny *Terminalia spinosa* grows in abundance. Black cotton soils throughout most of the well-frequented areas can prove to be quite a serious obstacle during the rains. The watercourses and riverine areas support different types of vegetation from the drier stretches of the reserve. Another impressive borassus palm species, *Borassus aethiopum*, is the tallest of the indigenous palms and with its bulging trunk is certainly the most distinctive. It can be recognized by its large fan-shaped leaves, and it bears a large, round, orange fruit that has edible pulp. After the rains wildflowers abound throughout the reserve, filling the land with colour.

Selous' wildlife

Selous is famous for its elephant. Though recent years have seen a decline in population, the reserve and surrounding ecosystem probably still harbour the highest elephant population in Africa. Generally seen in small herds composed of females, adolescents and young, elephant are often encountered on the move through the reserve.

Another major feature of the Selous is the large number of hippo and crocodile that can be seen in and around the lakes and rivers. The crocodile often bask on a ridge or the shoreline, while the hippo generally stay in deeper waters, occasionally raising their massive heads out of curiosity or during play.

The reserve has an enormous variety of ungulates such as Maasai giraffe, buffalo, Burchell's zebra, eland, common waterbuck, impala, hartebeest, and both the Nyasaland gnu (occurring south of the river) and the brindled gnu (occurring north of the river). Predators are found throughout the reserve, the most commonly seen being lion and spotted hyena. Known to exist in the park, though not seen regularly, are leopard, cheetah and hunting dog. Formerly present in great numbers is the black rhino, whose plight has attracted worldwide coverage; it still occurs, though rarely seen.

The Selous is a haven for bird-watchers: over 300 species have been recorded. You will often see brilliant flashes of colour swoop past, as many of the birds in the reserve are brightly feathered, such as the Lilacbreasted, Broadbilled, Cinnamon, and Racket-tailed rollers. Various sunbirds, and bee-eaters, such as the Little, Whitefronted and Böhm's, can also be seen; from December to April, you may catch sight of the distinctively marked Carmine bee-eater. Waterbirds, in particular, are worth spending some time observing as their variety and numbers are staggering. The African skimmer, Whitebacked night heron, and the Rock, or Whitecollared, pratincole all occur in the Selous. Birds of prey are abundant and the elusive Pel's fishing owl is not an uncommon sight.

Guided safaris on foot, by boat and by four-wheel-drive

A unique advantage of the Selous is the variety of game-viewing options available, especially to visitors staying in permanent camps and lodges. Game drives are always on offer, but many guests take advantage of viewing the wildlife by boat along the river or on the lakes. This not only enables visitors to view wildlife as it approaches the water, but also allows a close-up look at the animals living in the many watercourses, which teem with hippo and crocodile throughout the reserve.

Crocodile (TOP RIGHT) *and hippo* (RIGHT) *are found in large numbers in the Selous.*

BUFFALO

The buffalo species found in Africa is the Cape buffalo *(Syncerus caffer)*. It is muddy brown to black in colour and often has a fringe edging its ears. Males weigh up to 900 kg (1,764 lb). Both males and females have strong, heavily bossed, inward curving horns, which are much smaller in the female. The buffalo's sense of sight and sound is adequate, its sense of smell excellent. Buffalo occur most commonly in family groups, sometimes small ones of up to five members, sometimes 500–600 members and, occasionally, thousands. Herds generally consist of females, their young and males, although the older males do tend to go off on their own, remaining in heavily wooded areas, mostly near a constant source of water. Solitary males should always be treated with extreme caution.

Spending most of the morning, evening and night-time grazing (perhaps because of their poor ability to regulate body temperature they avoid overactivity during the heat of the day), buffalos need to drink daily and there-fore stay close to water. Their enemies include lion and hyena. Cattle egrets and the brightly marked Yellowbilled oxpecker are normally seen in the vicinity of buffalo herds, the oxpeckers often hitching a ride on the back of a buffalo while eating insects off its hide.

Buffalo are a common sight in Tanzania.

The walking safaris led by trained armed guards are also special. This exciting experience brings the bush much closer to guests, giving them the opportunity to stretch their legs and look at aspects of the African wilds they may not have noticed before.

For self-driving visitors, game-viewing drives along the main reserve road between the Matambwe and Mtemere gates, which is a direct three-hour route of approximately 85 km, or 53 miles, can provide good sightings of the prolific wildlife in the area. Numerous tracks meander in and around the reserve, but there are no bollards indicating circuits or places of interest. This fact can make navigation a little difficult; the hiring of a reserve escort is recommended to ease this difficulty.

Stiegler's Gorge

Named after a German explorer who was killed in the area by an elephant, Stiegler's Gorge is located roughly 44 km (27 miles) from the Matambwe Gate at the northwestern border of the reserve. A turnoff to the right approximately 1 km (half a mile) after the gate winds its way eventually to the gorge. At the gorge itself the Rufiji River, lying about 100 m (328 ft) below (having joined up with the Great Ruaha) snakes impressively through the mountain rock for about 8 km (5 miles).

Lake Tagalala and the Hot Springs

Situated in the Beho Beho area, Lake Tagalala is an ideal place for leisurely game-viewing and bird-watching. The road leading to this

area can be picked up about 13 km (8 miles) from the Matambwe Gate. You will have to cross the Beho Beho River about 11 km (7 miles) along the road (the river is dry for most of the year and, when in flood, generally recedes quickly). If you enter through the Mtemere Gate (at the northeast corner of the park) to reach the area, continue along the main road for 49 km (30 miles), at which point a road cuts in from the left. The Beho Beho area should be reached on this route after about 20 km (12 miles). The road to Lake Tagalala cuts into the main road south

ABOVE: *A game drive in the Selous Game Reserve.*
BELOW: *Selous' hot springs are worth visiting.*

of the airstrip. Be warned that the 14-km (9 miles) drive from here to the lake takes approximately an hour!

The turning for the hot springs is about 12 km (7 miles) from the airstrip, on the right-hand side. Look for a stream of clear water as a landmark. The springs concealed in the thick vegetation and graced with shimmering dappled light are truly worth a visit. The travertine mineral deposits and rock formations add a unique charm to the beauty of the calm, restful waters, as do the various pieces of petrified wood (formed as a result of exposure over the years to calcium-carbonate in the area). The sulphurous water that cascades into shallow pools and trickling streams is extremely inviting and is sure to ease away any of the day's stresses.

UDZUNGWA MOUNTAINS NATIONAL PARK

Near the northwestern corner of the Selous, in the south-central parts of Iringa and Morogoro, this 1,900-km^2 (729 sq. miles) area of land was gazetted in 1992. The Udzungwa Mountains and the Uluguru and Usambara mountains form Tanzania's 'eastern arc'.

The eastern escarpment is dominated by the forest canopies of lowland through montane forest which rises to over 2,000 m (6,562 ft). These fertile forests and their canopy hold plant species that range from the minute to the massive, including a newly discovered tiny African violet, ferns, orchids and soaring trees that stretch for 30 m (98 ft). Some plant species are found nowhere else in the world (among these is the tiny African violet). These enchanting forests and plateaux are worth visiting as they represent a fascinating habitat that is fast diminishing.

The park is designed for walking and hiking and, although it is not mandatory to have an armed escort, visitors need to be extremely cautious as elephant and buffalo do roam freely throughout the area. Specially appealing is the 170-m (558 ft) drop of a particularly lovely waterfall on the Sanje River. The walk to this first waterfall is roughly an hour and a half and meanders through ever-changing lush vegetation and beautiful scenery. Other waterfalls and pools can be reached further along the trail. Some sections of the walk can be moderately steep and narrow – a walking stick is helpful and sturdy, comfortable shoes are a must. Also special in the Udzungwa Mountains National Park are the wooded grasslands and mountain views.

Six primate species occur in the park, among them the Iringa red colobus monkey and the Sanje crested mangabey, both endemic to the area. Within the plateau region, which can be reached by walking through the forest, there are herds of elephant, buffalo, eland and waterbuck. Seen often are elusive creatures of the forest such as bushbuck and duiker.

Bird-watching in the forest takes a fair amount of patience but can be most rewarding. Large numbers of birds including endemic species have been recorded; in fact, the Udzungwa's forests qualify as one of the top three important zones for bird conservation in Africa. Several new species have been discovered during recent research, including a new member of the francolin family.

IRINGA

Situated to the southwest of Morogoro (and west of the Udzungwa Mountains park), the city of Iringa is perched on a plateau amid the luxuriant greenness of southern Tanzania's highlands. The drive to Iringa winds through a spectacular escarpment and, if you are approaching from the south, you will be surrounded by richly yielding agricultural lands and a beautiful pine forest (part of a forestation programme) before reaching the city. Iringa is a centre for business and trade, and has a unique character. It is a mixture of old and relatively new buildings, impressive churches and an old mosque. Its architecture also reflects its Germanic influences. Outside the city centre, the tobacco fields are probably the largest source of capital, though small farms are dotted throughout the area. The region's fertile soils have attracted settlement for many years and it harbours a past that's rich in history. The people who live here are predominantly members of the Hehe ethnic group. It was their famous chief, Mkwawa, who was responsible for building up the reputation of the Hehe people as a formidable force and who battled fiercely – once successfully – against German colonial forces in 1891. However, in a conflict in 1894 at Kalenga, just beyond Iringa, the Hehe people were overpowered by the Germans despite their building a new stone-and-mud fort (yet unfinished at the time of the defeat), said to have had 2.5-m-high (8 ft) walls and to extend for 3.5 km² (1 sq. mile).

A roadside stall selling pots on the road to Iringa.

A general supplies store in Iringa.

Iringa is the last opportunity to buy basic supplies and fuel before heading into the Ruaha National Park, 120 km (75 miles) off. The city market is interesting, offering a colourful insight into life in this growing community. You may park at the police station across the street (a safe option). The market is packed with a wide variety of fruits, vegetables and dried beans and can also provide items ranging from cassette tapes to tea kettles and clothing. If you would like to go for a meal, try Lulu's or the Taj Lodge, both in the city centre. Petrol and diesel are readily available in Iringa. The water in the city is not suitable for drinking and should be obtained elsewhere. (If you are heading to the Ruaha National Park, drinking water is available from the park headquarters.)

Isimila Stone Age Site

About 20 km (12 miles) south of Iringa on the main road to Mbeya, is a signposted turning to the Isimila Stone Age Site. Following the road for 1 km (half a mile), you will come to the site's office. If you are lucky, you may meet Celima, the caretaker for the area. He first came to the site in the 1950s, working with archaeological teams who arrived; he has remained at the site, and now guides visitors around, informing them about the area.

Some of the richest finds of Stone Age tools yet known may have been exposed at Isimila. It is nothing less than incredible physically to see the massive numbers of hand-cut stones that lie in the sand, exposed by the elements. The prehistoric implements found in the area are referred to as Acheulean (taken from St. Acheul, the suburb in France where tools of a similar type, believed to have originated during the palaeolithic period in Europe, were first discovered). The site was discovered in 1951 by D. A. Maclennan of the St. Peters School in Johannesburg, South Africa. Excavations carried out by scholars from the University of Chicago in the late 1950s, and the University of Illinois in the late 1960s and early 1970s, provided a wealth of knowledge as to the reasons why such vast numbers of tools have been left resting here, possibly for as long as 60,000 years.

It is believed that much of the area was at one time covered by a small lake created by a landslide that slipped into a valley west of the site. Not very deep, the lake measured roughly 1 km (half a mile) by 1.5 km (1 mile). It was fed by a stream in the east and contained some sections of reeds and marsh. The fast-moving water from the stream carried with it silt together with gravel and sand. At the point where the stream met the lake, the flow of water was slowed to a halt and the sediment quickly fell to the bottom, eventually building up in mass. When the lake began to dry up, a stream from the Kipolwi River in the west started to cut back towards the dried depression, creating the present korongo (dry watercourse) as it cut through the surface deposits and lake beds. Though the stream is now almost always completely dry, the years of erosion resulting from its seasonal passage have exposed the primitive tools: hand-axes, cleavers, scrapers and spheres. These can all still be seen throughout the central korongo.

Stone Age man is believed to have camped along the lake shore and the many streams, where he gathered water or hunted animals as they came to drink. It is here that he worked diligently, fashioning his tools – proof of which is not only the multitude of tools found in the area, but also the blocks, cobbles and boulders that served as part of his production process. Also found are the flakes chipped off his tools in this prehistoric factory. The stone from which the tools were fashioned was mainly granite and quartzite. Many fossilized bones have also been found in the area, among them those of elephant and a mammal related to our modern-day giraffe, but having a much shorter neck, Sivatherium. Still found in the korongo are the fossilized remains of an extinct hippo, H. gorgops, which had unusual periscope-like projections as eyes.

Natural Pillars

Beyond the Stone Age site, a path leads through corn fields and cassava to what the locals refer to as 'Mnara', or 'church steeple'.

Isimila's uniquely beautiful stone pillars.

As you head along the path, people working their crops take little notice as they are accustomed to curious visitors. A quick walk of approximately 10 minutes reveals a fantastic, timeless display of natural art in the form of massive pillars, shaped by wind and erosion. If you descend into the dry riverbed, these exquisite columns, some 18 m (60 ft) tall, tower gracefully above, casting shadows that dance about you.

Visits to the Stone Age site and the Natural Pillars are best undertaken during the early morning and late afternoon, since midday temperatures can be uncomfortably hot. There is moderate walking involved and a couple of semisteep slopes, but if they are taken slowly they can be navigated by most visitors.

A covered picnic area is situated at the main entrance to the site. At the time of writing there was no entrance fee but a minimal fee may be introduced in future. Many stones from the area can also be viewed at the National Museum in Dar es Salaam.

Kalenga's Museum

Driving 12 km (7 miles) out of Iringa towards the Ruaha National Park, you will meet the village of Kalenga. A signpost indicates the direction of the museum, which is just under 1 km (half a mile) off the main road. It may be necessary to ask for the caretaker to be called, but this usually takes only a few minutes. Besides a building that houses a few local artefacts, the on-site museum consists of two burial sites belonging to former Hehe chiefs. The most spectacular item is the skeletal head of Chief Mkwawa, the fierce warrior who stood up to the colonial Germans in the late 1800s. Records state that, when Mkwawa's fort was seized, the Germans hired 400 porters to carry away the Hehe chief's ivory stores and close to 13,650 kg (30,000 lb) of gunpowder. After Mkwawa's death, his head was sent to Germany in 1898; it was not returned to Tanzania until 1954 at the insistence of Governor Edward Twining. Sadly many of the artefacts in the museum have been stolen, but the story of Mkwawa, his leadership and courageous struggle as told by the current Hehe residents is worth hearing. Outside, beyond a maize field, stands the house of the current Hehe chief, built in 1957 by the Roman Catholic Mission in Tosamaganga and paid for by an imposed local tax.

RUAHA NATIONAL PARK

West of Selous National Park and just south of central Tanzania lies a hidden treasure that few visitors take the time to experience. Ruaha National Park, the second-largest national park in Tanzania has captivating landscapes and impressive animal populations. It is a transition zone containing wildlife and vegetation types of both East and southern Africa. A count of plant species occurring in the Ruaha ecosystem has revealed 1,650 varieties. Many of these recorded species produce flowers; the best time to see these is March and April. The

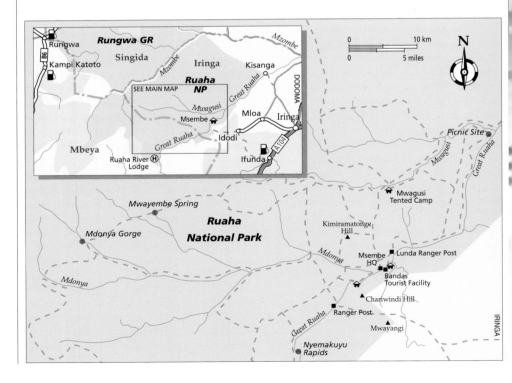

Sunrise over the Great Ruaha River.

park's special qualities as a transitional zone are emphasized by East Africa's annual grasses and scrub, which are found here in their southernmost environment, and southern Africa's different varieties of legumes and perennial grasses, occurring here in their northernmost environment (they are not seen in Tanzania north of this point). The virtually untouched wilderness of the Ruaha National Park is a major attraction; visitors seldom see other vehicles while in the park. Remote and secluded, it is the quintessential African bush.

In 1910 the area was secured as part of the Saba River Game Reserve, and in 1964 it was gazetted as a national park. Today the park boundaries encompass 10,300 km² (3,931 sq. miles) and, together with the Rungwa-Kisigo Game Reserve in the northwest, form the 45,000-km² (17,345 sq. miles) Ruaha ecosystem. It is estimated that 90% of visitors use only 6% of the park. This is due mainly to the fact that the majority of the park is elevated above the Rift Valley on a thick miombo-covered plateau, 100 m (328 ft) higher than

the riverine area. These plateaux are for the most part inaccessible, but there may be plans in the future to include walking treks which are more suited to this type of habitat and will have a minor ecological impact. The park does, though, have a network of well-developed roads.

The name Ruaha is derived from the Hehe word for river, 'luvaha'. The Rift Valley river of the same name flows approximately 160 km (99 miles) along the eastern border of the park, and provides some of the best game-viewing opportunities along its length. The Great Ruaha River is fed by the Usangu flats 50 km (31 miles) southwest of the park. The Ruaha and the Mzombe River (to the north) meet, flow through the Mtera and the Kidatu dams to the east of the park before joining up with the Rufiji River in the Selous Game Reserve, which then heads finally towards the Indian Ocean. The dams were developed in the 1970s and 1980s to provide electricity for Dar es Salaam and a great deal of the country; however, recently the Great Ruaha River has begun to dry up towards the end of the dry season. The remaining pools are rich with hippo, crocodile and fish, but research is underway to investigate the change in the river's pattern and the resultant long-term implications. The river, which usually peaks in April, hosts 38 identified species of fish which provide food both for the communities that live along the river and for the sizeable crocodiles that occur in and around the park.

A bridge on the way to Ruaha National Park.

The Ruaha's wildlife

Wildlife in the Ruaha is unique in terms not only of its numbers, but of the extraordinary variety of species. There is a meeting of fauna typical to East and southern Africa (Grant's gazelle is common to northeast Africa but can be seen in its southernmost territory towards Lunda in the northeast of the park, while roan antelope, mainly a southern African species, also occur in the Ruaha). Though shy and elusive, the sizeable eland is seen regularly, as are both greater and lesser kudu, sable, dik-dik, impala, Lichtenstein's hartebeest, Burchell's zebra and Maasai giraffe. Elephant and buffalo are a main feature of the Ruaha, but the oribi, klipspringer and steenbok are also present.

Hunting dogs are occasionally spotted, and may be found around the kopjes of the old airstrip close to bollard 21. Other predators, such as lion, leopard, cheetah, bat-eared fox and spotted hyena, are frequently seen. The striped hyena and the side-striped jackal also occur in Ruaha National Park, as does the serval, although sightings of these animals are rarer.

There are five recorded types of mongoose in the park, among them the Egyptian and the white-tailed species. As for the smaller species, keep your eyes open for spring and Cape hares, rock and tree hyrax – and, in the waterways, the Cape clawless otter.

The crocodile and hippo numbers are vast and these animals can be viewed right through the year. Monitor lizards with their prehistoric appearance are seen regularly and, without fail, visitors are entertained by the bright pink and blue agama lizard as it scampers along the kopjes.

A recent bird count undertaken in the area revealed over 400 species; this includes residents as well as northern and southern migrants. Among the many species of hornbill present, a glimpse of the Palebilled hornbill perched in the *Brachystegia* trees is extremely rewarding as they are not sighted as often, while the haunting morning call of the Ground hornbill is a recognizable sound of the Ruaha. The feathered hues of the region's avifauna usually provide the colour in the wilds. Six species of starling have been recorded in the area, the most conspicuous of which is the exquisitely coloured Superb starling and the less attractive Ashy starling. The Rufous crowned roller can be spotted among the branches as can the Lilacbreasted and the rarer Racket-tailed species. You will no doubt catch a flash of red from the commonly occurring Whiteheaded buffalo weavers, along with greenbuls and cliffchats. Doves are plentiful; often seen flying off the road as vehicles approach is the streamlined Namaqua dove. You are also likely to see the Blackbellied bustard moving through the grassland plains, where the distinctively marked Redcrested bustard occurs too.

There are plenty of waterbirds along the river courses and at the seasonal swamps and marshes – egrets, herons, geese and storks and, if luck is on your side, you may be able to identify the unique Whitecrowned plover by its long, bright yellow wattles and loud, sharp, repetitive call. Birds of prey are numerous: often seen are the Bateleur, Longcrested and Fish eagles. Rare sightings of the Black eagle are possible and, in December and January, the migrant Eleonora's falcon.

Game drives in the Ruaha

Slightly different from most optimum game-viewing times in Tanzania, there seems to be a great deal of activity mid-morning in the Ruaha. Unlike most of the country's national parks, the road system in the Ruaha is excellent; it is well maintained, and there are clearly marked bollards at crossroads and junctions. Vehicles are permitted to move within the park from 06:00 to 19:00, allowing plenty of time to explore the terrain.

After passing through the main gate (from Iringa) and crossing the bridge you will come to bollard R8A: if you wish to head to the hippo pools, turn left and immediately turn right at bollard R8. Follow this track for a short distance, then the hippo pools come into view, with lovely shaded areas and picnic sites in and around the kopjes. Often seen here are large family groups, or pods, of hippo, crocodiles impressive in size and number, waterbirds and wildlife as it comes to the water. This is a superb spot and worth checking out at various times of the day to see what activity is going on.

The main track comes to a crossroad at bollard R7. From here you can go straight towards the far side of Kimiramatonge Hill in the north-central area of the park, left (upstream) towards the Ruaha River Lodge 10 km (6 miles) away, or right (downstream) towards the Msembe area, the campsites, and the park headquarters 8 km (5 miles) away. When heading towards Msembe there are some superb panoramic viewpoints both from the main road and from signposted turnings. Roan antelope can often be seen

Elephant are often seen in the Ruaha.

Some baobabs may be thousands of years old.

along this drive. Several well-marked circuits in the Msembe area offer stunning views with plenty of game and birdlife.

If you head upstream towards the lodge, at the crossroads the road winds through dense thickets of *Combretum* where kudu and elephant are often seen. There is a sense of intrigue about this area, especially in the dry season when the animals camouflage themselves in the shade of lone baobabs as they make their way to the river to drink. When it is dry, most of the wildlife is usually seen closer to the river, so heading towards the lodge gives visitors a good chance of seeing a variety of birds and animals since the road meanders along the river's edge for about 4.5 km (3 miles) before it reaches the lodge. The road continues on along the river and eventually turns back inland, forming a pleasant circuit of roughly 19.5 km (12 miles).

The Ruaha River Road, heading downstream, is an excellent drive for its game-viewing and riverine vegetation – in the wet season it can be particularly rewarding. The valley through which the Ruaha flows is noted for its figs, acacias, tamarinds and palms. If you turn right at bollard R22, this wonderful track skirts the river's edge for approximately 14 km (9 miles). As you head to the northeast, keeping the river on your right, the rolling grassland plains on your left often reveal large numbers of plains game. Also in this area are patches of entrenching black cotton soil and gentle undulating hills. As you come up to the next bollard, you will have arrived at the confluence of the Great Ruaha and the Mwagusi Sand rivers. The rolling hills continue to the north and the vegetation changes to the bristly combretum-commiphora woodlands.

The tracks leading to and around the Mwagusi Sand River often reveal large numbers of buffalo, elephant and Maasai giraffe. The Mwagusi is dry most of the year, but after the rains it flows at a fast pace into the Great Ruaha. Gradually, as the season changes, the river once again starts to appear dry. But, just beneath the surface, dams form which enable animals to dig for the water. Elephant, in particular, are quite adept in reaching the hidden water catchments, using their feet and tusks. The soft rolling terrain around the Mwagusi Sand River, marked by the contorted branches of baobabs and *Combretum* and *Acacia* species, is part of the diversity that makes the Ruaha so special. The baobabs found throughout the park are enormous, some with perfect holes carved through the centre by elephant damage.

A distinctive sound of the Ruaha is the morning call of the Ground hornbill.

ROAN AND SABLE ANTELOPE

SABLE ANTELOPE (*Hippogragus niger*) This is an impressive animal which frequents dry, open woodland with medium to tall grasses. The sable antelope has magnificent, heavily ringed, scimitar-shaped horns which occur in both sexes but are larger and more pronounced on the male. Sable are an overall chestnut brown, although older males will turn jet black; they have white undersides and their facial masks feature a streaky white patch from muzzle to eye as well as along the side jawline. A mane runs from the neck to beyond the shoulder. Herds averaging 10–30 members comprise either a single male with females and their young or bachelor herds; nursery herds also occur, led by a dominant female. Males often mark their territory by breaking the tops of branches with their sweeping horns, and they are known to drop to their knees to take part in fierce territorial battles, sometimes with fatal results. The sable antelope is most active in the early morning and late evening and, although extremely shy, can be viewed at waterholes as it must drink water daily.

ROAN ANTELOPE (*Hippotragus equinus*) The movements of this antelope have been associated with those of a wild horse, hence its scientific name. Its colouring is a greyish-brown with a darker mane running from the neck to the shoulder; it also has a rough beard from the lower neck to the foreleg and its long ears are fringed. Its distinctive facial markings show a white patch around the muzzle and a white streak from the muzzle to above the eye. Both males and females carry ringed, curved horns, though not as large as those of the sable antelope. Roans appear in small herds of between six and 12 members, usually bachelor herds or cows and their calves led by one male. They are commonly found in open, wooded grassland areas and their diet consists mainly of grass, leaves and roots. Enemies include lion, leopard and hyena.

Sable antelope occur in dry woodland areas.

As you head northwest from the Mwagusi Sand River towards Mpululu, there are several tracks that lead into the dense and bewitching combretum thickets and miombo woodlands – mainly made up of *Brachystegia* – on the rising plateau (which forms the majority of the park). Look closely for the regal sable antelope that occurs in this area. Though difficult to spot, it is exquisite in colour and form with its graceful horns that curve back in an impressive arc. The wildlife is not as prolific here as elsewhere in the park, and the presence of tsetse fly makes itself quickly felt.

The western regions of the park include submontane forests and evergreen uplands, but at present remain inaccessible.

MBEYA TOWN

Lying southwest of Iringa and roughly equidistant from the Zambian and Malawian borders, the town of Mbeya was founded in 1927. With Mbeya Peak looming overhead, the town below keeps a fast pace, offering basic supplies, banking and fuel but little else. The town came into being because of the flourishing Lupa goldfields. The mines closed in the mid-1950s, but Mbeya was by this time well established and still today it remains a centre for trade in the southern highlands. It is the last major town before arriving at the borders of Malawi and Zambia. The town is set in a vast, fertile area with a backdrop of mountain ranges with misty crests and rolling foothills. The city centre, on the other hand, is untidy and not very well kept. There is limited accommodation available, but it is sufficient for overnight requirements. Throughout the southern highlands the temperatures can be extremely cold, especially in July, and it is suggested that visitors have a suitable jacket or heavy sweater with them while visiting the area.

Sights of interest in and around Mbeya

While in Mbeya, take a look at St. Anthony's Catholic cathedral, built in 1954 with an old-world style and character. If you are travelling from Zambia into Tanzania, a stop at the Mbozi Meteorite might be of interest. There is a signposted turning roughly 53.5 km (33 miles) from Tunduma on the Zambian border. Another 13 km (8 miles) along a bumpy road winds through small farms, eventually leading to another short turnoff. The meteorite is placed on a mounting, but it is obvious that previous visitors have attempted to hack bits of it away. There is also a covered picnic spot but, unless one has a keen interest in this type of geological find, it is one attraction that may not be worth the bumpy trip to see.

Spectacular viewpoints

Another relatively short journey is to the 'World's End' viewpoint. If you head north out of Mbeya towards Chunya, at the 21-km (13 miles) milestone there is a forest camp. A track off to the right leads to the sweeping viewpoint which encompasses the escarpment of the Great Rift Valley and the Usangu flats.

If you head south of Mbeya through the Poroto Mountains, the sightseeing opportunities are wonderful and certainly worth the effort. They can be enjoyed as part of a day trip from Mbeya or en route to or from the Malawi border. As you drive through this area, the lush expanse of the Kitulo Plateau unfolds, with Rungwe volcano and the Kipengere range rising in the distance.

Climbs and trails

Energetic visitors can indulge in some mountain climbing at Mbeya. Hikers generally head towards the challenging 2,809-m-high (9,216 ft) Mbeya Peak. There are two trails leading to the summit: the first is a gradual climb that starts in the north, about 13 km (8 miles) from Mbeya town on the road to Chunya. Turn at the signpost that says: Karateri Farm and Mbeya Peak. Follow the track until it ends; the walk begins at this point and should take approximately one to one-and-a-half hours. The second, more active trail is tackled from a coffee farm in Luiji north of Mbeya (ask for directions at a petrol station in Mbeya or at one of the lodges or hotels). This path involves scrambling through gullies and steep segments and could entail getting your feet wet from water and mud in the gullies, but the scenery is enchanting and, once you are at the top, the panoramic views are exquisite.

Local residents believe that Ngozi Lake, nestled in a volcanic crater south of Mbeya, possesses magical powers. It is termed a 'dead' lake since it was formed as a result of volcanic activity and sustains no life within its ashy depths. However, the surrounding cliffs and misty atmosphere around the lake are tranquil and certainly offer visitors a restful escape. Ngozi Lake can be reached from the main Mbeya/Tukuyu road, after turning into a signposted track roughly 35 km (22 miles) from Mbeya. Keeping on the *murram* track (dirt road) for another 4 km (2.5 miles), visitors reach the forest edge where they leave their vehicles and walk for about an hour through the forest before reaching the lake's rim. The walk can be steep in places and slippery if there has been some rain, but it is certainly pleasant.

God's Bridge and the Boiling Pot
The turnoff to these two delightful sights is 10 km (6 miles) north of the town Tukuyu, not far from the Malawian border. There are no signs directing visitors to these two areas of interest, so look for the sign to the Pentecostal Holiness Association Mission. If you are looking for a basic, no-frills place at which to camp, you can stay at the Pentecostal Mission approximately 2.5 km (1.5 miles) along the turning. Continuing on past the mission, stay on the main road for a total of 10 km (6 miles). You will come to a turning on your left with a signboard to Ujenzi; turn left here and you will drive a very short distance before the lovely God's Bridge comes into view. Spanning the Kiwira River, this unique land formation has a backdrop of babbling clear waters, waterfalls and mountain passes. Its formation was the result of the meeting some 400 years ago of molten lava from Rungwe volcano and the cold, fast-flowing waters of the Kiwira River.

The Kiwira River at God's Bridge.

To reach the Boiling Pot, continue on the main road which crosses a bridge a bit further upstream. Go over the bridge and stay to the right, following the signs to the 'Shule ya magereza', or the Police Training School of Prison Works. Continue up the road to the gate. Perhaps wondering what you may have got yourself into, tell the guard that you'd like to visit the Boiling Pot, or Kijunu. They may allow you to pass unescorted, or they may request you to take a guard with you. Either way is fine and, once through the gate, you continue on for another kilometre (half a mile). At this point there is an opening in the banana trees. Leave your car here and head off to the right on the footpath; you will come to the Kiwira River's edge and the amazing turbulent waters of the Boiling Pot. The river's breadth narrows, creating calm shallows at the edges, but forcing the mass of water into a powerful flow which drops into a churning brew below forming a natural cauldron, before edging out a hollow in the pot's side and filling another pool below. The violent waters bubbling and brewing in the pot force spray up to the rocks and moss thrives on the upper surfaces. The walk from the track to the river's edge is easy, but does have one short steep section that may require a slower pace or a helping hand.

LAKE NYASA (LAKE MALAWI)

Making your way southwards to Lake Nyasa (in Malawi, Lake Malawi), you pass through the town of Tukuyu, which at an elevation of 1,500 m (4,922 ft) may be the wettest in Tanzania. It has little to offer visitors save sufficient supplies of fuel. The Masoko Crater Lake on the Tukuyu–Ipinda road may be of interest; its blue waters (some say as much as 3 km/2 miles deep) are rumoured to have been used by the Germans to dump guns and vehicles. The road to the lake is not one of Tanzania's finest.

The northern part of Lake Nyasa's shores lie within the borders of Tanzania and, although they are not developed for tourism as they are in Malawi, the lake provides food for many of the inhabitants of the area and, from the north and western shores, there are spectacular views of the Livingstone range of mountains lying to the east.

Once you have turned off the main Mbeya road, the journey to the lake runs the whole gamut from good to extremely bad. From Mbeya the entire journey takes about two hours, during which you pass rolling expanses of tea plantations, many small villages where the local women are dressed in their brightly patterned khangas and, on clear days, panoramic vistas of the lake and surrounding mountain ranges will unfold before you. You can visit the quiet Itungi Port on the northwest edge of the lake, and the adventurous can book a passage for various

The trip to Lake Nyasa passes tea plantations.

excursions to the southern ports of Liuli (Wednesdays) on Lake Nyasa's eastern shores and, a little further down, Mbamba Bay (Mondays and Fridays).

Lake Nyasa rests about 480 m (1,575 ft) above sea level. It measures roughly 500 km (311 miles) north to south and 50 km (31 miles) east to west. The water line of the lake seems to be rising continuously as the problem of silting increases; this is the result of erosion caused by deforestation which deposits silt into the many rivers which then flow into the lake. What the long-term effect of this will be is yet to be seen.

The relative isolation of this southernmost Rift Valley lake has resulted in high numbers of endemic fish within its waters. Thirty per cent of the world's recorded cichlids (mouthbreeders) and over 400 species of the brightly coloured haplochromine fish occur in the lake. At the northernmost tip of the lake lies the village of Matema. The majority of the people living here are the Wa-Nyakyusa whose traditional homes, which are constructed of bamboo, plastered over with mud and uniquely painted, can still be seen. There is a small stretch of beach at which one can camp, but all provisions and camping equipment should be acquired first before arriving.

A visit to Lake Nyasa is an unhurried, enjoyable experience that leaves one with an overriding impression of the simplicity of life. One can watch the fishermen as they move along in wooden dugouts, or listen to the lapping of the waves and simply let time slip by.

ADVISORY: THE SOUTHERN CIRCUIT

CLIMATE
The Southern Circuit covers a vast area with wide temperature variations. Mornings and evenings are cool; daytime temperatures average 25 °C (77 °F) but are much lower in the highlands in July. Most of the area has one rainy season: December–May, with a break from mid-December to February. From June to November, days are drier, but humidity rises as the rains start in November. The rain pattern around Udzungwa and Mikumi national parks is more typical of the north: short rains in November and December, long rains in March–May.

BEST TIMES TO VISIT
Mikumi National Park In mid-August to October most temporary groundwater dries up, forcing animals to the hippo pools, the Mkata River, the spring below Mikumi Wildlife Lodge, and waterholes. Temperatures are pleasant, but a jacket is advisable for mornings and evenings. Mikumi is wonderful for bird-watching (October–April sees the arrival of the Eurasian migrants) but it may be hindered by rains. During the November/December short rains wildlife disperses as surface water becomes more available. It is possible to move around the park, but some roads may be inaccessible. Check road indicators with the rangers and on park map for the latest update. The park is lush and green in January and February; migrant birds are plentiful, wildflowers in bloom and wildlife is wide-spread. The wettest months are from March to May. Many roads in the park become inaccessible, as patches of black cotton soil inhibit travel in the low-lying areas. Some roads may still be impassable just after the rains, but overall travel should be unimpeded. Wildlife is easily seen and, although the migrant bird species have gone, there are many resident species in and around the park.

Selous Game Reserve and Ruaha National Park From June–November dry weather forces wildlife to waterholes and river outlets. Temperatures are pleasant until October, when days can be hot. There may be showers in November. With the onset of rain in December, it is advisable to fly in as some roads may be impassable. January to February can be a wonderful time in both parks. The wettest time is from March to May. Both parks are open all year, but many lodges and camps close temporarily. Wildlife is widely dispersed and many roads, especially in and around the Selous, become impassable.

MAIN ATTRACTIONS
Vast wilderness may be the biggest attraction of the area. Virtually untouched by humanity, the wildlife, bird species, varied vegetation zones, Stone Age sites, Rift Valley lakes, and the challenge of mountain-climbing are unsurpassed in Africa.

TRAVEL IN THE SOUTHERN CIRCUIT
The road network is good. *Murram* (dirt) roads are passable in the dry season, albeit dusty and bumpy. A 4x4 vehicle is recommended year-round. Fuel is available in most towns, but spares probably only in major cities. Air transport is recommended into Selous Game Reserve (ensure that transport to lodges/camps is prebooked). Coastal Travels in Dar runs weekly flights into southern parks. One can charter flights to southern Tanzanian destinations.

HEALTH HAZARDS
Take precautions against malaria. Be aware of potentially dangerous wild animals. Ensure you have sufficient fresh water before arriving in the Iringa area.

TRAVEL TO DODOMA
By road Dodoma is a 3-hour trip 242 km (150 miles) northwest of Morogoro. The tarmac road is in good condition, but starting to deteriorate. The 495-km (308 miles) drive from Arusha on the Arusha–Dodoma road takes 11 hours or more, an exercise in patience, dust inhalation in dry weather, and extreme care in wet. The rock paintings in Kolo, 165 km (103 miles) north of Dodoma (via the Arusha–Dodoma road), should not missed.
By rail Dodoma can be reached via the Central Railway linking Kigoma on Lake Tanganyika to Dar es Salaam. The journey is beautiful, but changes in schedule and delays make it unreliable.

ACCOMMODATION
Christian Council of Tanzania Conference and Training Centre Basic, clean, secure accommodation in the heart of Dodoma. Tasty, homely meals, with a local flair. Reasonable rates. SLP 372, Dodoma.
Dodoma Hotel (near station). The hotel is showing signs of fatigue; it has a bar, dining room and 24-hour room service. Credit cards not taken. Tel. (255) 61-22991/ 22042, fax 24595. PO Box 239, Dodoma.

TRAVEL TO MIKUMI NATIONAL PARK
By air There are no scheduled flights into Mikumi, but an airstrip accommodates up to 15-seaters. Ground transport should be arranged beforehand.
By road Mikumi, 288 km (179 miles) from Dar and is the capital's closest wildlife destination. Driving from Dar via Morogoro, 195 km (121 miles) away, takes 4 hours. Udzungwa National Park is 80 km (50 miles) southwest of Mikumi; Iringa 310 km (193 miles) from Mkumi. The Iringa–Dar es Salaam road is fair/excellent tarmac.

ACCOMMODATION
Morogoro

Mama Pierina Restaurant & Annex (Station Road): A friendly place for accommodation, a delicious meal, or just a drink in the bar. Twelve basic en-suite double rooms with ceiling fans and mosquito nets; there is a laundry service and rates are reasonable. Tel. (255) 56-2172. PO Box 338, Morogoro.

Morogoro Hotel Near the city centre, this hotel is used for conferences. It has 69 en-suite rooms, dining room and terrace, tennis courts and an 18-hole golf course. There is a disco on Friday and Saturday, and television/video Mondays, Tuesdays and Thursdays. Tel. (255) 56-3270/1/1, fax 4001, telex 55100 MOHOT TZ; or Bushtrekker Hotels, tel. (255) 51-31957, telex 41178. PO Box 5350, Dar es Salaam.

Mikumi National Park

Mikumi Wildlife Camp (through the park gate). En-suite bandas (no hot water) overlook the Mkata flood plain. Evening meals served outside, weather permitting. Tel. (255) 51-68062/3/4, fax 68631. Oyster Bay Hotel, PO Box 2261, Dar es Salaam.

Mikumi Wildlife Lodge south of the TANZAM Highway in the Vuma Hills, on a hillside with panoramic views. Fifty rooms with private bathrooms. The bar and dining area overlook a waterhole; barbecues are held at weekends. Tel. (255) 57-8502, fax 8221. Tanzania Hotel Investments.

Rest-house, guest-house, hostel, camping

Camping Three sites with pit latrines. Only Site One, near the gate, has a water tap. Site Two is on the Kisingura Circuit and Site Three in the south of the park, off the main road. Special sites available.

Rest-house, guest-house, hostel The rest-house has two double rooms, toilet, sitting room and kitchen. The guest-house has six double rooms with bar, dining room and kitchen. The hostel has 30 double and two single beds; cooking facilities and toilets nearby.

For all the above, contact the Park Warden, Mikumi National Park, PO Box 62, Mikumi.

TRAVEL TO SELOUS GAME RESERVE

By air Chartered and scheduled flights from Dar (45 minutes–1 hour). After landing ensure the pilot waits to confirm that transport is waiting.

By road A 4x4 vehicle is necessary. Roads can be erratic, especially during rainy seasons.

From Dar es Salaam The road south from Dar to Selous deteriorates rapidly. The trip to Kibiti (fuel and limited supplies available) is 120 km (75 miles) and takes approximately 8 hours. The 30-km (19 miles) dirt road to Mkongo can be better than the broken tarmac, but the 75 km (47 miles) to Mtemere Gate in the north is bumpy in the dry season, impassable in the rains. Total time (225 km; 140 miles) is between 14 hours and 2 days.

From Mikumi National Park A dry season track from Mikumi to Selous takes about three-quarters of a day to cover. Check with rangers for conditions.

By rail The TAZARA railway line runs west from Dar and cuts across the north of Selous, stopping at Fuga and Kisaki. Tickets can be bought from TAZARA in Dar; transport and accommodation in Selous must be booked separately. Another option is taking the Beho Beho Express, with accommodation at Beho Beho Camp. Book through the Oyster Bay Hotel in Dar. Travel time without delays is 5 hours.

ACCOMMODATION

Beho Beho Camp Bandas on a hill in Beho Beho area. Walking, fishing, boating, game drives and visits to World War I trenches. Transport by rail from Dar. Tel. (255) 51-68062/3/4, fax 68631. Oyster Bay Hotel, PO Box 2261, Dar es Salaam.

Mbuyu Safari Camp En-suite tents along the river. The bar and dining areas surround a baobab. There is an airstrip nearby. Wilderness walks, boating and game drives arranged. Tel. (255) 51-24896 (ask for Mbuyu), fax 24897. Southern Tanganyika Game Safaris & Tours, PO Box 2828, Dar es Salaam.

Mbuyuni Luxury Tented Camp Twelve screened en-suite tents with verandas. Bar/dining facilities in open tent; there is a *dungu* (game platform). Hippo, crocodile and birdlife abundant; walking, boating and game drives on offer. The camp is near an airstrip, and may close April–May, depending on the rains. Tel. (255) 51-28485/35638, fax 46980, telex 81016. Selous Safari Co, PO Box 1192, Dar es Salaam.

Rufiji River Camp Comfortable en-suite tents with verandas have wonderful views. The staff are accommodating, the menus international. Arrangements are made for walks, fishing, boating and game drives. The camp may close from April to May, depending on the rains. An airstrip is nearby. Tel. (255) 51-3680/ 71610, fax 75165, telex 41685 TAIR TZ.

Sand Rivers Selous An exquisite lodge situated on the banks of the Rufiji River. The six stone and thatch cottages all have private views. Activities include swimming, hiking, game-viewing by boat, 4x4 outings, and fly camping (a temporary camp). The camp is powered by solar energy. There is an airstrip nearby. The lodge generally closes from mid-April to the start of June. Tel. (255) 51-46862 or 811-324341 (cellular), fax 46863. Nomad Safaris, PO Box 70192, Dar es Salaam.

Camping Check with gate rangers for location and accessibility. Tel. (255) 51-32680. The Warden, Selous Game Reserve, PO Box 25295, Dar es Salaam.

TRAVEL TO UDZUNGWA MOUNTAINS NATIONAL PARK

By road The gate and headquarters are on the Mikumi–Ifakara road, 60 km (37 miles) from

Mikumi village; look for a signposted turning off the Iringa–Morogoro road (TANZAM Highway). Road conditions are relatively good.

ACCOMMODATION

Twiga Resort Near the gate, this guest-house has basic rooms, en-suite facilities, wholesome meals.
Camping Three sites in the park, no facilities. Obtain supplies before arrival. Warden, Udzungwa Mountains National Park, PO Box 99, Mang'ula.

TRAVEL TO IRINGA

By air There is an airstrip for chartered aircraft.
By road Iringa is 310 km (193 miles) southwest of Morogoro, a spectacular 4-hour drive (good tar road). Take the Iringa turnoff from the main road; at the T-junction, turn left (the old cemetery on your left) towards Kalenga village and Ruaha National Park (no sign). The 4-hour drive to Iringa from Mbeya is on 330 km (205 miles) of good tarmac.

ACCOMMODATION

Huruma Baptist Conference Centre Immaculately clean, moderate, secure lodgings; wholesome food (no alcohol); small apartments with kitchen and appliances. Camping possible. Turn onto Mkwawa Road from the main Iringa road. Drive 2 km (1 mile) along this bumpy dirt road, and turn left. The gate to the centre is under half a kilometre further, on the right. Tel. (255) 64-2579. PO Box 632, Iringa.
Isimila Hotel City centre; dining room, bar, 48 en-suite rooms. Tel. (255) 64-2605. PO Box 216, Iringa.

TRAVEL TO RUAHA NATIONAL PARK

By air Charter and scheduled (three times weekly) flights from Dar es Salaam land at a park airstrip.
By road The all-weather road (passable all year) from Iringa (120 km/75 miles) takes 3 hours. After 60 km (37 miles), you reach a Y-junction: both roads lead to Ruaha. The right road is recommended; flanked by miombo woodland, it lives up to its nickname of 'never-ending road'. A left turn will take you through the villages. Though interesting, with glimpses of locals going about their daily life, it can be a struggle as the road is not well maintained.

ACCOMMODATION
Lodge and tented camp

Mwagusi Safari Camp Intimate tented camp on the banks of the Mwagusi Sand River. Each of the eight double tents is thatched, with a bathroom and river view. Two library and two dining bandas. Mwagusi has efficient staff, and good home cooking. Elephant often pass the camp. Game drives are conducted by the knowledgeable camp manager. 4x4 vehicles can be hired. The 30-minute drive to or from the airstrip is a game drive in itself! The camp may close in April or May depending on the weather. Tel. (255) 51-37479/80, fax 46045, telex 41150 CSITZ. Coastal Travels, PO Box 3052, Dar es Salaam.

Ruaha River Lodge On the banks of Great Ruaha River. Stone/thatch bandas among kopjes or along the river. Bandas have private bathrooms, verandas or patios and dining and bar enclosures. 4x4 vehicles can be hired. The lodge is open all year. Tel. (255) 51-37479/80, fax 46045, telex 41150 CSITZ. Coastal Travels, PO Box 3052, Dar es Salaam.

Bandas and camping

Bandas Basic accommodation near headquarters – from sheets and pillows to cooking utensils. Showers and toilets need maintenance.
Camping Two sites in the park offer panoramic vistas of the Ruaha River, shady trees and firewood. There are pit latrines and water can be obtained at the bandas' site. Special campsites can be arranged. Write to The Warden, Ruaha National Park, PO Box 369, Iringa.

TRAVEL TO MBEYA

By air There is a small airport on the outskirts of Mbeya town, but no scheduled service.
By road All roads into Mbeya are good tarmac. The 330-km (205 miles) drive from Iringa takes four hours. Tunduma, on the Zambian border, is 104 km (64 miles) from Mbeya. The Malawi border is 116 km (72 miles) south of Mbeya.
By rail Mbeya can be reached via the Uhuru Railway, or TAZARA, linking Zambia and Tanzania.

ACCOMMODATION

Karibuni Centre Just outside city centre, off the Zambia road; clean and secure. The toilets and showers are immaculate; hot/cold water. Wholesome meals (no alcohol; restaurant closed Sundays). Tel. (255) 65-3035, fax 4178. PO Box 144, Mbeya.
Mt. Livingstone Hotel Situated near the city centre, moderate accommodation, bar and dining room. Barbecues are held in an attractive garden, with a disco on Wednesdays, Saturdays and Sundays. Tel. (255) 65-3331/3, telex 51173 LIVIN TZ. PO Box 1401, Mbeya.
Utengule Country Resort in the foothills of the Mbeya range. Turn north at Mbalizi (11 km/7 miles, southwest of Mbeya); 9 km (6 miles) along the dirt road, turn right at the sign to the resort. Comfortable en-suite rooms. Squash, volleyball, tennis, table tennis, mini-golf, billiards, a fitness room and swimming pool. Safaris and day trips to the Lupa River hot springs, and Kanga Lake for bird-watchers, can be arranged. Fax (255) 65-2768. PO Box 139, Mbeya.
Lwika, Lake Rukwa Delightful, off-the-beaten track. Erling Schaug Johansen, PO Box 2983, Mbeya.

THE WEST AND NORTHWEST

Western and northwestern Tanzania cover vast expanses of wilderness, with high concentrations of wildlife. This part of the country flaunts dramatic mountain ranges, spectacular scenery and two of Africa's largest lakes – Tanganyika and Victoria.. Poor road conditions ensure low numbers of annual visitors to the parks and game reserves, thereby slowing development and ensuring an unmatched 'bush' experience with minimal disturbance to the environment.

TABORA

Tabora (originally called Kazeh), roughly equidistant from Lake Victoria and Lake Tanganyika, was founded in 1820, and was an important stop for trade caravans. About 800 km (497 miles) from the ocean, the town grew quickly as a trading centre for slaves and was a base for explorers Richard Burton and John Hanning Speke; Tabora was also a temporary home for David Livingstone and Henry Morton Stanley. Today there is a museum on the site where Livingstone lived.

The area around Tabora is hot and dry. The people, mainly the Nyamwezi, who were once a fearsome tribe under Chief Mirambo, are today a peaceful community, growing crops, raising livestock and keeping bees.

KATAVI NATIONAL PARK

To the southwest of Tabora and adjacent to Lake Tanganyika, Katavi covers 2,253 km² (864 sq. miles). The Katavi-Lake Chada area was designated as a game controlled area in the 1800s by the Germans; it became the Lake Rukwa Valley area in 1932, and in 1951 the Katavi Plains Game Reserve was established. It was upgraded in 1974 to national park status. Located in the western arm of the Great Rift Valley, the park consists of the valley floor, the foothills, the escarpment

The red colobus monkey, an unusual looking inhabitant of forested areas.

rising to the east, and high plateaux. Lying in the high-altitude flood plain are Lake Katavi to the north, Lake Chada to the southeast and the Katesunga Swamp between the two.

The vegetation is a mixture of eastern and southern African savanna and miombo woodland, and short-grass plains dotted with acacias, while palm trees surround Lake Chada. The grassland plains support high concentrations of larger mammals (buffalo and elephant, as well as sizeable herds of Burchell's zebra, Maasai giraffe, gazelles, waterbuck, roan antelope and topi). Also seen is the rare puku, a honey-coloured antelope that seldom occurs in Tanzania (it is found more in south-central Africa). The lakes host enormous pods of hippo and massive crocodiles. Over 400 bird species have been recorded, among them a substantial number of waterbirds.

Large areas of Katavi have black cotton soil, making travel on the park's limited tracks very difficult. Visitors should plan their journey during the drier periods, from July to October or December to February

UGALLA RIVER GAME RESERVE

This little-visited 5,000 km² (1,927 sq. miles) reserve lies 90 km (56 miles) northeast of Katavi National Park. Access roads into the reserve poor; although marked on most maps, they are virtually nonexistent! The reserve consists of the ubiquitous miombo woodland with lovely riverine valleys. Sable antelope are a highlight in the area. Visitors must be fully self-sufficient in everything from fuel to food. This is a true wilderness experience, to be undertaken by the adventurous only.

LAKE TANGANYIKA

Fishing boats, dugouts and canoes glide on sparkling waters rimmed by mountain ranges: these are all part of the atmosphere of Lake Tanganyika. The longest freshwater lake in the world, it runs north to south for 675 km (419 miles) and is the world's second deepest, with depths beyond 1,440 m (4,725 ft).

The lake is believed to be 20 million years old. Its shores were explored by famous intrepid travellers who firmly believed that this

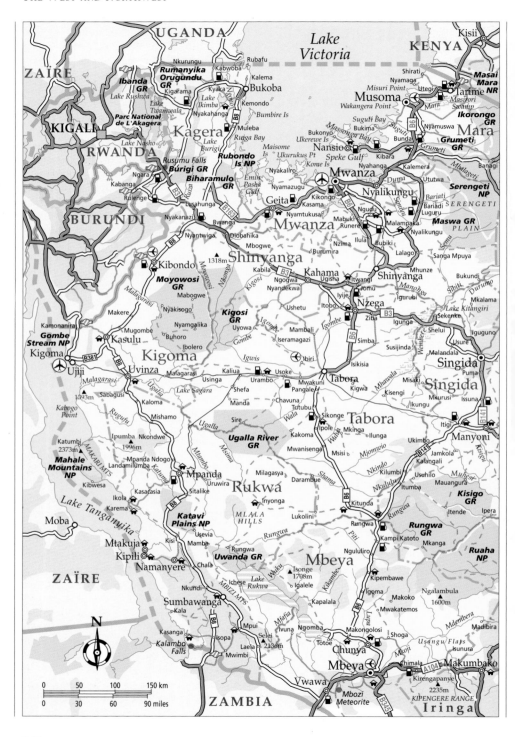

was the source of the Nile. Interestingly, only the top 200 m (656 ft) of the lake is utilized by the resident fish species. The remaining depths are considered 'dead' waters, as they contain little oxygen and strangely do not mix with the upper layers of water. There are 250 species of fish in the lake – most of them endemic – which makes Tanganyika a biologically fascinating study. Over 200 species are the brightly coloured cichlids, or mouth breeders. The dagaa *(Stolothrissa tanganyikae)* is a fish that is of great commercial use, and is caught at night using lights to attract the small silvery creatures to the surface. The fish are netted by the fishermen, sun-dried and sold in large quantities locally and for export.

The movement of the water in the open shoreline areas of Lake Tanganyika indicates little presence of bilharzia, and the daily temperature of 23 °C (73 °F) makes snorkelling in the clear waters a real treat for those who don't mind braving the unimaginable depths. The amazing colours and patterns of the cichlids, along with the Lake Tanganyika jellyfish, freshwater crabs and the rarely seen water cobra, are well worth seeking out.

KALAMBO FALLS

Most easily reached from the Zambian side, these spectacular 212-m (695 ft) falls on the Tanzanian–Zambian border are well worth a visit. The forest on the edge of the falls is full of gnarled trees and unique tiered termite mounds. The pools at the top are wonderful for swimming and can be crossed if the river is not in flood – keep away from the edge! The walls on either side of Kalambo Falls and the canyon below are breathtaking, with the sheer rock cut into grooves. A nature trail in the area affords magnificent cliff-edge views of the falls. Camping is permitted for a nominal fee.

MAHALE MOUNTAINS NATIONAL PARK

Perched halfway along Lake Tanganyika's length, on its eastern edge, Mahale Mountains is home to 1,000 chimpanzees and several other primate species and mammals. Covering about 1,613 km² (615 sq. miles), the park is roughly 30 times larger than

Vendors on Lake Tanganyika, which is the second-deepest lake in the world.

ABOVE: *A laden cargo boat on Lake Tanganyika.*
LEFT: *A campsite in the remote and pristine Mahale Mountains National Park.*

Gombe Stream National Park to the north. The park remains remote and unspoiled as it has no road access and can only be reached by air or by ferry on Lake Tanganyika. Only walking treks are possible within the park boundaries. Formerly home to the Waholo-holo and the Batongwe peoples (although it never supported large numbers of residents), the area was gazetted in 1980.

Mahale Mountains has seven vegetation zones, ranging from grass steppe, acacia savanna and baobabs to miombo woodland, riverine forest, rainforest and montane forest. The miombo is made up primarily of *Brachystegia*, *Isoberlinia* and *Julbernardia* tree species and covers most of the area. At 1,800 m (5,906 ft) a mixture of bamboo bushland and montane forest – neither of which is seen in Gombe – begins. The montane forest is generally composed of *Podocarpus* (yellowwood) species), *Macaranga* and *Croton megalocarpus* species. Above 2,300 m (7,546 ft) the forest is replaced with montane grassland.

The main attraction in the park is the experience of being able to come into contact with the chimpanzee families. Research on the chimpanzees by Japanese teams has been under way since 1961; the family groups are well habituated to people and are approachable. This is one of the last places in Africa – and in the world – where it is possible to watch chimps in their natural habitat and observe their daily lives in close proximity. Children under the age of 10 are not permitted to visit the chimpanzees, likewise any individual who potentially has a contagious disease or ailment.

Besides the chimps, Mahale Mountains has several other types of primates, including yellow baboons, Angolan colobus monkeys, the black-and-white and red colobus monkeys, as well as the savanna, blue and red-tailed species. In the eastern woodland areas you can find elephant, zebra, buffalo, warthog, roan and sable antelope, and Maasai giraffe. Even lion are known to be in the area and they occasionally prey on the chimpanzees. In the lowland forest areas look for the brush-tailed porcupine and the giant forest squirrel. Bird-watching in the park can be extremely rewarding, given its variety of spectacular vegetation zones. Be sure to look for the Whitespotted pygmy crake and the Crested malimbe.

The Study of Chimpanzees

The behaviour of chimpanzees *(Pantroglodytes schweinfurthii)* has been closely studied for 30 years. Their use of tools, family interaction, hunting and feeding habits and so on have been monitored, and they show amazing dissimilarities from the chimpanzees in Gombe. If you sit quietly, it is possible to interact with these fascinating creatures. As with humans, chimps are distinguished by their faces, shapes and voices, and by the way they move. Individual personalities are also distinguishable. They feed for about six hours a day on fruit, flowers, leaves, stems, bark and seeds. They have been seen to use sticks to gather termites and fierce safari ants. Renowned primatologist Jane Goodall made one of her most important discoveries in 1960, when she came upon a chimp eating a baby bushpig. Chimps have also been seen to eat the carcass of a bushbuck and are known to hunt red colobus monkeys. Another unsettling discovery, made by Goodall, in 1975, was that chimpanzees may resort to cannibalism. One female in Gombe killed another's infant and, together with her daughter, ate its flesh. This ritual was repeated several times over a two-year period.

Chimpanzees live in comunities of between 20 and 100 members, and share a home range. They will generally separate as they move about their area looking for food, keeping in communication with other members through loud calls and hooting. When on the move, they keep to the ground, using well-worn paths in single file.

At the end of the day, the chimps take to the treetops, making nests of branches and leaves in tree limbs. Mothers share a nest with their suckling young, while the rest of the community nests in the same tree if space allows, or in nearby trees. Unlike most primate species, males form the centre of the community, spending their entire life in the group to which they were born. Banding together, the males patrol their area, warding off intruders by chasing and even attacking them, sometimes with fatal results. The young females do not only mate with one

Mahale Mountains National Park is renowned for its chimpanzee families.

male but with several, sometimes breeding with members of other communities. When in oestrus, they show definite signs of their state with an obvious anogenital swelling. As the female ages, she may tend to breed only with certain males. Often a male suitor will lead an older female away from the group, sometimes for two weeks or longer. This generally gives him exclusive rights over the female and offers better chances for the production of his offspring.

Chimpanzees are very vocal, expressing emotions, greetings and warning calls. The most commonly heard vocalization is the 'pan-hoot' which is given in chorus to announce their presence. The discovery of new food sources is expressed with irregular barks, while loud screams alert the group that a member of the community is being threatened or attacked. Though unable to formalize words, intelligence is apparent; chimpanzees will sometimes suppress vocalization when rich food sources are found to conceal its location. In captivity several chimps have learned symbolic languages and communicate through the use of the American Sign Language system, creating new signs and using them constantly to form grammatical sentences and ask questions.

147

KIGOMA

Kigoma is a major port on Lake Tanganyika, not far from Tanzania's border with Burundi. It is the final destination on the Central Railway line from Dar es Salaam on the east coast and is the starting point for trips into Gombe Stream National Park. The harbour was developed by the Germans, who even before the outbreak of World War I made use of the lake, and who felt, similarly with caravan leaders of the trade routes, that Kigoma was a town of great strategic importance.

During the war the Germans, in an attempt to secure their position in the lake region, had the *Graf von Goetzen*, a 1,300-tonne steamship, sent piece by piece to Kigoma on the railroad line they had had constructed all the way from Dar es Salaam. The ship never embarked on a voyage for the Germans as she was bombed by Belgian air forces before she could do so. The Germans later intentionally sank the ship, which remained at the bottom of the lake until 1924 when the British salvaged her and renamed her the *Liemba*. The ship later became even more famous when she played a starring role in the film *The African Queen*. Currently, together with the younger *Mwongozo*, the *Liemba* continues to service the lake; trips moving between the northern end of the lake to the southern sector are regularly scheduled, transporting passengers and cargo, and stopping at several ports along the eastern coast. The entire journey from Burundi to Zambia is a colourful experience: the locals are always dressed in vibrant cloths; fruits, vegetables and fish are often carried on board; and the scenery is dramatic. The trip lasts about four days, provided there are no breakdowns or delays.

Today Kigoma is a fast-paced town; the harbour is a hive of activity, with cargo being loaded and unloaded, and passengers making their way to and from the ferries. Basic supplies, banking and postal services are all available in the town. There is a market, and next to the harbour is the old railway station built by the Germans in 1914.

A Visit to Ujiji

This historic town is located just 6 km (4 miles) south of Kigoma. Arab influence is evident here in the architecture and a few beautifully carved doors. Acting at one time as the terminus for the caravan routes, the city still bustles with activity. It was here that Henry Morton Stanley greeted David Livingstone, uttering the now famous words, 'Dr Livingstone, I presume?' This historic meeting is marked by a monument at the cultural centre on Livingstone Street. Burton and Speke, too, spent time at Ujiji, resting and preparing for their journeys into the territory around Lake Tanganyika.

GOMBE STREAM NATIONAL PARK

With Lake Tanganyika abutting its western edge (although the lake shore is outside park boundaries), Gombe Stream National Park is close to Tanzania's border with Burundi. Kigoma lies 16 km (10 miles) to the south. The park covers only 52 km² (20 sq. miles), its eastern edge bordering the Great Rift Valley escarpment. Gombe Stream's altitude ranges from 773 m (2,536 ft) above sea level to 1,500 m (4,922 ft) at the top of the escarpment. In the park are 13 steep-sided valleys. The reserve was created in 1943 to protect the vegetation and the resident chimpanzee populations, both of which have seen some destruction. Sponsored by Dr Louis Leakey, primatologist Jane Goodall arrived in 1960 to begin research on the chimpanzees. There are four communities in the park, and Goodall's research focussed mainly on the Kasakela and Mitumba groups. Research continues, although Goodall left in 1985. In 1968 the reserve was upgraded to a national park and is Tanzania's smallest protected park.

Gombe Stream can be reached only by boat. A landing is made by the larger ferries at Mwamgongo just north of the park, where guests either walk to the park or hire a boat.

The many vegetation zones in Gombe Stream provide great opportunities for game-viewing and bird-watching, experienced on a completely different level as there are no vehicles in the park, and the forests remain virtually primeval. The park has six habitats. Though a good portion of the region is miombo woodland *(Brachystegia)*, the park's lakeside location and high mountain ranges attract enough rain to support more extensive forests, especially in the northern sections. The well-watered valley floors support tall evergreen forest with moderate layers of shrub. The valley slopes support dry forest, a buffer zone between the evergreen forest and upper woodlands. This low canopy of miombo woodland is extensive and most commonly found in the southern section of the park. The highest elevations are on the Rift escarpment and covered in moorland grasses.

Most visitors come to Gombe Stream to see our closest animal relative, the chimpanzee. Watching the chimps' behaviour is fascinating and rewarding. Olive baboons will often be spotted foraging on the beach, and vervet, blue, red-tailed and red colobus monkeys are also present. Bushbuck, bush duiker and bushpigs are common, as are three mongoose species (marsh, slender and white-tailed). The clawless and spot-necked otter occur near streams and waterways, as well as the ground pangolin, the crested porcupine and the ratel (honey badger).

Gombe's birds vary greatly from zone to zone and occur in impressive numbers. The lakeshore is a good place to spot Giant and Pied kingfishers, the Palm-nut vulture and the Fish eagle. The forest can reveal Livingstone's and Ross's turaco, the Redchested cuckoo, Redcapped robin chat, Goldenrumped tinker bird and Doubletoothed barbet. Gombe's insects are of particular interest: masses of butterflies come to the shores to drink water from the sand; ants are common, among them 'singing', weaver and safari ants.

GOMBE STREAM NATIONAL PARK RULES

• It is essential to have a guide with you whenever you enter the park. Groups may not exceed six people, including the guide. Children under seven are not allowed.

• Visitors are requested not to smoke or to deviate from the main trails. If conversation is necessary, keep voices very low.

• Although baboons have been studied for almost 30 years and are used to people, they are still wild animals and caution should be taken on encountering them. Never stare directly at a baboon, especially a large male. If one threatens you, look away, turn your back and slowly move off. Never frighten an infant, as adults can race to their defence.

• Do not eat outside, secure all food, and never leave windows, doors or tents open. Do not leave personal items unattended. If a baboon grabs something from you, do not try to retrieve it; call a park guide for assistance.

• Dispose of rubbish appropriately.

• Remember that although chimpanzees are also used to the presence of humans they, too, are wild animals. A unique trust has been achieved over many years and this delicate relationship should not be compromised. Stay with your group and do not spread out or surround the chimps. Sit rather than stand and, if photographing them, do not use a flash or artificial light. One should not attempt to attract their attention. Do not get closer than 5 m (5.5 yd) to a chimp or 8 m (8.5 yd) if it is being observed by researchers. Do not follow the chimps if they move off the main path.

• If visitors have any suspicion of colds, sore throats or any infectious ailments, an attempt to visit the chimps should not be made. Humans are capable of infecting them with their diseases, just as chimps are capable of passing their ailments on to us. For this reason, too, visitors should keep their distance.

• Many of the locals are of the Muslim faith; out of respect for their customs and beliefs, visitors are asked to refrain from nudity on the beaches, and to ask permission before taking photographs of the local community residents.

The Kakombe Waterfall in the east of the park, a 30-minute walk from the feeding station, is worth a visit. Although the tracks that lead from the beach along the shore of Lake Tanganyika to the Rift Valley escarpment give on to spectacular scenery, they should be attempted only by those in extremely good physical shape.

LAKE VICTORIA

After years of searching and much struggle and hardship, Lake Victoria was declared the source of the Nile by John Hanning Speke on 3 August 1858. The largest lake in Africa, it is dotted with many islands and hosts waterbirds, fishermen and pleasure-seekers alike. Roughly 70 m (230 ft) deep, Lake Victoria lies in a depression between the western and eastern arms of the Great Rift Valley.

BELOW: *The distinctive balancing Bismarck's Rock at Mwanza's waterfront.*
BOTTOM: *Mwanza is Lake Victoria's largest and most successful port.*

Its beauty is boundless and its abundant fish life is of high commercial value. Tilapia, members of the cichlid family which grow up to 2 kg (4.5 lb), are regularly caught in great numbers by local fishermen. Also found in the lake is the lungfish, an unusual-looking creature with a narrow, streamlined body. Thought to be about 300 million years old, it uses lungs instead of gills to breathe. Commonly seen is the *Protopterus aethiopicus*, an aggressive fish which lies dormant in times of drought by burrowing into the mud and sealing itself in a shell of mucous, allowing for a tiny breathing hole. The Nile perch preys voraciously on other species and reaches weights that can exceed 225 kg (496 lb). The fish was reintroduced in the mid-1950s, in an attempt to boost the food supply for local fishermen, since it was larger and smaller catches would therefore be required. But the local people found the fish unpalatable and difficult to cook or sun-dry. Presently, the cichlids and other species in the lake are fast diminishing, with the Nile perch making up 85–90% of all catches.

The three main ports of Lake Victoria are Bukoba, Mwanza and Musoma. All three towns can be reached by ferries that cross the lake from Uganda and Kenya. Bukoba is on the northwest side of the lake, but it doesn't really have much to offer the tourist. Mwanza, on Victoria's southern shores, is probably the largest and most successful of the lake's towns. It profits considerably from fishing, and has also become an agricultural centre for the Sukuma people, Tanzania's largest ethnic group who specialize in maize, cassava and cotton. While you are in Mwanza, make sure you see the waterfront's Bismarck's Rock, which is famous for its unusual formation and balancing act. The Sukuma Museum may be another interesting place to explore, as it portrays the lifestyle, handicrafts and culture of the Sukuma people. Basic to moderate accommodation can be found in Mwanza. Although a quiet port, Musoma, north of Mwanza on Lake Victoria's northeastern shores, is a pleasant place from which to view the lake and the surrounding area.

SITATUNGA

The sitatunga is a highly adaptive animal which lives in swampy areas of tall reeds and papyrus. Standing about 1 m (3 ft) at the shoulder, the secretive sitatunga's pelage is reddish- to dark-brown, with transverse stripes and spots on its rear flanks. Females are generally lighter in colour and their markings more visible. Their coats are made up of long wispy hair that is slightly oiled and water-resistant. The antelope's hooves are unusually long and splayed, adapted to allow the sitatunga to move with agility through the wet, swampy vegetation it inhabits. Only the males sport large, thickset horns that are gently spiralled.

Sitatungas are most active at dawn and dusk, and rest in flattened reedbeds. They graze on aquatic vegetation (they will forage on woodland vegetation if it is available). Excellent swimmers, sitatungas spend a good part of the day in water; when disturbed or pursued, they submerge themselves up to their nose.

The shy and elusive sitatunga.

Most commonly seen are herds of a male with females and young, although solitary animals and adolescent herds do occur. Calves are born after a 220–225-day gestation period. Birth takes place on a higher, drier platform of reeds prepared by the mother, where the calf will remain for about a month. It will become an impressive swimmer before it can properly walk. The sitatunga has a good sense of hearing and smell. Man is the sitatunga's main enemy, followed by leopard, crocodile, python and, in drier areas, lion.

Wildlife at Lake Victoria

There are two wildlife areas of interest at Lake Victoria. The first, the Saa Nane Island Wildlife Sanctuary, admittedly does not teem with wildlife, but it boasts some lovely views. The second, Rubondo Island National Park, was gazetted as a national park in 1977. It contains a combination of resident as well as introduced animal species, such as Maasai giraffe, black-and-white colobus monkey and chimpanzee.

Rubondo island covers an area of 240 km² (90 sq. miles), and is mainly forested. It can be reached only by boat or chartered air service. Rubondo is a delightful and quiet place for relaxing. One of its resident species is the aquatically adapted sitatunga, which derives its scientific name *Tragelphines spekei* from the explorer, Speke. As the island can be explored only on foot or by boat, it provides excellent opportunities for bird-watching.

Residents and migrants alike flock to the pools, marshes and forests. Entomologists, too, are in for a treat as butterflies and creepy crawlies abound.

The island takes some time to reach. From Mwanza, visitors must drive 300 km (186 miles) to Nkome, where they catch a boat across to the island. The boat trip takes about 2 hours. A faster option is to fly by charter service directly to the island. Campsites are available on Rubondo, but all supplies and equipment must be brought along.

There are several other game reserves in the northern and northwestern corner of Tanzania, namely the Biharamulo, Burigi, Ibanda and Rumanyika Orugundu game reserves. Inaccessibility and a lack of development – there is little funding for roads and infrastructure in these areas – make them attractive to poachers, and the reserves are therefore heavily exploited by them.

ADVISORY: THE WEST AND NORTHWEST

CLIMATE

From June to October the days are generally sunny and warm (29°C/84°F), but most evenings are cool, so visitors are advised to pack a jacket or sweater.

BEST TIMES TO VISIT

Visit this area from June to October. Heavy rains during the rest of the year can cause poor road conditions, making travel slow, tedious and miserable.

MAIN ATTRACTIONS

Huge herds of buffalo roam the unspoiled Katavi National Park. At the Gombe Stream and Mahale Mountains national parks chimpanzees and other primates can be observed at close hand. The range of vegetation is superb and the scenery breathtaking. Only walking is permitted within these parks. Lake Victoria and Lake Tanganyika are worth exploring for their serene beauty and their large numbers of endemic fish.

TRAVEL IN THE WEST AND NORTHWEST

Travel in this areas is slow and difficult, so it is best to visit Gombe and Mahale by rail, boat or charter aeroplane. Lake Tanganyika can be crossed via the ferries MV *Liemba* or MV *Mwongozo*, which can accommodate most vehicles. The ferries make regular stops up and down the lake. At certain places along the lake the ferry will pull into a bay and dugouts, canoes and small motor boats make their way to it from the shore. Disembarking and boarding passengers clamber over many of the little boats to reach the one they wish to use.

Bookings for the ferries can be made in Mpulungu, Zambia, at Cosy Enterprises near the boat jetty, at Bujumbura, Burundi, at the NASCO office, or at the Tanzania Railways Corporation offices, near the port in Kigoma, Tanzania. Fares and port fees (for vehicles) are generally asked to be paid in US dollars.

There is a weekly passenger service between Mwanza and Kisumu, Kenya, on Lake Victoria, with first-, second- and third-class accommodation. Tickets (non-residents must pay in US dollars) can be purchased at the Kisumu and Mwanza piers.

HEALTH HAZARDS

Take precautions against malaria and guard against bilharzia, especially around Lake Tanganyika and rivers and slow-moving streams. In areas where tsetse fly is present, wear long sleeves and trousers. When in close proximity to chimpanzees and primates, follow all rules and regulations. Always be aware of potentially dangerous wild animals.

TRAVEL TO KATAVI NATIONAL PARK

Air Tanzania has regular flights into Tabora, but delays and overbookings can make this service unreliable. Air charter services are available. Transportation from the airport should be confirmed before arrival. Charter flights land at Tabora, Sumbawanga and Mpanda, or in the park, which has two airstrips – one for small aircraft, the other for larger planes (up to 10-seaters).

By road Access by land can be painfully slow. Though the roads are officially recorded as being all-weather, 4x4 vehicles are highly recommended. The 200-km (124 miles) Mbeya–Tunduma–Sumbawanga road may be an option as it has recently been resurfaced. The route from the north via the Kigoma–Uvinza– Mpanda road (approximately 432 km/268 miles), should be attempted only in the dry season. The park can be accessed from the Ruaha to the east, but the going is slow. These tracks are extremely remote, so visitors should make sure they take plenty of provisions along with them.

By train There is a scheduled train service into Tabora and Mpanda, but it is highly unreliable due to schedule changes and delays. Further transportation must be arranged prior to arrival.

ACCOMMODATION
Tented camp

Katavi Tented Camp This camp has been designed for those visitors who fly in and offers them a unique bush experience graced with an old-world charm. Each of the spacious tents have individual hot showers and pleasant views. Meals, which include candlelit dinners, are served in a mess tent or out in the open. Walking and game-viewing drives can be arranged, and lightweight fly camps (temporary camps that are usually set up under a tree for a day or two) are available. All-inclusive trips that incorporate visits to Mahale Mountains National Park can be arranged from Katavi. Tel. (254) 2-502491/506139, fax 502739/503391. Greystoke Safaris, PO Box 56923, Nairobi.

Rest-house and camping

The park manages a self-catering rest-house with six beds; there are no ablution facilities provided. The Chief Park Warden, Katavi National Park, PO Box 89, Mpanda. There are basic lodgings in Mpanda and Sumbawanga.

TRAVEL TO MAHALE MOUNTAINS NATIONAL PARK

By air The best way to travel to the park is via an air charter service. Air Tanzania has scheduled flights into Kigoma, on the northern lake shore, but visitors have to arrange boat transport down Lake Tanganyika to the park. Check with the Mahale

Mountains Wildlife Research Centre (ask for directions) or with Sunset Tours in Kigoma to find out about available transport.

By boat Two ferries, the MV *Liemba* and MV *Mwongozo*, run on Lake Tanganyika between Bujumbura in Burundi and Mpulungu in Zambia. Passages can be booked at the Kigoma railway office near the port. The ships sail every week, stopping at Kigoma and Mugambo. From Mugambo, visitors have to take another boat to the park headquarters. The journey from Kigoma takes 9 hours.

ACCOMMODATION
Tented camp

Mahale Mountains Tented Camp This exclusive camp has been established on the beach. There are excellent walks and treks through the park. Tel. (254) 2-502491/506139, fax 502739/503391. Greystoke Safaris, PO Box 56923, Nairobi.

Guest-house and camping

There is a public campsite near the park headquarters at Kasiha, and a small guest-house near Kasiha village, but visitors should bring their own supplies. The Park Warden, Mahale Mountains National Park, PO Box 3134, Arusha.

TRAVEL TO KIGOMA AND GOMBE STREAM NATIONAL PARK

By air Kigoma can be reached via Air Tanzania's scheduled service from Dar es Salaam, but the service is unreliable. Charter flights are easily arranged, though these can be expensive.

By road The roads from the interior to Kigoma are in a bad state and it can take from two to four days to drive from Mwanza to Kigoma. In the wet season the roads can become impassable. Four-wheel-drive vehicles are recommended.

By boat Kigoma and Ujiji can be reached on the weekly ferries MV *Liemba* and MV *Mwongozo*. Immigration and customs formalities are handled

on board. Boats can be arranged along the coast, but immigration must be handled at the border.

Gombe Stream National Park can be reached by boat only. Larger ferries call at Mwamgongo, just north of the park, and guests can walk to the park, or hire a small boat. Travellers can make their way from Kigoma or Ujiji by water taxi, rather crowded and taking 3 to 6 hours. One can hire a boat for one's sole use, for a large fee.

By rail There are several weekly trains from Dar es Salaam on the coast to Kigoma. One can buy a ticket from Mwanza on Lake Victoria to Tabora and connect with the Central Line into Kigoma. The constant delays and schedule changes are frustrating and the trip can take from 2 to 6 days. Food is available on the train, but it is a good idea to take your own food and drinking water.

ACCOMMODATION IN AND AROUND GOMBE STREAM NATIONAL PARK
Kigoma

Aqua Lodge Two kilometres (1 mile) from the city centre, this lodge offers nine double rooms with en-suite facilities, facing Lake Tanganyika. Watersports such as snorkelling, wind-surfing, water-skiing, boating and fishing are available. Arrangements can be made to visit the Mahale Mountains and Gombe Stream national parks. Tel. (255) 695-2408, fax 3707. Sunset Tours, PO Box 34, Kigoma.

Lake Tanganyika Beach Hotel offers moderate lodgings and is centrally located. Tel. (255) 695-2694/3633. PO Box 9, Kigoma.

In the park

Hostel and camping In the park there is a hostel which can accommodate 10 people. Camping is permitted on Lake Tanganyika's shores (speak to the park guards). Baboons can pose a problem and supplies must be properly secured. Visitors should use mosquito nets. Basic supplies can be obtained in Kigoma. The Park Warden, Gombe Stream National Park, PO Box 3134, Arusha.

THE COAST

The 800 km (500 miles) of palm-lined beaches along Tanzania's east coast, its spectacular dive sites and the romantic allure of the Spice Islands contribute to make this area a popular tourist desination.

DAR ES SALAAM

Modern-day Dar es Salaam is busy and fast-paced, the base for the country's largest port, administrative capital and commercial centre. It is quite different from the sleepy, village of Mzizima (as it was known) that greeted Zanzibar's ruler, Sultan Seyyid Majid, when he first visited the mainland shores in 1866. Captivated by the beauty and serenity of the Kurasini Creek and surrounding area, he set about obtaining the land from the local Zaramo and Shomvi people, and built himself a palace. In Swahili Dar es Salaam

OPPOSITE: *Bagamoyo on Tanzania's north coast boasts lovely, unspoilt beaches.*
ABOVE: *Ras Kutani Beach Resort south of the capital, Dar es Salaam.*

means 'haven of peace'. It was the sultan's intention eventually to move his capital from Zanzibar to the security and tranquillity of Dar, but due to his untimely death his plan

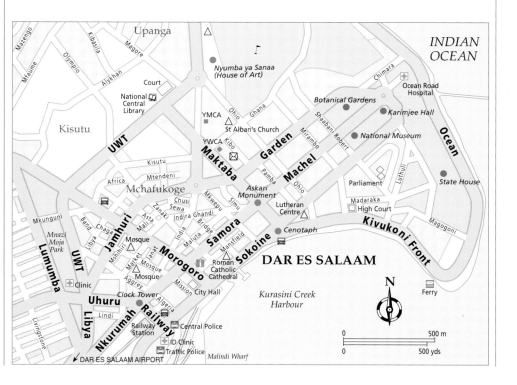

155

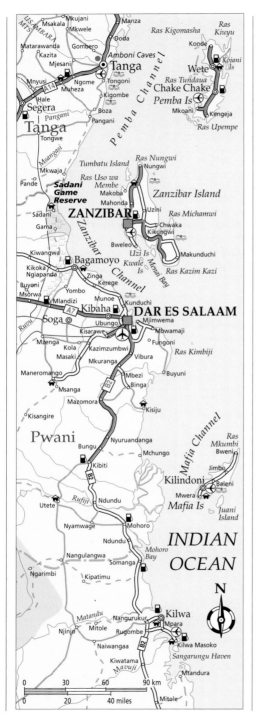

was never executed. He was often in dispute with his successor, Sultan Seyyid Barghash, and as a result this move of government never took place, and further development of Dar es Salaam was temporarily put on hold.

By 1877, Sir William Mackinon and Sir Thomas Fowell Burton, with Zanzibar's British consul, Dr. Sir John Kirk, had begun efforts to bring legitimate trade from the interior to the coast with the construction of a road linking Dar es Salaam with Lake Malawi (Nyasa). The road progressed painfully slowly, and the project was finally abandoned in 1881, after the completion of only 112 km (70 miles). Dar did not see any new development until the arrival of the Germans, who originally chose Bagamoyo as their administrative capital; this idea was eventually rejected and Dar was decided on due to the depth of the natural harbour in Kurasini Creek.

Dar es Salaam saw sudden rapid growth during this time and, by the beginning of World War I, it was the country's commercial centre. After the war, under the new British rule, Dar es Salaam continued to grow.

Today, the diverse ethnic cultures that have played a role in the development of this city are visible, influencing the city's appearance and flavour. The architecture displays a myriad styles – Swahili whitewashed arches, classic German touches and modern high-rises of glass and metal. Two of the city's oldest buildings are its cathedrals, the Lutheran Church which was consecrated in 1902, and the Roman Catholic St. Joseph's Cathedral, started in 1898 and consecrated in 1903.

Dar's streets are abuzz with activity as the people move to or from work, wait for the *daladalas* (buses), or buy items at the kiosks lining the roadsides. Splashes of colour fill the streets with a unique and appealing mixing of old and new — women often appear in modern clothes, but also combine these outfits with brightly patterned traditional khangas. The harbour is a hive of activity as the ferry moves across the creek, enormous cargo ships sail in and out of the busy docks and the beautiful, classic lines of the dhows slowly drift across the coastal waters.

Sights of interest in and around Dar es Salaam

Though Dar es Salaam is constantly active because of its countless embassies, High Commissions and governmental offices, there is not a great deal in the city centre for the average tourist to see. However, there are several places of interest on the outskirts of the city and in its outlying areas – which is a decidedly better option for visitors. If you do choose to explore the city, walking tours are often the best option due to constant traffic congestion and difficulties in securing parking. As with many major cities of the world, Dar es Salaam has fallen victim to crime and car theft, so caution should be taken when touring around, no matter what your mode of transport is.

The **National Museum**, at the corner of Sokoine Drive and Shaaban Robert Street, is well worth a visit for a look at Tanzania's archaeological history. Displays include the famous excavated finds from Olduvai Gorge as well as African, Arab, Oriental, German, and British artefacts. Some of Tanzania's most famous explorers are discussed, and the country's road to independence is plotted for visitors. The original museum building to the back of the complex, established in 1940, has an exquisite entry way with an impressive Swahili door and colourful tile work. The current main museum building is the site on which President Julius Nyerere signed his famous Arusha Declaration in 1967. Fees are payable at the entrance gate.

The **Gymkhana Club** and **Botanical Garden** are further north on Shaaban Robert Street. The garden, dating back to 1906, is relatively small but quiet, and plant species are clearly labelled. The Gymkhana Club offers temporary membership and is equipped with an 18-hole golf course, tennis and squash courts, and football and rugby fields.

Passed often as people rush around Dar is the **Askari Monument** at the corner of Samora Machel Avenue and Maktaba Street. This was once the site of a German monument to Commissioner Herman von Wissman, who played a key role in German

Public transport takes on a whole new meaning.

development of Dar es Salaam. The askari, or soldier, now standing with rifle at the ready, commemorates the African soldiers who lost their lives while serving in World War I.

Facing the harbour on Sokoine Drive are the spires of **St. Joseph's Metropolitan Cathedral** and the **Evangelical Lutheran Church**, together with the old **post office**. Along the harbour front you will find the many ticket offices for the ferries to Zanzibar, Pemba, Mafia, and Mombasa in Kenya. Photographing the harbour is frowned upon in Dar es Salaam and may lead to a confrontation with local police. Also in the area is the famous **Sno-Cream** ice-cream parlour but, for the best ice-cream around, a trip out along the old Bagamoyo Road to the **Ice Cream Fountain** is recommended for its delicious home-made ice-creams and gelatos.

At the corner of Upanga Road and Ohio Street, near the Sheraton Hotel, is the **Nyumba ya Sanaa** ('house of art'), a unique non-profit cooperative of student artists who sell their work during training. Crafts include batiks, carvings, paintings and pottery, although new artistic directions and fresh ideas are continually being explored. The original concept and centre was established in the early 1970s by a Maryknoll missionary sister to benefit young urban residents, particularly the handicapped. Today the centre includes a restaurant and offers visitors a mix of African talent in a pleasant setting.

A vendor selling carved seats near Tanga on the north coast.

North of the city, on the 'new' Bagamoyo road, is the village of Mwenge and its **Makonde carvers**. The Makonde people are originally from the southeast corner of Tanzania and are famous for their traditional 'tree of life' carvings which portray unique characters moving through life and experiencing its celebrations or grievances. In Mwenge's many shops, there is a wide range of carvings from candlestick holders to enormous Zanzibar chests. The hardwoods used are generally olive, ebony and mvuli. This excursion can be a fun-filled experience, whether visitors become involved in shopping or just watch the many carvers at work. Prices are negotiable, so bargaining is a must!

Other places with carvings and local crafts further along the new Bagamoyo road are the **Karibu Gallery** and the **Village Museum**. An excellent execution of Makonde work stands outside the gallery, while inside is a good selection of paintings, carvings, musical instruments, jewellery and basketry. The Village Museum is another shopping outlet including traditional homesteads of different Tanzanian tribes; unfortunately the museum has recently fallen into a state of disrepair.

Dar es Salaam offers excellent **diving** and **snorkelling**; excursions can be arranged through most moderate and upmarket hotels. Many reefs have been damaged by explosives used by local fishermen, but there is still ample opportunity to see the beauty of the underwater life at the offshore coral reefs and islands. **Beaches** north and south of Dar are lovely, but more enjoyable and secure if you stay at one of the many beach resort hotels. Beaches and coastal waters edging the city centre are not clean. Deep-sea and sport **fishing** are on offer, but the options are limited. However, as tourism develops throughout Tanzania and along the coast, sport fishing is seen as a potentially growing market.

NORTH COAST: BAGAMOYO

Bagamoyo is 72 km (45 miles) north of Dar es Salaam. In the 14th century the Shirazi Arabs were the first traders to settle in the area, south of Bagamoyo at Kaole – the ruins today provide a fascinating glimpse into the past. As the Shirazis integrated with the coastal African peoples, the germination of the Swahili culture came about. The Shirazi presence was diminished by the arrival of the Portuguese, later ousted by the Omani Arabs. They established a garrison in Bagamoyo in the 19th century, and the town quickly developed. The sudden increase in the demand for slaves and ivory from the interior meant Bagamoyo gained in importance and prospered. Trade caravan porters named the town Bwagamoyo, 'lay down the burden of your heart', as their arrival in the town signified the end of their strenuous labour in the interior. As the slave trade grew, the town was used as a terminus for thousands of captives heading for Zanzibar and beyond. Aware of their fate and what lay ahead, the slaves renamed the town Bagamoyo, 'crush your heart'.

Many famous explorers used Bagamoyo as a starting point for their adventure-filled journeys into the interior. The first Catholic mission was erected in 1868; it was here that David Livingstone's body was brought, after a journey of almost a year from Zambia where he had died, sick and weary from his efforts to establish the source of the Nile. Eventually an orphanage was established at the mission for those children who were spared a life as slaves. The Holy Ghost fathers also established the Catholic Freedom Village, where they ransomed thousands of slaves, granting them a free existence.

The German colonial presence in the late 1800s saw much conflict and unrest and, with the Germans eventually overpowering the Arabs, the German East Africa Company came into being. Bagamoyo was initially selected as the German administrative capital, but proved unsuitable for shipping and docking purposes. Commissioner von Wissman then settled on Tanga, but in the end decided on Dar es Salaam.

Modern-day Bagamoyo, considered a 'new' Swahili town (established or rebuilt in the 18th or 19th centuries in contrast to older towns of the 14th and 15th centuries), is a quiet coastal town whose dismal history is never forgotten, yet children play cheerfully in the narrow streets amidst whitewashed buildings and heavily carved Swahili doors. It has several small shops and kiosks, a modest city market and a petrol station. Dhows are hand-built and cured in Bagamoyo, and fishermen gather their nets on the sand beaches.

Sights of interest in and around Bagamoyo

If you'd like to trace the past of Bagamoyo, a visit to the **Catholic Mission** just north of the town may be a good place to start. A small, well-laid-out museum was started at the mission site by a resident priest in 1969. The museum presents a concise history of the settlement in the area, beginning in the 12th and 13th centuries, progressing to the days of the slave trade and into the colonial era. The story of the establishment of the mission and its historic role in its battle against slavery is also told through freedom papers, ancient shackles and old photographs. Also on exhibition is a display of local musical instruments, biographies of some of the famous explorers, information on the town's historical buildings, a description of the Swahili door carvings, and artefacts dating back to colonial days and earlier.

The mission site itself is a wonderful collection of old buildings: the original church, the new church, the cemetery and a grotto built in 1876 by ex-slaves in appreciation to the mission for their freedom. The original

KUNDUCHI RUINS

The extraordinary Kunduchi Ruins lie 21 km (13 miles) north of Dar es Salaam. Reputed to be some of the most exceptional examples of 18th- and 19th-century Arabic tombs on the eastern coastal shores, Kunduchi has a unique feel about it. Several grave sites have distinctive coral stone pillars or large, ornately carved coral stone tombs inset with decorative Chinese celadon and blue-and-white porcelain bowls. Different theories attempt to explain the presence of the porcelain, one of which suggests that the bowls were purely decorative. Another puts forward the idea that they are indicators of the deceased's wealth and standing in the community. Kunduchi is one of the

last sites where many of the bowls are intact. If you plan to visit the ruins, you need to stop at the Mtongani Police Station and pick up an escort. To reach the ruins, drive into Kunduchi village and turn left at the big baobab.

The Kunduchi Ruins near Dar es Salaam.

church, which was built in 1872, is known as Livingstone's Tower. It is here that Livingstone's body was temporarily laid to rest in February 1874 after a monumental journey from Zambia, before being moved to Zanzibar, and eventually Westminster Abbey. His heart is said to have been buried under the tree where he died, near Lake Bangweulu; his body was then embalmed, prepared and carried some 1,500 km (932 miles) back to Bagamoyo by his faithful assistants. It is said that about 700 freed slaves came to pay their final respects.

In Bagamoyo several street vendors sell coins, many from the old German East Africa. Numerous historical landmarks, such as the **Customs House**, built in 1895 and still in use, and the old **German Store House**, completed in 1889, are close to the water's edge. The **German Boma**, built in 1897, houses government offices, and the old **Arab fort** – where slaves were held before being shipped to further destinations – was eventually taken over by the Germans, and then used as a police post until 1992. After being renovated and restored, it currently houses the **College of Antiquities**. The relocated memorial built by the Germans to commemorate their war heroes used to stand in front of the German Boma. The monument was dismantled by the British in 1946 and the plaques moved, but they have recently been completely removed.

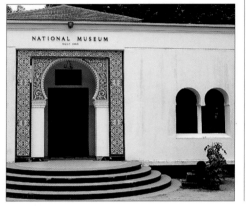

LEFT: *The courtyard door of the National Museum in Dar es Salaam.*
BELOW: *A dhow being built at Bagamoyo.*

Along the shoreline south of the Bedego Beach Hotel is an old German military cemetery with access from the beach and a covered picnic area just outside the cemetery boundary. The **College of Arts**, developed in 1990, is just south of the town and holds an annual festival in September. The infamous Hanging Tree, used by the Germans against those who flaunted their harsh authority, used to stand near the Bedego Beach Hotel, but it burned down in 1985.

The beaches around Bagamoyo are lovely and clean; not far south is Lazy Lagoon with excellent snorkelling and sunbathing.

Kaole Ruins

The Kaole Ruins, 5 km (3 miles) south of Bagamoyo, are worth visiting. The caretaker has worked at the site since the excavations were undertaken in the late 1950s and has a wealth of enthusiasm and knowledge to share.

Twenty-two graves featuring intricate designs, as well as a mosque dating from the 13th to the 15th centuries, are accessible to visitors. External steps at the mosque site were probably used by the muezzin as he called the faithful to prayer. The *mihrab* (an alcove indicating the direction of Mecca) is remarkably well preserved, although the ceiling of the building collapsed long ago. A well is also on site, used to provide water for foot baths. It still contains water and the washing basin is visible.

These old Shirazi ruins reveal the construction process used when the town of Kaole was being built. The processing of sand, coral and lime is lengthy but it produces a cementing material that has certainly withstood the test of time. Also at the site is an old Shirazi house and, 274 m (300 yd) away, a second mosque. A fee is payable to the caretaker.

SADANI GAME RESERVE

Roughly 60 km (37 miles) north of Bagamoyo lies the country's smallest game reserve. Road access into the park from any direction is usually on extremely rough road conditions and, during the wet season, roads can become completely impassable. The reserve

TOP: *Sleepy fishing villages are dotted all along Tanzania's coastline.*
ABOVE: *The Kaole Ruins are situated some 5 km (3 miles) south of Bagamoyo.*

receives few visitors although the vegetation is lush and the coastal shores pristine. Wildlife is present in the reserve and it has been reported that elephant have been seen on the beach and swimming in the ocean! Accommodation is minimal, consisting of two bandas in need of major renovations.

PANGANI

TANGA

The village of Pangani, on the mouth of a river by the same name, is situated north of Bagamoyo, while Zanzibar Island lies not far to the south. The area around Pangani is quiet and offers nothing to visitors except for lovely beaches, ocean views and the slow pace of coastal life. History tells us that the village once flourished and prospered when the trade caravans took advantage of its strategic position on the coast and its proximity to Zanzibar.

Today there is a ferry that crosses the Pangani River (the village is located on the north side of the river), but the coastal road to the south dwindles to a virtually impassable track. In the town itself , small kiosks sell the basics and the locals work on the boats. After being floated down the river from a plantation which is further upstream, coconuts are sorted and prepared at the river mouth for factories.

Coconuts are grown near Pangani.

Pangani and Tanga (a quaint if somewhat run-down coastal town 404 km/251 miles north of Dar es Salaam) are separated by 50 km (31 miles) of lush tracts of bananas, palm trees and sisal. The road to Tanga is not often graded and can be rough in places. Tanga's distinct architectural styles are a mix of Arab, Swahili and colonial influences. The town served a short-lived spell as the German administrative capital before this was moved to Dar es Salaam.

A railway line connecting Tanga to Moshi in the northeast was completed by 1911, though a small line had already been laid to the south between Tanga and Pangani. Tanga became the second-largest commercial port in Tanzania and at one time was the second-largest town in the country. The introduction of sisal, an important cash crop in Tanzania, relatively near to the town ensured that the port remained a commercial centre. Today Tanga has a well-stocked market, many small shops and a quiet tourist trade.

Sights of interest
in and around Tanga

Visitors may want to take a short drive around the town and the peninsula area as there are lovely old buildings and homes to see, displaying architectural influences, as well as a few old German monuments.

Just north of the town, almost 8 km (5 miles) further on the Tanga–Mombasa road, are the Amboni Caves, probably the most massive cave system in East Africa. The caves are reputed to be the dwelling place of a 'good' spirit resembling a snake; offerings such as rose water, perfumes, food and sugar are left in a small alcove near the entrance. Some locals who believe the water has medicinal properties come to the cave to drink the sweet water that drips from its timeless stalactites. Though used by the local communities for many years, the caves were not discovered by Europeans until 1922. Sadly, the outside walls of the caves and first few chambers have been covered with graffiti, but, deeper inside, the walls remain untouched and they enclose natural geological treasures – winding avenues of stalagmites and stalactites forming fantastic sculptures. It is estimated that the caves cover a total of roughly 230 km (143 miles). It appears as though the entire area was once covered in water as fossilized fish have been excavated here. Bats above keep their distance as you are guided through the passages, some of which require visitors to crawl a short length on their knees; other chambers are mammoth in size. A hole plunges to a depth of 400 m (1,312 ft), exposing a basin of sulphurous water believed to come from volcanic sources to the west. The walk through the caves is not difficult, but there is the short section that has to be crossed on hands and knees and there are also some short uphill sections. Visitors to the caves will be led around by a guide. To get to the Amboni Caves, head out of Tanga, drive past the sign for the cave, continuing for a short distance till you reach a sign marked: Ralliestated Ltd. Turn left and drive for 1 km (half a mile); turn left again and follow the curve left.

About 18 m (20 yd) further on turn right and there should be a sign indicating the Amboni Caves. Special rates for residents are offered.

Further along the Tanga–Mombasa road are the Galanos Sulphur Springs, exploited in the 1950s by a Greek sisal estate owner. Little remains of the constructed spa facility as it fell into a sad state and was badly vandalized.

If you head southwards out of Tanga for roughly 11 km (7 miles) along a bad road towards Pangani, you will find the Tongoni Ruins. The tombs – over 40 of them – and mosque site are estimated to be 600 years old. An ancient sacred feeling emanates from the coral stone structures. The pillars, *mihrab* and foot basin indicate where the old Shirazi mosque stood, and the tombs and pillars show traces of the rich number of Oriental bowls and fine relief work that were once set in the stone. A caretaker is on site although he has limited knowledge of the area, but visitors are free to enjoy the site on their own.

The Amboni Caves are about 8 km (5 miles) north of the town of Tanga.

SOUTH COAST: THE KILWAS

A collection of ancient ruins, remnants of the prosperous times of centuries ago, lies on the southern coast, 350 km (217 miles) from Dar es Salaam. These ruins, consisting of houses and once-impressive palaces and mosques, are reputed to be some of the finest examples of coral masonry on the East African coast. The oldest settlement here is Kilwa Kisiwani, 'Kilwa on the island' (where the small town developed). Commercial activity and the founding of a community occurred as early as the 9th century. By 1100 Kilwa was gaining strength over coastal towns further north, probably rivalled only by the island of Mafia; it is believed that the ruling sultan at that time held sway over both islands.

It is also said (there is some dissension) that the founders of Kilwa Kisiwani were Shirazi Arabs, from Shiraz in Persia. The Kilwa Chronicles, recorded on paper in 1550, suggest that a sultan named Ali bin al-Hasan was the first to arrive in Kilwa. Whether he was a sultan or not, it is believed that he established the dynasty referred to throughout history as Shirazi, which ruled over Kilwa Kisiwani for the next two centuries.

The island's position allowed quick, easy access to the mainland, but also provided security and a safe harbour. Between the 12th and 14th centuries, Kilwa saw rapid but steady growth as it gained control from Mozambique over the gold and ivory trade (in particular the hold that Sofala – a strategic port in Mozambique – had over the gold trade). The island's wealth was reflected in the surge of construction that ensued. This

DOORS OF THE PAST, MESSAGES FOR THE FUTURE

The architecture of Tanzania's east coast and its islands has a unique flavour inspired by the integration of many cultures and traditions. One such influence can be seen in the carved Swahili (or Zanzibar) doors. Throughout Zanzibar and along the coast, narrow streets twist and wind among whitewashed buildings and ancient shadowy mosques.

The carvings in the door frame and overhead panel, and on the narrow strip running down the centre panel (called a dume in Swahili and meaning 'bull'), have very specific meanings. At the time, the intricate handiwork expressed the hopes, ambitions and state of wellbeing of the individual who commissioned the door. The origins of these symbols and patterns stem from Egyptian, Syrian and Hebrew cultures. Chains or the links of a chain symbolized security, while the representation of smoke from frankincense indicated wealth. A date tree, or more commonly the fruit, brought

hopes of abundance or prosperity; the lotus flower characterized reproductive powers or the act of passing on to new generations. This complex art form underwent its own evolutionary process with pineapples being replaced by fish to signify fertility, which symbol later began to look more like a flower vase and, finally, a simple flower.

When you pass one of these spectacular doors, pause to examine each one's detailed story – hidden to most yet revealed to a few.

Door to the House of Wonders, Stone Town.

included building enormous houses with elaborate detailing and increasing the extent of the Great Mosque to over four times its original size. The mosque underwent construction again in the 15th century to shore up the previous building work when arches, domes and barrel vaults were added.

Kilwa Kiwisani was adversely affected by the arrival of the Portuguese in the early 1500s. The island was taken by force when the ruling dignitary refused to pay tribute to the new arrivals. The strength of the trade routes changed vastly since the Portuguese were intent not on ruling, but on controlling the commodities that were in such high demand on the international markets. Lacking further income, Kilwa fell into steady decline. By 1513 the Portuguese had withdrawn from the island, preferring their more strategically placed strongholds of Malindi in Kenya and Mozambique Island to the south of Tanzania. In 1587 Kilwa's fate worsened: the island was invaded by the cannibalistic Zimba tribe from Mozambique. Predictably, only a few inhabitants of the island survived.

The island had a slight reprieve with the arrival of the Omani Arabs from the Arabian Peninsula and the fall of the Portuguese in the late 17th century. Ousted from both the Tanzanian and Kenyan coasts, the Portuguese still maintained control over the gold trade in Mozambique. Despite the re-establishment of the caravan routes under the Omanis, Kilwa Kisiwani saw virtually no commercial growth.

The new Swahili town, Kilwa Kivinje ('Kilwa of the casuarina trees'), situated on the mainland north of Kilwa Kisiwani, took centre stage as it was better suited to handle the growing trade business in slavery. The splendour of the latter's buildings and mosques was taken over by the wealthy sultans and slave traders. Kilwa Kivinje today is a quiet, sleepy town with many reminders of its chequered past in its old buildings, exquisitely carved doors and a mosque.

Kilwa Masoko ('Kilwa of the market') is a small town situated south of Kilwa Kivinje, on the tip of a narrow peninsula, which still bustles with the activity of coastal commerce.

The Tongoni Ruins near Tanga house tombs that are estimated to be about 600 years old.

As its name implies, the city market is an important feature of the town, overflowing with fruits and vegetables and activity.

The islands of Songa Mnara and Sanje Majoma, to the south of Kilwa Kisiwani, are also worth a visit for their ruins of ancient stone towns wrapped in intrigue and still capable of stirring interest. Lindi and Mtwara are two typical coastal towns that receive few visitors yet are havens for beach-lovers and divers alike. Fishing is reputedly excellent. The Makonde people are prominent around Mtwara, giving visitors ample opportunity to learn more about this artistic tribe and to observe their world-famous carvings. Terrible roads force visitors to make use of Air Tanzania's erratic weekly service to both cities.

ZANZIBAR

Unguja is the correct name of what we today call Zanzibar, and it is unclear where exactly the name Zanzibar originated. As early as the 9th century the word 'Zanj' was used to describe black people – particularly from East Africa. In Persian and Hindi texts there is reference to Zanzibar and, more infrequently, Zangistan. Zanzibar's indigenous inhabitants were Bantu peoples, who had obviously migrated to the island from the mainland, but for centuries the island of Zanzibar has seen ancient seamen and traders descend on

Sunrise over a palm-lined beach.

its shores. The first mosque on the East African coast stands on Zanzibar at Kizimkazi in the extreme south, and is still in use.

Zanzibar has a long history of slavery. Before the arrival of the Omani Arabs in the late 17th century and the subsequent surge in the slave business, the 9th century saw Zanj slaves taken from East Africa to lower Iraq to drain marshes and to labour in the salt mines of Basra. With the settling of Omani Arabs on the island after their defeat of the Portuguese, Zanzibar gained in strength and also grew progressively wealthy. Sultan Seyyid Said's move of government from Oman to the island resulted in the subsequent development of caravan routes to the north and west of the country and, with his increasing influence, he eventually took them over. The Omani Arabs are thought to have been responsible for a great deal of the exploitation that continued right into the 19th century with the booming of the slave markets, and the continuous growth of the clove industry (the sultan himself had introduced cloves). The 18th century particularly saw the demand for labour grow, especially

in sugar-producing countries such as the West Indies and Brazil, and the French colonies and Middle East.

Although the island has a somewhat chequered history, it has produced a melting pot of cultures and a fascinating heritage. Reflected today in the oldest section of Zanzibar town, Stone Town, are its many facets: history, tradition and mysticism, all helping to create a magical place. The architecture reveals the influences of Arabia, Persia, the Orient, Egypt, Africa and Europe. The people remain generous and humble.

Travel across the 38-km (24 miles) by 85-km (53 miles) island can be accomplished quite easily as the main roads are good, but many access roads are in bad condition. Fuel is only available in Stone Town and on the north of the island in Kinyasini. The island's east coast is known for its excellent long stretches of beach, and its shoreline retreats that offer the bare essentials right through to luxury. East of Stone Town is the incredible Jozani Forest with an abundance of endemic plant species; it is also home to the red colobus monkey. Zanzibar's west coast is dotted with ruins and agricultural fields and, as you head up to the north, the large tracts of agriculture continue, eventually giving way to the pristine beauty of a tropical island that offers superb swimming and diving.

Stone Town

Stone Town breathes history and is alive with activity. It is most easily covered on foot or by bicycle. Entrance fees (usually minimal) are requested at some historical buildings. There are several maps available that supply adequate street information and identification of buildings; although you will probably get lost a few times, a map is a highly recommended purchase. Although Stone Town's narrow streets seem nothing more than a twisting network of endless shadowed passages, closer inspection reveals their charm: whitewashed buildings with massive arches, elaborately carved wooden doors, balconies with decorative latticework trim, graceful mosques and churches, palaces and ruins.

HISTORICAL HOTELS IN STONE TOWN

DHOW PALACE Located in the heart of Stone Town, this lovely hotel successfully blends the romantic style of old Zanzibar with the modern conveniences of today. The building itself, with its cool, whitewashed walls, is over a hundred years old and was the former residence of British Captain Poole of the ship *Pegasus*. The ten large rooms, of which three are suites, are all en suite and air-conditioned, and are stylishly decorated; local flair is evident in the antique furnishings and Swahili beds draped with mosquito nets. The dining room is set in a pretty courtyard and serves delicious local and international cuisine. No alcohol is served. The Tembo Hotel (*see* below) is owned by the same concern.

EMERSON'S HOUSE Guests immediately step into the past on entering the lobby of this hotel, which bursts with old-world charm and offers visitors to Zanzibar a unique experience. It is filled with antiques, and unusual and interesting artefacts. Eight stylishly romantic rooms, decorated in various colour schemes, create different moods; local materials and antique furnishings are used throughout. The staff are most accommodating and can assist with tours, cruises and special requests. Rooms are either en suite or share facilities, but even in the latter case are decorated and furnished with great care. There is even a bathtub on a private terrace for use by the guests! The dining room and bar create intimate atmospheres.

TEMBO HOTEL Also in Stone Town, this building is over 110 years old and looks out onto lovely ocean views (some of the rooms face the seafront). A pleasant dining room with an outside terrace is a magical spot to be in at sunset, although alcohol is not served. Thirty rooms with en-suite facilities are air-conditioned and feature the dark, heavy wood of Swahili beds and the nostalgia of mosquito nets. The hotel has a swimming pool.

Stone Town's elegant Tembo Hotel.

One of the fascinating buildings that point to Stone Town's historic past.

Don't worry about losing your way in Stone Town as the residents are always willing to help visitors. You may regard their kindness with suspicion at first, but you will quickly recognize their genuine intentions. You will often see the town's inhabitants dressed in traditional clothing – women in the vibrant colours of their khangas or the concealing folds of their jet-black buibuis (long, flowing robes that cover the head and partially the face). Men of all ages don white robes, or *kanzus*, and caps, or *kofias*. Be aware that the majority of people on Zanzibar are Muslim. In respect of their beliefs visitors, while in cities and towns, should refrain

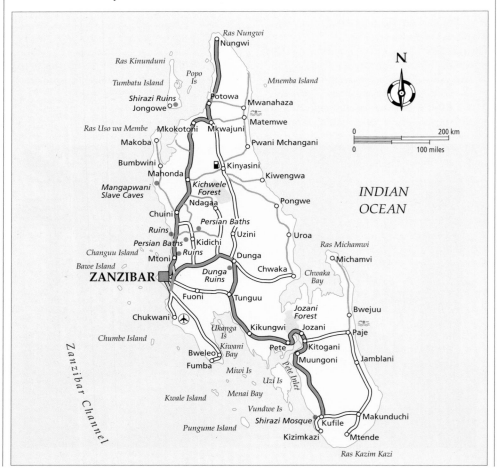

from wearing revealing clothing (extra-short skirts or tiny shorts, plunging necklines and bathing suits except on the beaches). It is also important always to ask permission before taking photographs of island residents, and not to insist when this is clearly an unwelcome imposition.

Stone Town is filled with captivating sights and it is possible to spend days threading through winding roads jammed with antique shops, gem-stone dealers, exotic, heady spices and fabric. Look out for traditional Zanzibar hand and foot painting in exquisite designs executed in wanje (ink) and henna. It is a good idea to shop with cash US dollars; credit cards are only just beginning to be accepted. Places of interest in Stone Town that should not be missed include:

THE DISPENSARY on Mizingani Road, the main seafront thoroughfare. Having recently undergone a face-lift, the old dispensary is a landmark with its extraordinary white lattice-work covering the building's entire façade.

THE PEOPLE'S PALACE, standing on the oceanfront, today housing a museum dedicated to the lives and history of the ruling sultans and their families. There are many pieces of furniture on exhibition along with a comprehensive chronology of the succession of the sultans. An entrance fee is payable.

BEIT EL-AAJIB (House of Wonders) next door was commissioned by Sultan Seyyid Barghash. Construction was started in 1880 and completed two years later. It earned its name because it was the first building on the island to have electricity. The clock tower once stood in the park across the street and the massive carved door is one of the island's finest. The guns on the steps are Portuguese and date back to the 16th century. Beit el-Ajaib, which until recently housed government offices, is undergoing renovation.

THE OLD ARAB FORT, just south of the House of Wonders, is itself an architectural wonder. The Omani Arabs built the fort on the rubble of a Portuguese chapel; it

TOP RIGHT: *Typical Stone Town architecture.*
RIGHT: *The nightly Forodhani festival.*

169

The People's Palace on Stone Town's waterfront.

was finished in 1710 and was eventually used as a prison for war criminals, then as army barracks, and during colonial times as the depot and workshop for the Bububu railway line (a 15-km/9 miles track leading out of Zanzibar town that never extended further and quickly fell into disuse). The courtyard of the fort was reconstructed in 1949 to become the site for the ladies' tennis club. In 1994 it was renovated further and the courtyard was opened as a theatre and cultural centre.

THE JAMITURI GARDENS are directly in front of these historical sites. Originally laid out in 1935 for King George V's Silver Jubilee, today they lack the maintenance that befits such a splendid site; but, come the evening, the gardens come to life with the nightly Forodhani. Each afternoon as the sun begins to set, the golden sky embraces the visitors and citizens of Zanzibar, welcoming them to a delicious, inexpensive and fun-filled twilight of grilled meats, seafood, Zanzibar pizza, fruit, and the most satiating ice-cold drink ever, sugar-cane juice (no alcoholic beverages are served). Free entertainment is provided by the local teens who take it in turns to dive wildly off the sea wall.

ST. JOSEPH'S CATHEDRAL'S two silver peaks can be seen from most areas in Stone Town. Built at the end of the 19th century, this Catholic church has wonderful detailing.

THE HIGH COURT OF JUSTICE on Kaunda Road is desperately in need of a coat of paint, but offers a unique melding of Arabic and Portuguese architectural styles. It is a relatively new building, built early this century by architect J. H. Sinclair. The clock that hangs out over the street is almost always working as the older gentlemen, usually seen across the street huddled in conversation, can attest to.

THE HOUSE OF PEACE stands at the corner of Kaunda and Creek roads. The National Museum, it was built in 1925 by the island's people in memory of the heroes of World War I. The main museum building houses a collection of old photographs that tell the island's pictorial history. African handicrafts are exhibited along with an exceptional 200-year-old carved Swahili door, information on the clove industry, and dhow-making. Shells are displayed and explorers discussed, and artefacts that belonged to Dr. Livingstone are on view. The museum, though relatively small, is worth a trip and your visit should not be rushed. Natural history displays are housed in an annexe to the museum, but animal and bird specimens are old and not in the best condition. An entrance fee is payable.

THE CHRIST CHURCH CATHEDRAL OF THE ANGLICAN CHURCH, one of the most visited places in Stone Town, is built on the site of the slave market, abolished on 6 June 1873 by Sultan Seyyid Barghash. Although the market was not used after that, the trade continued surreptitiously for quite some time. Part of the site was purchased by an English missionary, the Rev. Arthur Nugent West, while the remainder of the site was donated to the church by a Hindu merchant, Mairam Senji. Construction on the cathedral started on Christmas day in 1873. Plans were sent from England to Bishop Edward Steere, who worked diligently on the construction, and building was completed exactly seven years later.

The altar is situated in the exact spot where the whipping post stood, and behind it is the grave of Bishop Steere. The pipe organ, made in England in 1880, is still in working order; access is via an outside entrance. The mosaics near the altar were donated by Miss Caroline Thackeray, a teacher who taught from 1877 until her death in 1926; the round marble design in the floor is a reminder of the whipping post's trunk. Stained glass windows and plaques pay respect to David Livingstone, the seamen who lost their lives fighting against slavery, and the air reconnaissance pilots of 1917.

The small wooden crucifix to the left of the altar was presented to the Diocese of Zanzibar in 1901; it is said to be made from the tree under which Livingstone's heart was buried. The pillars at the rear of the church are upside down, which happened while Steere was on safari. Sultan Barghash donated the clock in the bell tower on the understanding that the tower was not to exceed his palace in height. It is said that the area to the rear of the church was used by women of Muslim origin who had converted (they conducted their religious observances separately from the men). The cathedral is still in use today and the complex also serves as a school and hostel. An entrance fee is payable.

THE HAMMAMNI BATHS, commissioned by Sultan Seyyid Barghash, were the only public baths on Zanzibar. For 10 cents people could bathe, have a massage, a haircut or partake of refreshments. The baths were used until 1927, when they were declared a national monument. Today, this fine old building stands empty, but it is possible to step back in time as you cross the marble floors in domed rooms while listening to an interesting lecture on the ingenuity of the plumbing and heating devices under the floor of the massage room and for the sauna. Visitors can access the roof where water collection channels and storage facilities are explained. The glassed-in windows on the domes, besides serving as protection from the rain, also provide the bath's only light source – even when the sun wasn't directly overhead, the sun's rays would reflect off the glass, creating light below. A fee is payable to the caretaker.

MOSQUES Stone Town has many mosques, varying in shape and size. Visitors are generally welcomed inside, but need to first ask permission. The Aga Khan Mosque is certainly a landmark in Stone Town, and has an elaborately carved door and a large following. Outside, the street opens out a little and children are often seen there playing football.

THE CITY MARKET nearby is a place of furious activity. Fruit and vegetables are piled in colourful banks. Meat and fish are sold in the

Diving is one of the favourite tourist attractions of Zanzibar and along the coast.

main market buildings; all around a maze of kiosks and shops offer goods from dried beans to rainbow-coloured plastic containers.

AT DHOW HARBOUR on the waterfront the dhows sail in and out all day, carrying passengers and cargo. Repairs are made and sails mended while crews prepare for the trip ahead or for shore leave. Many dhows are motorized now, but their speed won't break any records, and their distinct lines still evoke a feeling of romance and nostalgia.

DIVING AND SNORKELLING Stone Town, offers ample opportunity for excellent diving and snorkelling, for which Zanzibar is well-known. Larger hotels often offer equipment to hire and some have a dive master. Stone Town has three dive centres that offer day trips, equipment hire and instruction, namely Indian Ocean Divers and one other.

ZANZIBAR'S BEACHES The beaches on Zanzibar's east coast may be some of the world's finest. Mile after mile of powdery shores and warm, inviting waters relieve visitors of their worries and encourage them to indulge in the natural splendours. Providing a haven of palms and sweet-smelling frangipani, warm days are cooled by an ever-present sea breeze. Visitors can cool off while swimming, diving or snorkelling, especially on the north and northeast coastlines. Fishing and boating are also available.

This style of fishing boat is made of one solid piece of wood from a mango tree.

Fishing villages

Fishing villages along the coastline offer an intriguing look at a simple life, unhampered by the worry or frustration of modern conveniences. Residents may offer you a seat in the shade while they repair their fishing nets or continue their dhow-building. The people

A SCENTED ISLAND

Cloves were only introduced to Pemba and Zanzibar around 1820 by Sultan Seyyid Said (the spice originated from the Molukkas in Southeast Asia). Because of Pemba's fertile conditions for agriculture and its good rainfall, today it outstrips Zanzibar in its clove production. The island has three times as many clove trees as its counterpart.

The clove is a closed bud from the tree which, when the bud is left to blossom, produces bright, deep pink flowers. The buds are picked while green or just beginning to turn

red (the cloves are ready to harvest during the months of July to December). Pickers climb the clove trees with the aid of ropes and ladders, and fill baskets with masses of these unripened buds, which are then dried in great heaps in the sun until they turn a dark brown. After having undergone a sorting and grading process, they are exported via Zanzibar's harbour. Essential oils, which are used to scent tobacco in the East, are distilled on the island and it is during the harvest that the air is heavily scented with cloves and spice.

are friendly, warm-hearted and relaxed but, be warned, their attitudes can quickly change if attempts are made to photograph them.

Spice tours

These guided trips are designed to show visitors the many spices, vegetables and flowers cultivated on Zanzibar. Private tours can be arranged as well as groups of between 10 and 30 (one such tour is Mr. Mitu's spice tour, although he seldom conducts the tours personally). Most trips consist of a low-key, relaxing four to six hours in the 'country'. Lunch is usually provided and the journey well laid-out and informative.

Depending on the time of year, visitors are likely to see cloves, peppers, saspodilla (a natural chewing gum), cardamom, cinnamon, tamarind, ginger and neem (*arobaini* in Swahili which means 'forty', a reference to the 40 different ailments it is said to cure). The fertile soils of Zanzibar are well suited to crops such as rice, millet, maize, cassava and yams; but delicious fruits are also an important source of food. During the spice tour, guests see these exotic fruits growing and taste the unusual flavours. The medley may include star fruits, sour sop, jackfruit, pomelo, breadnut, breadfruit, Chinese apple and the strong-smelling but sweet and creamy durian.

Kizimkazi

If you plan to head out of Stone Town, you have the option of renting vehicles or motorbikes, but you should remember that you have to carry an International Driver's Licence. Visitors can also hire a taxi for the day or secure a seat on local transportation – one of the many *daladalas* (private buses) that move throughout the island.

In the south the roads are not good, but a visit to Kizimkazi may be of interest. It is said to be the site of the oldest mosque in East Africa. Still in use today, the original mihrab of this old Shirazi mosque reveals on the left an inscription with the Arabic date 500H – or AD 1107 – in decorative Kufic writing. The coral inscription on the right tells us that the

Mangapwani coral cave is situated about 25 km (16 miles) north of Stone Town.

mosque was partially rebuilt in 1800. The building itself is now in a sad state and has a tin roof, but the mihrab and graves outside may be of interest to those with a keen curiosity in this type of historical ruin. Communities of dolphins are a feature of the Kizimkazi coastline and visitors frequently swim with these remarkable creatures.

Jozani Forest

This delightful forest 35 km (22 miles) southeast of Zanzibar town is worth a day trip, time permitting. The reserve's vegetation encompasses ground-water forest, clumps of mangroves, saline grassland, evergreen thickets, artificial (exotic) forest and tracts of fern. Of the over 98 plant species, the most common are varieties of *Solanum, Diospyros* and *Sansevieria* as well as 26 endemic shrubs.

There is an enormous amount of birdlife to be seen in the reserve with common sightings of the Little greenbul, Redcapped robin chat and the Olive sunbird. Butterflies are profuse with 95 species recorded, nine of them endemic. The elephant shrew, furtive suni antelope, wild pig and Sykes' monkey all occur in Jozani Forest, but most people come to see the whimsical-looking red colobus monkeys. Once visitors have arrived at the headquarters, the closest troop of monkeys will be located and a group of people led by a guide will then track them on foot. Long trousers and closed shoes are recommended against nettles. A large family of colobus monkeys can generally be found within 20 minutes. These lovely creatures have black faces and wild white and red punk hairstyles. Typical of the *Colobus* species, they are thumbless, but move adeptly through the forest, their eyes peeking inquisitively from under their loony locks. Though the number of visitors to the park is low, the troop is remarkably used to people, moving carelessly about the lower tree branches and shrubs, foraging for food. Park fees are payable at headquarters.

Maruhubi Ruins

Just north of Stone Town are the splendid Maruhubi Ruins. Built by Sultan Seyyid Barghash, the palace was completed in 1882, taking only two years to build. The sultan reputedly had one wife, and 99 concubines, all of whom lived in this once-grand residence. Three bathing pools were outside the palace with water supplied via an aqueduct. The black-and-white marble floor is visible in several of the changing rooms and ablution areas. One room with a fine domed roof has a private pool. Outside, massive columns stand as sentinels – the wooded balcony they once supported burned down in 1899 when a fire broke out, destroying the entire palace.

Mangapwani Slave Chambers

Roughly 25 km (16 miles) north of Stone Town are the Mangapwani Slave Chambers and an unrelated coral cave. The main road is tarmac and in excellent condition but, from the turning onwards, the remaining 13 km (8 miles) are extremely slow-going. The caves were used after a ban on slavery in the early 1870s, when it was necessary to conceal the slaves until they were shipped off under cover of night. The caves contain a single free-standing stairway; at the time they were covered with wooden panels and limited ventilation was provided by slits cut into the top of the rock walls. A path from outside the chambers led to the shore where slaves were marched to the dhows.

Not far from the slave chambers is the Mangapwani Coral Cave, a protected historical monument. There are wild tales that this cave was also used to conceal slaves, but these stories are incorrect and there is no evidence to back them. Oral tradition spins a splendid tale of the cave's discovery.

The land in the area was owned by a wealthy Arab who employed several slaves to tend his goats. A young slave boy is said to have wandered off in search of a stray goat, and he eventually heard the goat's cries coming from somewhere below. The animal had fallen down a large hole that had become hidden by undergrowth. Once cleared, the coral limestone cave was revealed and with it the clear fresh waters of a natural spring. The cave is cool and damp and still provides water for the villagers in the area.

Prison and Grave Islands

From Stone Town one can make arrangements to go to Prison and Grave islands. The boats usually ask a set price for the fare, so the best value is to go as a group or join with other passengers to reduce individual costs.

Prison Island is the site of an old ruin that, though intended for use as a prison, was used instead as a hospital and quarantine station. Little remains now, but a pleasant walk around the island takes about 20 minutes. Today, the famous inhabitants of Prison Island are tortoises, slow-moving giants quietly covering the island at leisure. There is presently a breeding programme in progress. Also on the island are peacocks and night herons. Typical vegetation consists of fig trees, euphorbias and fragrant frangipanis. A fee must be paid to the caretaker.

Less than 10 minutes away from Prison Island is Grave Island, so-named because of the many graves of European sailors who died in valiant attempts to interrupt the passage of slave dhows. The grass grows tall over rows of headstones that bear numbers instead of names. Sufficient names remain to remind all of the darkness that once prevailed in these now calm waters. A fee is payable to the caretaker.

COLOURFUL KHANGAS

Throughout Tanzania (in fact, East Africa) women can be seen wearing brightly coloured cloth covered in bold designs. These cloths are khangas, usually worn as a pair with one piece of fabric tied about the waist and the other used as a shawl or head covering. The khanga is thought to have originated on the East African coast around the mid-19th century, when women bought a number of kerchiefs, sewed them together to the appropriate size and began to wear them much as they do today. The patterns and designs on the cloths, roughly measuring 117 cm by 145 cm (44 in by 57 in), are often based on a theme or motif. The name 'khanga' is said to come from the Swahili word for 'guinea-fowl', perhaps used to describe the patterns used on the earlier styles. Although it has evolved considerably since its early beginnings, there is usually a Swahili saying along the bottom of the cloth, a tradition started early this century. Sometimes it will be a proverb, sometimes a riddle – but you are sure to receive different interpretations, depending on where and whom you ask.

Wearing a khanga and using it to its full potential is an art form in itself. It is worn by women of all ages and, depending on body proportions and personal taste, can be wrapped around the lower and upper torso either in one piece or in combinations. Often, Western clothing is worn underneath the khanga; at other times, the khanga becomes a fashionable accessory. Colour-combining is not essential, and often friends or family members will split a pair between them. It is used to bundle up belongings and is then balanced on the women's heads, or it can be rolled into a doughnut shape and placed on their heads to cushion a cumbersome load. Babies are carried in soft slings made from khangas; the colourful cloths can also provide protection from the sun or will prettify a table. The versatility of the khanga is undisputed – whether used in traditional or nontraditional fashion, it always makes a colourful statement. Men wear a similar garment around the lower torso known as a 'kikoi'.

Local women in their colourful khangas.

PEMBA ISLAND

Lying 25 km (16 miles) north of Zanzibar and accessible by ferry or dhow, Pemba is also known as the 'green island'. Sixty-eight kilometres (42 miles) long and 23 km (14 miles) wide, it is a lush and fertile paradise of rolling hills, mangroves and coconuts. A historic past has left timeless ruins as reminders, and the smell of cloves often hangs in the air.

Pemba island has at different times been inhabited by Bantu-speaking people from the mainland, Shirazis from the Persian Gulf, seafaring Portuguese and Omani Arabs. As a result, a unique mix of traditions and cultures has evolved; for instance, bullfights are held from December to February. Pemba is said to be the world's highest producer of cloves and essential oils, and at harvest time, the entire island works together. An oil distilling plant

ABOVE: *Scuba diving off Zanzibar Island.*
TOP RIGHT: *Cardinal fish among staghorn coral.*

is in Chake Chake, on the west coast halfway along the island. Travel around the island can be difficult; it may be necessary to take a taxi or the local daladala. Northeast of Chwaka is the burial ground of Haruni, son of the cruel ruler of Pemba, Muhammad bin Abdulrahman (or Mkame Ndume, 'exploiter of men').

More ruins linked to the evil Muhammad bin Abdulrahman can be found at Pujini, 11 km (7 miles) south of Chake Chake. The buildings have been razed to the ground, making the ruins difficult to comprehend. The finest ruins on Pemba are at Ras Mkumbuu, on a western promontory halfway along the island. The tombs and a mosque were probably built in the 8th and 9th centuries.

People generally come to Pemba to dive, snorkel and deep-sea fish. It is still possible to enjoy the shimmering waters and its living treasures in virtual seclusion. Visibility ranges from 30–60 m (100–200 ft) with frequent sightings of turtles, manta rays and reef sharks. Nearby Misali Island has wonderful coral displays and a rainbow of tropical fish. Visitors must bring all their own equipment.

MAFIA ISLAND

Mafia Island lies 160 km (99 miles) south of Zanzibar and is just opposite the mouth of the Rufiji River. Its attractions lie in its captivating scenery – a tropical paradise awaits a small yet steady number of annual visitors – and the island's spectacular reefs are thrilling for snorkellers and divers alike.

Mafia is the largest in a cluster of islands (394 km²; 151 sq. miles); its name is thought to derive from the Arabic word *morfiyeh*, for 'group'. Similar to many lands along the East African coast, Mafia has experienced foreign settlement on its shores for centuries: Shirazi, Portuguese, German and British seafaring explorers have all left their mark. One of the islands southeast of Mafia, Juani, has 14th-century ruins. Boats visit the island. World War I saw Mafia being used by the British to assemble aircraft for reconnaissance flights. One of their finds was a German ship *Königsberg* in the Rufiji River Delta. The ship was attacked and sunk in 1915.

The people of Mafia are predominantly fishermen, though coconut farming is also an important industry. Just off Chole Bay, on the southeast side of the island, lies Jibondo Island where it is said the finest dhows in Tanzania are made. The glistening waters of Chole Bay and its deeper waters fanning out further afield are famous for deep-sea diving and fishing, offering catches of kingfish, marlin, sailfish and rock cod. An amazing variety of marine life and coral also occur here.

ADVISORY: THE COAST

CLIMATE
Hot, humid, temperatures 28–40 °C (82–105 °F). October–February monsoon Kaskazi blows north to east, rest of year Kusi blows south to east. Long rains March–May, short rains November–December.

BEST TIMES TO VISIT
Visit here from June to September when it is warm but less humid, with a sea breeze making the days enjoyable. Fishing is best from September to March.

MAIN ATTRACTIONS
Beaches, ocean, diving, snorkelling, fishing, boating and ruins. Stone Town, Zanzibar, with its romantic setting, old buildings and maze of shops, mosques.

TRAVEL ALONG THE COAST
Travel is virtually problem-free unless one uses the coastal road south from Dar as the road is appalling. Preferably book accommodation. Fuel available in most major towns. Diving equipment can be hired in Dar and at larger hotels, but bring your own mask, buoyancy compensator (BC), fins and wetsuit.

HEALTH HAZARDS
Carry insect repellent. Take precautions against malaria. Always wear sunscreen, wide-brimmed hat. Drinking water almost always available in hotels and larger supermarkets, tap water often runs out, as does electricity, particularly in major cities such as Dar.

TRAVEL TO DAR ES SALAAM
By air Airport is not far from city centre. Transport to city should be prearranged; there are shuttle buses and taxis, but make sure you first agree on the fare.
By road Easy to reach by tarmac road. Larger cities are Arusha 650 km (404 miles) northwest, eight hours via Moshi on a good tarmac surface, Morogoro 195 km (121 miles) west, Tanga 351 km (218 miles) north. The drive south can be very slow.
By rail All Tanzania's rail lines converge in Dar. Rail services are erratic. Though fares are reasonable, bedding facilities and food services are limited.

SPECIAL EXCURSION
Deep-sea fishing Dar to Latham's Island. Licences arranged, tackle supplied. Catches include yellowfin tuna, sailfish and marlin. Tel./fax (255) 51-72808. Grubu's Ocean Safaris, PO Box 727, Dar es Salaam.

ACCOMMODATION
Hotel Agip Central. 57 air-conditioned, en-suite rooms, dining room, bar, snack bar. Conference facilities, room service. Tel. (255) 51-23511/3, fax 39833, telex 41276 MOTAGI. PO Box 529, Dar es Salaam.

Hotel Karibu 62 air-conditioned rooms. Dining areas, beer garden, poolside bars, gym, conference room, shops. Tel. (255) 51-67760/1, fax 68254, telex 81038 MALAIK TZ. PO Box 20200, Dar es Salaam.
Kilimanjaro Hotel 200 rooms, bar, restaurantss, swimming pool, etc. Periodically has no water. Tel. (255) 51-46529/30, fax 46762, telex 41061. PO Box 9574, Dar es Salaam.
New Africa Hotel Central. 240 rooms, restaurant, grill, casino, gym. Tel. (255) 51-29611/9, fax 29610, telex 81049 AFRHOT. PO Box 9314, Dar es Salaam.
Oyster Bay Hotel Over 40 air-conditioned en-suite rooms, bars, dining areas, swimming pool, shopping arcade. Tel. (255) 51-68062/4, fax 68631, telex 41573 JAMBO TZ. PO Box 2261, Dar es Salaam.
Sheraton Dar es Salaam Hotel Fine dining and conference facilities. Tel. (255) 51-4411, fax 44847. PO Box 791, Dar es Salaam.

WHERE TO EAT
The Rickshaw, Msasani Peninsula. Chinese food.
The Alcove, Samora Machel Avenue. Indian food.
Open House, ask for directions. Indian food.
Casanova, Toure Drive. Italian food.
Agip Snack Bar, corner Sokoine Drive and Pamba Street. Casual light meals.
Ice Cream Fountain, Old Bagamoyo Road.

ANNUAL EVENTS
International Trade Fair Held annually in Dar during the first week of July.
Bagamoyo Art Festival Takes place in September. Tanzania Tourist Board, tel. (255) 51-27672/3, fax 46780. PO Box 2485, Dar es Salaam.

ACCOMMODATION BEYOND DAR
North Coast
Bahari Beach Hotel 25 km (16 miles) north of Dar, 100 rooms with air conditioning, mosquito nets, bar, dining area, swimming pool, tennis courts, diving/snorkelling. Tel. (255) 51-47101/2, telex 41185. PO Box 9312, Dar, or Bushtrekker Hotels, tel. (255) 51-31957, telex 41178. PO Box 5350, Dar es Salaam.
Silversands Beach Hotel 25 km (16 miles) from Dar, 35 air-conditioned rooms, bar, dining room. Basic camping facilities. Tel. (255) 51-35437, fax 44568. Savannah Tours, PO Box 20032, Dar es Salaam.
White Sands Hotel 20 km (12 miles) north of Dar, 88 air-conditioned rooms, balconies, television; bar with tables on beach; casino; watersports, boating. Tel. (255) 51-44484/35801, fax 39885/44476, telex 41540 SEAROCK TZ. PO Box 3030, Dar es Salaam.

South Coast
Amani Beach Club Luxury en-suite, air-conditioned bungalows. Swimming pool, tennis/squash courts, watersports. Tel. (255) 51-411437, fax 40752. Val Investments, PO Box 1547, Dar es Salaam.

Ras Kutani Beach Resort 25 bandas, no hot water. Bar, dining area, watersports. The resort is closed from mid-April to mid-May. Tel. (255) 51-28485, fax 46980, telex 81016. Selous Safari Co, PO Box 1192, Dar es Salaam.

Campsites

Camping is difficult at best. Silversands Beach Hotel has site with poor ablution facilities. Salvation Army site on Nelson Mandela Road has basic ablution facilities. Area quite secure, with swimming pool, good meals and refreshments. Donations in lieu of fees. The Salvation Army, PO Box 1273, Dar es Salaam.

TRAVEL TO BAGAMOYO

By land Bagamoyo is roughly 72 km (45 miles) north of Dar. For half the distance, the road is all-weather *murram* (dirt) and bumpy and dusty.

By sea Transport by dhow can be arranged between Bagamoyo and Zanzibar, quite long and rough.

ACCOMMODATION
Lodges and hotels

Bagamoyo Beach Resort Not all 18 en-suite rooms air conditioned. Huts with mosquito nets. Watersports, volleyball, mini-golf. Tel. (255) Bagamoyo 83. PO Box 250, Bagamoyo.

Bedego Beach Hotel Some rooms en suite, all have mosquito nets. Pleasure boat; bring diving equipment; no dive master. Camping facilities available. Tel. (255) Bagamoyo 22. PO Box 261, Bagamoyo.

Lazy Lagoon Lodge 15 en-suite rooms. Swimming pool, boating, watersports. PO Box 5, Bagamoyo.

Traveller's Lodge All 15 rooms (8 en suite) have mosquito nets. Camping facilities, watersports; no dive master or hire equipment. Tel. (255) Bagamoyo 77. PO Box 275, Bagamoyo.

Camping

Camping facilities at Bedego Beach Hotel and Traveller's Lodge (*see* above).

TRAVEL TO PANGANI AND TANGA

By air Air Tanzania runs regular, though erratic, service to Tanga. Charter flights available.

By road Main access routes from Moshi, 360 km (224 miles) northwest, from Dar, 404 km (251 miles) south via Segera–Chalinze road, good tarmac. Mombasa roughly 150 km (93 miles) north. The coastal road from Pangani slow and bumpy.

By rail Tanga via Moshi–Dar es Salaam line. Erratic.

By ferry Weekly service between Dar es Salaam, Tanga and Pemba.

ACCOMMODATION
Lodges and hotels

Pangani Lodge Air-conditioned bungalows. Bar and dining. Twice-weekly barbecue. Tel. (255) 51-27840, fax 46668. PO Box 8293, Dar es Salaam.

Mashado Game Fishing Lodge 40 luxury rooms. Watersports, deep-sea fishing, river cruises. Tel. (255) 51-27840, fax 46668. PO Box 8293, Dar es Salaam.

Kingfisher Lodge Watersports, campsites. Tel. (255) 53-42491, fax 46573. Private Bag, Tanga.

Mkonge Hotel 50 air-conditioned rooms. Bar, dining areas. Swimming pool, tennis court. Tel. (255) 53-44542/6, fax 43637, telex 45020. PO Box 1544, Tanga, or Bushtrekker Hotels, tel. (255) 51-31957, telex 41178. PO Box 5350, Dar es Salaam.

Motel Panori 15 air-conditioned, en-suite rooms, inside and al fresco bar and dining room. Tel. (255) 53-46044. PO Box 672, Tanga.

Camping

Facilities at Hotel New Era off Hospital Road and Kingfisher Lodge on the Pangani road.

TRAVEL TO THE KILWAS

By air Air Tanzania offers an erratic air service to south coast. Expensive charter flights available.

By road The road from Dar to the south coast may well be the worst road in Africa and should only be tackled by adventurers who will not be put out by 350 km (217 miles) of teeth-jarring, broken tarmac.

By sea The Tanzania Coastal Shipping Lines on Sokoine Drive in Dar run a fortnightly service from Dar. Dhow trips can be arranged. Tel. (255) 51-26192, telex 41532. PO Box 9461, Dar es Salaam.

SOUTH COAST ACCOMMODATION

The area offers limited accommodation; camping is recommended, but visitors should bring supplies. Fresh food can be purchased locally.

Ruvula Camp Luxury camp, focus on diving. Water sports and fishing. Airstrip close by. Fax (255) 57-8547. Zama East Africa, PO Box 49, Arusha.

SPECIAL EXCURSIONS
Diving Excursions (Zanzibar)

One Ocean Snorkelling, diving excursions, cruises, diving courses. Modern, well-maintained equipment for hire, tank-filling facilities. Contact the Zanzibar Dive Centre, tel. (255) 54-33816, fax 33816. PO Box 608, Zanzibar.

Indian Ocean Divers Day trips. Tel. (255) 54-33860, fax 54-33860. PO Box 2370, Zanzibar.

Note: Valid certificate of good health, record of qualifications and log books may be required.

TRAVEL TO ZANZIBAR

By air Coastal Travels (*see* p. 179) and Air Tanzania run regular services via Dar International Airport; air charter available. International airlines also fly here

By sea Daily ferry by hydrofoil, hovercraft and catamaran between Dar and Zanzibar. Take passport and health card. Fares and taxes payable in US dollars Dhows can be hired in Dar (*see* above). First fix price.

Moderately well-maintained main roads. Car/ motorbike hire, taxis, local buses *(daladalas)*. Bicycles may come in handy for exploring Stone Town.

ACCOMMODATION
Stone Town

Dhow Palace Air-conditioned en-suite rooms. Tel. (255) 54-33012, fax 33008. PO Box 3974, Zanzibar.
Garden Lodge 8 rooms with mosquito nets, some en suite. Tel. (255) 54-33298. PO Box 3413, Zanzibar.
Mazson's Hotel Clean, moderate accommodation. The dining room does not serve alcohol. En-suite rooms all have air conditioners and satellite television. Tel. (255) 54-33694, fax 33695. PO Box 3367, Zanzibar.
Mbweni Ruins Hotel 12 air-conditioned en-suite rooms, mosquito nets and terraces. Bar and dining area, tours and boat trips can be arranged. Tel. (255) 54-31832, fax 30536. PO Box 2542, Zanzibar.
Tembo Hotel En-suite rooms. Terraced dining room, swimming pool. Tel. (255) 54-33005, fax 33777. PO Box 3974, Zanzibar.
Tufaah Inn There are 8 en-suite rooms; some of them with air conditioning. Tel. (255) 54-30728. PO Box 1029, Zanzibar.
Zanzibar Reef Hotel Rooms air-conditioned, mosquito nets. Bar, restaurants, swimming pool. Watersports. Tel. (255) 54-30208, fax 30556. PO Box 2586, Mazizini, Zanzibar, or tel. (254) 11-473034, fax 471349. PO Box 82234, Mombasa, Kenya.

West Coast

Lala Salama/Bububu 10 rooms with air conditioning, satellite television; dining room/bar; diving, snorkelling. Major credit cards accepted. Tel. (255) 54-32512/33767, fax 32512/33098, telex 57380. Air Zanzibar, PO Box 1784, Zanzibar.
Mtoni Marine Centre Split club/village: club air-conditioned en-suite rooms; village rustic en-suite rooms. Watersports, boating, tours. Club tel. (255) 54-32540, village tel. (255) 54-30285. PO Box 992, Zanzibar, or **Coastal Travels** in Dar es Salaam, tel (255) 51-37479/80, fax 46045, telex 41150.

North Coast

Lala Salama/Nungwi The focus is on diving and-watersports. Rooms with balconies, dining room and bar. Tel. (255) 54-32512/33767, fax 32512/33098, telex 57380.
Mnemba Club 10 en-suite cottages with mosquito nets. Watersports and deep-sea fishing. Tel. (255) 57-3303/3530, fax 8268, telex 22082. Conservation Corporation Africa, PO Box 751, Arusha.

East Coast

Matemwe Beach Bungalows Bungalows with mosquito nets, some en suite. Volleyball, snorkelling, diving. Closed mid-March to mid-April. Tel./fax (255) 54-31342. Mkune Sini, PO Box 3275, Zanzibar.

Tamarind Beach Hotel Thatched dining area and bar. 20 en-suite bungalows with mosquito nets, fans terraces. Good dive shop; PADI instruction available. Fishing trips arranged and tackle provided. Tel. (255) 54-33041, fax 33042. PO Box 2206, Uroa, Zanzibar.

WHERE TO EAT IN STONE TOWN

Clove Restaurant, Hurumzi Street. Rooftop position.
Emerson's Hurumzi Street. Probably the best food in Zanzibar, rooftop dining; reservations essential.
Fisherman's, Shangani Street. Known for seafood.
Floating Restaurant, Jamituri Gardens. Delicious homemade ice creams.
Forodhani, Jamituri Gardens. Vegetables, seafood, grilled meats and more; no alcohol.
House of Spices, Khad Bazaar (Kiponda). Rooftop dining, seafood; spice shop.
La Lampara, Victoria Street. Italian food.
Luna Mare, Gizenga Street. Excellent local fare.
Omani, ask for directions. Local food.
Spice Inn, Changa Bazaar. Tea shop.

TRAVEL TO PEMBA

By air Air Tanzania runs an erratic service from Tanga to Pemba. Charter flights available.
By sea Several ferries from Dar es Salaam, Tanga and Zanzibar; schedules erratic. Can cross by dhow.
The island is best traversed by taxi.

ACCOMMODATION

Kiweni Marine Resort Luxurious resort, diving. Tel. (cellular) (255) 0811-325367, fax (cellular) (255) 0811-325368. PO Box 215, Chake Chake, Pemba.
Camping Camping a good choice; most hotels and guest-houses offer basic lodgings and dining service.

SPECIAL EXCURSIONS

Live-aboard yacht MY *Kisiwani* 5 air-conditioned cabins, 3–4 dives per day. Snorkelling, wind-surfing, tours. Tel. (254) 11-313749/225417, fax 316875. Pemba Diving Ltd, PO Box 86952, Mombasa.

TRAVEL TO MAFIA

By air Coastal Travels (*see* this page) in Dar most reliable. In Zanzibar, book at airport.
By sea Regular, though erratic, service from Dar. Check with Tanzania Coastal Shipping Lines on Sokoine Drive in Dar. Tel. (255) 51-26192, telex 41532. PO Box 9461, Dar es Salaam.

ACCOMMODATION

Kinasi Camp Luxury lodge for 20. Diving, snorkelling, fishing arranged. Coastal Travels (*see* this page).
Mafia Island Lodge 40 rooms with verandas. Island trips, diving, snorkelling and fishing arranged. Tel. (255) 57-8502/2711, fax 8221.

PART THREE

VISITOR'S DIGEST

The very nature of Tanzania – its greatly appealing vast tracts of unexploited wilderness populated by impressive numbers of wildlife – embraces the fact that immeasurable distances separate the country's renowned and well-visited parks. For this reason, and the fact that areas can differ immensely from season to season, it is wise to plan your trip well ahead with a reputable safari operator.

This section of the book aims to advise visitors on the best way to tackle their trip to Tanzania, as well as giving information on suitable safari companies and advice on the best mode of travel, including air charter and tips for the self-sufficient four-wheel-drive traveller, such as border formalities, vehicle papers and fees, as well as currency, banks and medical information.

LEFT: *Plains game such as Burchell's zebra occur in abundance in Serengeti National Park.*
ABOVE: *A diving dhow off Zanzibar Island.*

VISITOR'S DIGEST

ENTERING TANZANIA

VISAS All foreign visitors except for citizens of the Commonwealth, of Scandinavian countries and the Republic of Ireland require a visa. They are obtainable from Tanzanian embassies, High Commissions and main ports of entry. The visa fee depends on the type of passport held. A visitor's pass is also required for all travellers; this can be obtained free of charge from any Tanzanian diplomatic mission or point of entry. However, it is always better to secure your visa before arriving in the country.

HEALTH REQUIREMENTS Vaccination against yellow fever is mandatory, and health certificates are often requested at ports of entry. Cholera is no longer a requirement, but is sometimes still asked for at borders. The threat of malaria exists throughout the country and prophylactics should be started two weeks prior to your arrival in the country (*see also* Medical Services). A tetanus shot is also recommended; consult your local physician.

FIREARM LICENCES If you plan to bring in guns for hunting purposes, it is best to discuss this in detail with the hunting company you have chosen. Reputable companies have expert knowledge on the lengthy processes involved in the handling of firearms brought in for temporary use.

VEHICLE PAPERS When entering Tanzania in a private vehicle, ensure your papers are in order. Vehicles need a valid *carnet de passage* and are subject to a road tax. Third party insurance may be required, but this may vary from border to border. All vehicles undergo a customs and sometimes a police search.

Drivers must hold an international driver's licence. Getting through frequently used borders such as Namanga or Lunga Lunga between Kenya and Tanzania is fairly quick and painless.

CUSTOMS Personal effects, including binoculars, cameras and film, may be temporarily imported duty free. A customs bond may be demanded from visitors bringing in video or filming equipment, radios, tape recorders and musical instruments to ensure that they are take back out of the country. Visitors may bring in the following duty free: 200 cigarettes, 50 cigars or 250g (9 oz) of tobacco, one litre (2 pt) of wine or spirits, and 250 ml (8 fl. oz) of perfume.

CLOTHING While on safari, the dress code is relaxed and easy. Loose-fitting cotton clothing is a good choice; stay away from bright colours and whites. Clothing should be in neutral shades and of sturdy fabric, able to withstand wear and tear. Shorts, trousers and skirts all come in handy; very brief shorts are uncomfortable on hot days. In the coastal areas it is advisable to be conservative in one's dress so as not to offend the predominantly Muslim local inhabitants. Laundry facilities are on offer in most lodges or accommodation units, with most items being returned the same day on request. Pack light and efficiently. Take the following:

Tracksuit or sweats
Windbreaker/jacket
One comfortable smart-casual outfit (often a clean pair of trousers or a skirt will suffice)
Comfortable walking shoes and sandals
Cotton socks, underwear and swimwear
Hat, sunblock, lip balm; eye drops
Sunglasses, regular glasses (contact lenses may not be suitable for rough travel)
Toiletries, moisturizer, face cloth, towel
Prescription drugs, malaria tablets, contraceptives, first-aid kit, insect repellent, boiled sweets
Pocket knife, flashlight with extra batteries, matches or a lighter
Camera equipment, batteries, film, cleaning materials, bags for dust protection, binoculars (8 x 35 or 10 x 40)
Pencils, pens, notebooks, envelopes, a book
Passport, health certificates, vehicle papers, traveller's cheques, cash (US dollars), credit cards

ARRIVING BY AIR International flights are handled by Kilimanjaro International Airport, which services both Arusha and Moshi. On the coast, international flights land at Dar es Salaam International Airport as well as Zanzibar Island.
Kilimanjaro International Airport, tel. (255) 55-2223.
Dar es Salaam International Airport, PO Box 543, Dar es Salaam; tel. (255) 51-42111.
Zanzibar Airport, tel. (255) 54-32001/872.

Airlines flying to Tanzania are: Air Tanzania, Aeroflot, Air Zimbabwe, Air India, Air France, British Airways, Egypt Air, Ethiopian Airlines, Gulf Air, Kenya Airways, KLM, Royal Swazi, Swissair and Zambia Airways. There is an airport departure tax payable; from Zanzibar, travellers heading to destinations within Tanzania are charged a fee; all tickets issued in Zanzibar are subject to a 10% tax.

ARRIVING BY RAIL Since the railway link between Kenya and Tanzania was resumed again in early 1996 (after a break of 18 years) there are now two points of entry to Tanzania by rail. A connecting passenger train between Nairobi, Kenya, and Moshi, Tanzania, crosses the border once a week at Taveta, while the second entry point is via the TAZARA line connecting Zambia and Tanzania at Tunduma. This mode of travel can be frustrating as the service is often delayed and schedules are not adhered to. Line maintenance is lacking and bookings, though reasonably priced, are handled inefficiently. First class is the only real option, but even then you should be equipped with your own food and bedding.

Tanzania-Zambia Railway Authority, PO Box 2434, Dar es Salaam; tel. (255) 51-64191; telex 41466 TAZARA TA.

Tanzania Railways Corporation, PO Box 468, Dar es Salaam; tel. (255) 51-26241; telex 41308 RAILS TZ.

Kenya Railways, PO Box 30121, Nairobi, Kenya; tel. (254) 2-221211; fax 2-34009; telex: 22254 RAIL KE.

ARRIVING BY ROAD Tanzania is most easily accessible by road from Kenya (border posts at Namanga, Taveta and Lunga Lunga), Malawi (Kasumulu) and Zambia (Tunduma and, by ship, Mpulungu on Lake Tanganyika). Be well prepared with your documentation; a good attitude is also important! From Uganda, Rwanda and Burundi you can expect lots of hassles and you need lots of time.

MONEY

CURRENCY The Tanzanian shilling (Tsh) equals 100 cents. There is no limit on the importation of foreign currency and currency declaration forms are no longer required. Changing money in major towns and cities is usually fairly painless and requires a small portion of your time. The best rates are usually offered by the foreign exchange (forex) bureaux. Be extremely cautious of black market exchange dealers; they are amazingly fast, and can pull hoaxes that can be quite costly. Smaller towns may require some patience as the paperwork and availability of cash can become somewhat irritating. On Zanzibar Island, cash in US dollars is favoured.

BANKS There are several banks, both local and international, and forex bureaux in Tanzania. Banking hours are 8:30–12:30 Mondays to Fridays and 8:30–11:30 on Saturdays. Some branches in the larger cities are beginning to extend their hours from 14:30 to 16:50 on weekday afternoons.

CREDIT CARDS AND TRAVELLER'S CHEQUES Credit cards such as MasterCard, Visa, American Express, Eurocard and Diners Club are becoming more widely accepted in Tanzania; they can generally be used in most larger hotels and shops, otherwise cash is the best option.

TIPPING Larger hotels and restaurants include a service charge on the tariff. If it is not included, however, and you feel you would like to add something extra, 10% is generally accepted. Likewise with drivers, attendants and game-rangers, tips are acceptable but visitors should keep these to a reasonable value. Many lodges have a staff tip box.

ACCOMMODATION

Tanzania is an expensive holiday destination. Distances are vast, and the cost to transport people and commodities is high. The government is taking advantage of this factor and is attempting to promote the country as a low-volume, high-cost destination. Most hotels, despite their varying quality, are reasonably expensive (even camping fees are a sizable amount), generally restricting budget travellers to substandard lodgings in cities and towns, or with organizations such as the YMCA. The main forms of accommodation offered in the reserves range from luxury lodges and tented camps complete with en-suite facilities (and often running on solar energy) through to self-catering bandas and the most basic of campsites with little more than a water tap and pit latrine. (For more specific accommodation information, refer to the Advisory at the end of each chapter.)

PETS Domestic animals are not allowed in national parks and game reserves. They should be left at home as there are no kennels or other forms of accommodation for them.

TRAVEL WITHIN TANZANIA

TRAVELLING BY ROAD In Tanzania traffic keeps to the left; road signs are international. If conditions allow, major roads can generally be covered at speeds of 100–120 km/h (60–75 mph). Travel in national parks and reserves is restricted to a maximum of 50 km/h (30 mph), but for the best game-viewing opportunities speed should be kept between 30 and 40 km/h (15–25 mph). Allow plenty of time for travel as scenery can be stunning, but distances can also be vast. A park fee per vehicle is payable. A guide can be enlisted at a fee.

Most of the main roads through the northern, eastern and southern sections of the country are generally in fair to good condition with recent grading or tarring having taken place; but the road network established in the west is appalling and requires much time and patience. The road south out of Dar es Salaam into the Selous Game Reserve and further south to Kilwa is horrendous; the road between Dodoma and Arusha is back-wrenching and, depending on the time of year, is either dusty or wet and slippery.

For off-road driving, and even for driving on secondary roads, a four-wheel-drive vehicle is recommended, particularly in the wet seasons; it is also better for driving throughout the parks. Driving after dark is not permitted in any of Tanzania's national parks and reserves.

MAPS Current, up-to-date maps of Tanzania are not easy to find, while road signs on major thoroughfares are few and far between. Look in book shops and curio stores for the maps listed below, but, when in doubt, just ask the local residents: *Central and Southern Africa* #955 by Michelin; for a little more detail, *The Road Map of East Africa* by the Text Book Centre Limited, PO Box 47540, Nairobi, Kenya; *Globetrotter Travel Map of Tanzania* by Struik Publishers.

FUEL Petrol and diesel are available in most major towns and cities, but less so once you're off the beaten track. Make sure you ask the price of fuel, no matter what the pump states!

CAR HIRE Vehicles can be hired in Tanzania, but this can be a very costly exercise. Four-wheel-drive vehicles are always hired out with a driver. Saloon cars are available for use in towns and cities, but hiring a taxi may be a cheaper method. If you are thinking of hiring a car, discuss this in great length with your tour operator or travel agent beforehand. The following car-hire firms can be contacted:
Monason Limited (Europcar Car Hire), PO Box 208, Dar es Salaam; tel. (255) 51-44358; fax 44579.
Hertz, PO Box 20517, Dar es Salaam; tel. (255) 51-25753/35413; fax 44568; telex: 46762 KILIMA TZ.

BREAKDOWNS Unless there is a dire emergency, it is a good idea to stay with your vehicle. Ensure that you always carry sufficient water with you as well as supplies to tide you over until someone comes to your aid.

TRAVELLING BY RAIL As already said earlier, this is an economical way to travel through the country, but it is time-consuming and rather unreliable.

TRAVELLING BY AIR There are airstrips throughout Tanzania. Most lodges, wildlife parks and reserves can accommodate aircraft ranging from 6- to 10-seaters. Air travel is a costly measure, but it provides a good means of covering the enormous distances required throughout the country and does make for a much more pleasant journey. A disadvantage of air travel is that it does not allow travellers to observe day-to-day life as overland treks do. However, the convenience of speed and comfort makes it without doubt a choice mode for travellers.

For further information contact the following:
Air Tanzania, PO Box 543, Dar es Salaam; tel. (255) 51-46643/44111; telex: 42137.
Air Zanzibar, PO Box 1784, Zanzibar; tel. (255) 54-33098; telex: 57380.
Coastal Travels, PO Box 3052, Dar es Salaam; tel. (255) 51-37479; fax 46045; telex: 41150 CSI TZ.
Fleet Air, tel. (255) 57-8126/2420.
Northern Air, PO Box 2782, Arusha; tel. (255) 57-8060; fax 8059.
Precision Air, PO Box 1636, Arusha; tel. (255) 57-6903; fax 8204; telex: 50008 and 42148.

PUBLIC TRANSPORT IN CITIES Buses, *matatus* and *daladalas* operate in and between all major cities. They are a cheap mode of transport used extensively by the local residents, but should be used with caution; these vehicles are often overloaded with people and parcels, and are often involved in accidents. Be prepared for lots of squeezing in and bouncing around. Taxis are also available, and, although the prices are a little higher than the bus fares, they are more reliable. Be sure to set the fare before entering the taxi and starting your journey.

TOURISM AND PUBLICITY OFFICE
It is difficult to get any information on Tanzania. The best place to begin is the Tanzanian Tourist Board (Dar es Salaam), PO Box 2485, Dar es Salaam; tel. (255) 51-27672/3; fax 46780 or (Arusha) PO Box 2348, Arusha; tel. (255) 57-3842 or 3843; fax 8256.

GENERAL INFORMATION
CLIMATE The Tanzanian climate is tropical. The central plateau is dry and arid with hot days and cool nights, while the northwest highlands are cool and temperate. The long rains occur from March to

May and the short rains from October to December. June to September is the cooler season, with the hottest period from October to February.

At the coast the long rains also occur from March to May, while the short rains are during November and December. The coast is hot and humid although sea breezes are a welcome relief; they are very pleasant from June to September.

ELECTRICITY Tanzania's power system is 230 volts AC, 50 Hz. Plugs are both round two-pin and square three-pin, with the square pin being the more predominant. Hotels, lodges and tented camps usually have sockets in the tents; sometimes they only have them in common areas or offices for visitors to charge their batteries.

ENTERTAINMENT AND ART Most entertainment is limited to what is provided in the hotels and lodges, this generally being traditional dance and music. Dar es Salaam and Arusha both have cinemas, while there are all types of bars and restaurants in any of the towns or cities.

The National Museum in Dar es Salaam has art exhibitions from time to time, and checking with international cultural centres can be rewarding.

FOOD AND WINE These days virtually everything is available in Tanzania in terms of food and beverages. Wines are generally imported from South Africa, with a reasonable selection on offer, but be prepared for high price tags. Spirits are readily available and can be purchased in most shops (they can actually be more affordable than wine). Soft drinks are reasonably priced, and are most often still served in glass bottles. For self-sufficient travellers it may be worth buying several bottles, paying the deposit and then exchanging the empties for new drinks while travelling through the country. Towards the end of your stay, simply return your remaining empties to any shop and your deposit will be given back.

Foodstuffs can be purchased in all major towns and cities, with fresh vegetables available almost everywhere. Roadside stalls and city markets offer the best prices for fresh produce; make sure you wash all purchases thoroughly in clean water. Most often seen at roadside stalls are potatoes, tomatoes, onions, cabbage, maize, beans, oranges, pineapples, bananas and cassava. You may have to wait for the larger towns and cities to buy fresh meat such as beef, pork, lamb and chicken.

Food at hotels, lodges and camps runs the gamut from basic, homecooked meals to international menus and fine cuisine.

ICE AND WATER One may order ice in restaurants, lodges and hotels, although it may not always be available. However, drinks are generally served ice-cold. It is not possible to purchase blocks or bags of ice for cold boxes; these simply are not available.

Water supplies at most accommodation units is clean and thermos flasks holding drinking water are kept filled. Bottled water may be purchased virtually anywhere. Tap water in most cities can be drunk, but should be first boiled or treated with water purification tablets. The water in Iringa is not clean and should not be drunk under any circumstances.

LANGUAGES Tanzania's official language is Kiswahili, but most business at an international level is conducted in English. There are over 120 tribal vernaculars found throughout the country.

MEASUREMENT Tanzania uses the Imperial system.

MEDIA Newspapers Tanzania's English language papers are: *The Daily News*, *The Guardian*, *The Express* (a bi-weekly), the *East African*, and the *Kenyan Daily Nation*.
Radio The country's local stations are Radio Tanzania, Radio One and Radio Tumaini. Frequencies for international broadcasts, although they can change, are as follows:
BBC World Service: MHz 21.47 17.885 15.42 9.63
Voice of America: MHz 21.49 15.60 9.525 6.035.
Television Stations offered are ITV, DTV, CTN and Television Zanzibar.

MEDICAL SERVICES Basic medical emergencies can be handled throughout Tanzania. Dar es Salaam and Arusha both have large hospitals, but visitors requiring extensive medical treatment are best flown out to Kenya or alternative destinations. Health insurance is advisable. Visitors can obtain temporary memberships for air service evacuations and additional medical requirements should the need arise. For further information contact:
African Air Rescue (K) Ltd, PO Box 41766, Nairobi, Kenya; tel. (254-2) 71-5319, fax 5328. In southern Africa, check with International SOS Assistance.
The Flying Doctors' Society of Africa, PO Box 30125, Nairobi, Kenya. tel. (254-2) 50-1300/1/2/3/ 50-0508; fax 2699. This service offers tourists air

rescue on two levels: the first encompasses visitors that are within a 500-km (300 miles) radius of the Flying Doctors' Nairobi base at Wilson Airport, which includes the northern section of Tanzania; the second encompasses those visiting areas within a 1,000-km (600 miles) radius of the Wilson Airport base, which includes most of the remaining Tanzanian areas.

Pharmacies can be found throughout the country and most available items can be bought over the counter. It is a good idea, however, to bring ample supplies of any necessary prescription drugs as stocks can be limited, especially in the rural areas and on Zanzibar Island. Visitors should also have basic first-aid supplies, although these items can be purchased a little more easily throughout the country.

Aids Aids and other sexually transmitted diseases are prevalent. Blood for transfusions is screened regularly for the HIV virus, and needles and syringes are not re-used. Visitors may find it more reassuring to travel with their own needles and transfusion kits. Unprotected sex always carries a high risk.

Bilharzia *(schistosomiasis)* Bilharzia can occur in streams, rivers and dams throughout Tanzania. It is caused by a microscopic, water-borne parasite that requires both a tiny freshwater snail and a human host during its life cycle. The parasite buries itself in human skin and works its way into the intestine walls, liver or bladder where it lays its eggs; from here the parasite is released again through urine and faeces, making it important not to urinate or defecate near any water sources. The snail prefers quiet sunny waters or generally slow-moving pools, which are often choked with reeds at the banks. In many cases, volcanic lakes do not show signs of bilharzia as the alkaline waters prove difficult for the parasites to live in. Symptoms take roughly six weeks to manifest themselves, but victims usually show signs of fatigue and overall ill-health. Blood may appear in the urine and/or stool.

Malaria Protection against malaria is an important factor in planning your trip. Prophylactics are readily available through medical doctors, and can make an enormous difference to the outcome of your safari. There are several strains of malaria, for which certain medications are better than others, so it is wise to discuss with your doctor exactly where you will be travelling and for how long.

The rainy season will obviously mean more mosquitoes as breeding grounds are prevalent throughout the country. It is the *Anopheles* mosquito – and only the female – that infects humans; simple precautions can increase your chances of not being bitten. Visitors should cover up in the early mornings and evenings. Wearing socks, long trousers and long-sleeved shirts will make a difference. Sleep under a mosquito net, keep the lights off and use a mosquito-repelling coil or bug spray if necessary.

Malaria begins to show seven to 10 days after you have been bitten. Some indicators may be a headache, chills and/or fever, shaking and sweating, stiff and sore muscles, and flu symptoms. Seek medical attention immediately if malaria is suspected and drink lots of fluids. The longer one waits, the worse the illness becomes.

Hepatitis A and B The 'A' virus (resulting in jaundice and an enlarged liver and spleen) is highly contagious and can occur in Tanzania. Visitors can be immunized for a short duration before arriving in the country. Hepatitis B is much more severe than 'A' and is spread by blood and body secretions. Immunization is possible, but this strain is rather uncommon in Tanzania.

Sleeping sickness *(trypanosomiasis*, or 'tryps') This disease is transmitted by the bite from an infected tsetse fly. Tanzania has a huge infestation problem with the tsetse fly, but most do not carry 'tryps'. If visitors are bitten, they generally only have some swelling and soreness for a couple of days.

Stomach problems Some visitors encounter a day or so of stomach problems which generally clear rapidly but should be handled appropriately: do not drink water that has not been boiled; do not drink milk, liquor or soft drinks; avoid fatty or fried foods; try to eat some plain rice or potatoes, and get plenty of rest.

Sun and heat While in Tanzania you are close to the equator, and the sun's wrath. Make sure you wear a hat and sunglasses, even on cloudy days. Cover up with sunscreen, not forgetting ears, lips and nose. Drink plenty of water. Try wearing a shirt with a collar and sleeves that can be rolled up or down.

Dehydration can occur with outward signs of dizziness, fatigue and nausea. To remedy this, increase your water as well as your salt intake. Rehydration powders can be purchased in pharmacies. Treat any sunburn immediately with a soothing lotion and do not continue to expose burned areas to the sun.

PHOTOGRAPHY Before photographing any people, do them the courtesy of asking their permission. Photographs of military units, police stations, train stations and the State House are strictly prohibited.

POSTAL SERVICES The postal service is slow but fairly reliable. Do not mail thick envelopes or packages containing money. Most cities and towns have post offices with morning and afternoon services on weekdays and Saturday mornings.

PUBLIC HOLIDAYS The start of Eid Al-Fitr and various Muslim festivals is timed according to local sightings of the moon. The dates for the Christian holiday of Good Friday and Easter Monday also vary.

January 1	New Year's Day
January 12	Zanzibar Revolution Day
April 26	Union Day
May 1	Labour Day
August 8	Peasants' Day
August 19	Prophet's Birthday
December 9	Independence Day
December 25	Christmas Day
December 26	Boxing Day

RELIGIONS The main religions are Islam, Hinduism and Christianity, as well as traditional beliefs.

SAFARI OPERATORS When it comes to choosing a safari operator there are hundreds of choices. The list below includes travel agents that should offer sound advice.

Arusha

Let's Go Travel, Adventure Centre, PO Box 12095, Arusha; tel. (255) 57-7111; fax 8997.

Abercrombie & Kent, PO Box 427, Arusha; tel. (255) 57-8343/7; fax 8273; telex: 42005.

Bushbuck Safaris Ltd, PO Box 1700, Arusha; tel. (255) 57-7473; fax 8293.

Hoopoe Adventure Tours Tanzania Ltd, PO Box 2047, Arusha; tel. (255) 57-7011/7541; fax 8226; telex: 42103.

Leopard Tours, PO Box 1638, Arusha; tel. (255) 57-8442/3; fax 8219; telex: 50002.

Ranger Safaris, PO Box 9, Arusha; tel. (255) 57-3738; fax 8205; telex: 42017.

Tanganyika Wildlife Safaris, PO Box 2231, Arusha; tel. (255) 57-6021; fax 8072.

The Safari Company, PO Box 207, Arusha; tel. (255) 57-8060; fax 8059.

Unique Safaris, PO Box 2189, Arusha; tel. (255) 57-8456; fax 8256.

UTC, PO Box 2211, Arusha; tel. (255) 57-8844; fax 8222; telex: 42110 UTC TZ.

Wildersun Safaris, PO Box 930, Arusha; tel. (255) 57-8848/9; fax 8223; telex: 42126.

SPECIALISED SAFARIS

Gibb's Farm Safaris, PO Box 6084, Arusha; tel. (255) 57-6702; fax 8310; telex: 42041 PANKER TZ.

Greystoke Safaris, PO Box 56923, Nairobi, Kenya; tel. (254) 2-502491; fax 502739.

Ker & Downey Safaris (Tanzania), PO Box 2982, Arusha; tel. (255) 57-8434; fax 8435; telex: 42013.

Mashado Luxury Tented Camp, PO Box 14823, Arusha. No telephone number available.

Mountain Bike Africa, c/o Adventure Centre, PO Box 12095, Arusha; tel. (255) 57-7111; fax 8997.

Pemba Diving Limited, PO Box 86952, Mombasa, Kenya; tel. (254) 11-313749; fax 316875.

Tanganyika Film & Safari Outfitters, PO Box 49, Arusha. No telephone number available.

Tropical Tours Tanzania, PO Box 727, Arusha; tel. (255) 57-8907/8353.

Wilderness Africa, PO Box 3052, Arusha; tel./fax (255) 57-8182.

Dar es Salaam

Coastal Travels, PO Box 3052, Dar es Salaam; tel. (255) 51-37479/480; fax 46045/44075; telex: 41150 CSI TZ.

Grubu's Ocean Safaris, PO Box 727, Dar es Salaam; tel./fax (255) 51-72808.

Nomad Safaris, PO Box 70192, Dar es Salaam; tel. (255) 51-46862; fax 46863.

Savannah Tours, PO Box 20517, Dar es Salaam; tel. (255) 51-35437/13; fax 44568; telex: 46762 KILIMA TZ.

Selous Safari Company, PO Box 1192, Dar es Salaam; tel. (255) 51-34802; fax 46980; telex: 81016.

Moshi

ZARA International Travel Agency, PO Box 1990, Moshi; tel. (255) 55-54240; fax 53105; telex: 43095 ZITA TZ.

Zanzibar

Ocean Tours (also represent Abercrombie & Kent), PO Box 3075, Zanzibar; tel. (255) 54-3342.

Zambro Tours, PO Box 152, Zanzibar; tel. (255) 51-31033.

SAFETY AND SECURITY Petty theft involving pedestrians and vehicles is commonplace in larger cities and towns. Vehicle doors should be locked, even with someone sitting in the car. While in the towns, make sure your vehicle is secure at all times; try to leave it in fenced areas that are also protected by security guards. Do not wear expensive jewellery or reveal items such as radios or cameras when walking around. Don't allow yourself to be rushed in shops and stores; ensure that your change is right. Keep an eye on all your luggage while you're in town, and guard your handbags. Hotel and lodge staff are normally extremely trustworthy; however, avoid tempting them by not leaving money or other valuables lying around in the rooms or tents.

SHOPPING Most shops are open from 08:30 or 09:00 to 12:00 or 12:30 and then open up again at 14:00 until 17:30 or 18:00 Mondays to Fridays, and on Saturdays from 08:30 or 09:00 to 12:30. In areas where there is a strong Muslim following, shops may be closed on Friday afternoons.
Food and household items There are some locally made products, but items are generally from South Africa and Kenya. Food prices on imports are not as high as one would suspect.
Crafts, curios and souvenirs Local items can be found throughout Tanzania with different ethnic cultures specializing in different trades. In Maasailand beadwork is available, and carvings and baskets can be purchased all over the country. Fabric is a special purchase and large pieces of khanga and kitenge cloth are displayed in colourful array. Near Dar es Salaam and the southern coast, look for the magnificent Makonde carvings in heavy woods and the intricately carved Zanzibar chests.

Caution should be used if buying anything made with animal skin. Export permits may be required for hide other than cowhide. Be prepared to bargain in markets and some shops – it is considered part of the process and is highly appreciated. Think, too, about bartering with goods you can bring along to trade with. Cash or, even better, cash dollars work well in the smaller shops as only the more expensive places accept credit cards, though these are gaining in popularity. However, credit card users may find an extra charge of 10% being added on to their purchase price.

TELEPHONE Tanzania's telephone service is improving all the time. International direct dialling is possible, but calls are staggeringly expensive; collect calls are not permitted. Local calls are reasonably priced. The country code is 255; below is a list of city codes. If dialling from outside Tanzania, drop the '0'.

Arusha 057
Bukoba 066
Chake Chake 155
Dar es Salaam 051
Dodoma 061
Iringa 064
Kigoma 0695
Kilimanjaro 0575
Lindi 0525
Mbeya 065
Morogoro 056
Moshi 055
Mwanza 068
Tabora 062
Tanga 053
Zanzibar 054

TIME Tanzania is three hours ahead of GMT.

TOILETS The public toilets in Tanzania leave a lot to be desired. Toilets in hotels, lodges and larger restaurants are a better option. Always carry toilet paper with you; if you use the bush as an alternative (which is often the cleaner option), make sure you dig a hole at least 30 cm (1 ft) deep. Burn toilet paper wherever possible.

VENOMOUS CREATURES Scorpions and spiders Make sure you shake out your boots, shoes and clothing before putting them on. When gathering wood for a fire, check it carefully; also check areas where you are digging a latrine. The sting from a scorpion's tail can be very painful (or even, in some cases, fatal). To relieve the pain of both scorpion and spider bites, put a cold compress on the affected area and take aspirin.
Snakebites It is essential to remain calm and to keep the victim calm. Popular remedies of cutting around a snakebite or applying serum or a tourniquet can often cause more harm than good. The best option is get medical attention for the victim as quickly as possible. If the snake has been killed, bring it along for identification.

BUSH AND CAMPING TIPS
Camping may be the finest way to see Tanzania. By following some simple guidelines, it can become a fun-filled wilderness experience.
• If you decide to camp 'unofficially', stay out of sight of the roads and do not attract attention.
• If local people do show up, they are usually there simply out of interest and not to cause any harm. If you are really off the beaten track, be courteous and offer them a cup of sweet tea.
• Sleep in a tent and use mosquito nets. Ensure that ground-level tents are well secured in case of animals visiting during the night.
• Don't feed wildlife and keep all food tightly secured (ensure that you have ample food supplies

with you). Make sure you pack away all food items before retiring for the night. All gear should be stowed in the vehicle or underneath it.

● Fires should be properly tended and monitored. In drought-stricken areas a fire is probably not a good idea. Keep fires small and only collect the amount of wood you need. Before you leave your site, embers should be extinguished.

● When using tinned food, burn the can and then crush it before placing it in your rubbish bag; this helps to eliminate old food smells and allows for more efficient storage.

● Dig 'bush' latrines at least 30 cm (1 ft) deep; burn paper and cover properly with earth.

● Make sure your drinking water is readily available by installing 'cycling' water bottles in your vehicle.

● There are generally ample water supplies throughout Tanzania unless you embark on an extensive off-the-beaten-track excursion; 50 litres (11 gal) is more than enough for two people at any one time. 'Drinkable' water purification tablets or drops should generally be used.

● Take a bucket along for laundry; don't forget a washing line and pegs.

● When drawing water from rivers, be on the lookout for crocodiles; don't venture into thick bush in case of hippo or buffalo.

● If you make use of a village's water supply, first always ask permission.

● Avoid dry riverbeds in case of flash flooding.

● Check your vehicle every day. Make sure you have a good supply of spares, fan belts, fluids, patches and tubes (or plenty of tubeless-tyre repair-adhesive, which is not available anywhere in Tanzania).

● Ensure that the gear in your vehicle is tied or strapped down as roads can be very bumpy.

● Cadac gas tanks are available in Kenya, but cannot be purchased in Tanzania, so ensure you have enough gas for the duration of your stay. Shell and BP gas is readily on sale.

● Do not wander off or jog in wilderness areas. Do not roam about after dark.

● Always keep your children within sight.

● Burn what rubbish you can safely, remove all other items from campsites and deposit in the nearest city refuse bin.

● Share sightings of animals and points of interest with other campers (they will probably reciprocate).

● Offer assistance with breakdowns or mishaps.

● Leave radios and television sets at home; the reception is never good and the bush offers its own natural entertainment.

DIPLOMATIC REPRESENTATION

Most foreign countries represented in Tanzania have missions in Dar es Salaam. Diplomatic representation includes the following countries: Albania, Algeria, Angola, Argentina, Australia, Belgium, Botswana, Brazil, Bulgaria, Burundi, Cambodia, Canada, China, Cuba, Cyprus, Czech and Slovak republics, Denmark, Egypt, Finland, France, Germany, Guinea, India, Indonesia, Iran, Ireland, Italy, Japan, Kenya, Korea, Libyan Arab Jamahiriya, Madagascar, Malawi, Mexico, Mozambique, Netherlands, Nigeria, Norway, Pakistan, Poland, Romania, Russian Federation, Rwanda, Somalia, Spain, Sudan, Sweden, Switzerland, Syrian Arab Republic, Turkey, Uganda, the United Kingdom and the United States of America.

Some of Tanzania's missions abroad are listed:

Belgium 363 Ave Louise, 1050 Brussels; tel. (32) 2-640-6500; fax 646-8026; telex 046-63616.

Canada 50 Range Road, Ottawa, Ontario KIN 8J4; tel. (1) 613-232-1500/9; fax 232-5184.

Germany Theaterplaz 26, 5300 Bonn 2; tel. (49) 228-35-8051/54; fax 35-8226; telex: 041-885569.

Japan 21–9 Kamiyoga 4, Chome, Setagaya-Ku, Tokyo 158; tel. (81) 3-425-4531/3; fax 425-7844; telex: 072-j22121.

South Africa PO Box 56572, Arcadia 0007, Pretoria; tel. (27) 12-323-9041; fax 323-9042.

Sweden Oxtorgsgatan 2-4, 103-89 Stockholm; tel. (46) 8-24-4870; fax 10-9815; telex: 054-10514.

United Kingdom 43 Hertford Street, London WIY8DB; tel. (44) 171-499-8951; fax 491-9321; telex: 051-262504.

United States of America 2139 R. Street, NW Washington DC, 20008, USA; tel. (1) 202-9396125/6/7; fax 7977408; telex: 032-64213; or 205 East 42nd Street, Room 1300, New York, New York, 10017; tel. (1) 21-972-9160; fax 682-5232; telex: 023-234702.

Zambia Ujamaa House, Plot No. 5200, United Nations Ave, Lusaka; PO Box 31219, Lusaka; tel. (260) 1-211422.

Zimbabwe Ujamaa House, 23 Baines Ave, Harare; PO Box 4841, Harare; tel. (263) 4-721870/724534.

INDEX